Navigating Complexity

A Practice Guide

Second Edition

Project Management Institute

Library of Congress Cataloging-in-Publication Data

Names: Project Management Institute issuing body
Title: Navigating complexity : a practice guide / Project Management Institute.
Description: Second edition. | Newtown Square, Pennsylvania : Project Management Institute, [2026] | Includes index. | Summary: "Navigating Complexity: A Practice Guide-Second Edition equips project and program professionals with the frameworks and mindset needed to manage nonlinear, unpredictable environments through systems thinking and adaptive strategies. This updated edition explores the six types of project complexity, provides guidance on developing leadership competencies for decision-making amid ambiguity, and offers practical approaches for building enterprise agility and resilient teams. By distinguishing true complexity from mere complication, the guide helps practitioners embrace uncertainty as an opportunity for project success"— Provided by publisher.
Identifiers: LCCN 2026016609 (print) | LCCN 2026016610 (ebook) | ISBN 9781628258899 paperback | ISBN 9781628258905 epub
Subjects: LCSH: Leadership | Communication in management | Critical thinking | Strategic planning
Classification: LCC HD57.7 .N385 2026 (print) | LCC HD57.7 (ebook)
LC record available at https://lccn.loc.gov/2026016609
LC ebook record available at https://lccn.loc.gov/2026016610

Published by:

Project Management Institute, Inc.
18 Campus Blvd., Ste. 150
Newtown Square, Pennsylvania 19073-3299 USA
Phone: +1 610 356 4600
PMI.org
Online Support: www.pmi.org/about/contact

The paper used in this book complies with the Permanent Paper Standard issued by the National Information Standards Organization (Z39.48—1992).

10 9 8 7 6 5 4 3 2 1

Notice

The Project Management Institute, Inc. (PMI) standards and guideline publications, of which the document contained herein is one, are developed through a voluntary consensus standards development process. This process brings together volunteers and/or seeks out the views of persons who have an interest in the topic covered by this publication. While PMI administers the process and establishes rules to promote fairness in the development of consensus, it does not write the document and it does not independently test, evaluate, or verify the accuracy or completeness of any information or the soundness of any judgments contained in its standards and guideline publications.

PMI disclaims liability for any personal injury, property or other damages of any nature whatsoever, whether special, indirect, consequential or compensatory, directly or indirectly resulting from the publication, use of application, or reliance on this document. PMI disclaims and makes no guaranty or warranty, expressed or implied, as to the accuracy or completeness of any information published herein, and disclaims and makes no warranty that the information in this document will fulfill any of your particular purposes or needs. PMI does not undertake to guarantee the performance of any individual manufacturer or seller's products or services by virtue of this standard or guide.

In publishing and making this document available, PMI is not undertaking to render professional or other services for or on behalf of any person or entity, nor is PMI undertaking to perform any duty owed by any person or entity to someone else. Anyone using this document should rely on his or her own independent judgment or, as appropriate, seek the advice of a competent professional in determining the exercise of reasonable care in any given circumstances. Information and other standards on the topic covered by this publication may be available from other sources, which the user may wish to consult for additional views or information not covered by this publication.

PMI has no power, nor does it undertake to police or enforce compliance with the contents of this document. PMI does not certify, test, or inspect products, designs, or installations for safety or health purposes. Any certification or other statement of compliance with any health or safety-related information in this document shall not be attributable to PMI and is solely the responsibility of the certifier or maker of the statement.

Table of Contents

List of Figures and Tables

Figures

Tables

Introduction

Navigating Complexity: A Practice Guide—Second Edition is a complementary document to the foundational standards of PMI. This introduction describes the purpose of the practice guide, its audience, and the relationship between this practice guide and other PMI standards and products. It also includes an overview of the structure of the practice guide.

Navigating Complexity: A Practice Guide—Second Edition supports project practitioners and organizations in recognizing and navigating projects and programs that are impacted by complexity. While the presence of complexity does not change the foundational practices of project and program management, it does necessitate more attention to interdependence, connectivity, emergence, nonlinearity, and multidimensionality. Complexity necessitates essential competencies, decision-making models, stakeholder engagement skills, and leadership strategies to enhance the likelihood of project success.

Purpose of *Navigating Complexity: A Practice Guide*—Second Edition

This practice guide provides a means to assess and navigate complexity in projects and programs. The purpose of this practice guide is to help project practitioners and organizations navigate complexity to deliver sustained value. It does this by providing the following:

- An introduction to complexity
- A means of categorizing complexity
- Practices for working effectively with people involved in complex projects
- Case studies, tools, techniques, frameworks, and assessments
- Organizational enablers for navigating complexity

Information in this practice guide draws on both relevant literature and the views of experienced project practitioners. While there are numerous elements associated with complexity, this practice guide addresses those elements that are commonly associated with projects and programs. The topic of complexity is limited to projects and programs; portfolio complexity is not addressed.

Audience for This Practice Guide

This practice guide provides a reference for project practitioners involved in projects that include elements of complexity. The information in this practice guide applies regardless of industry, location, size, or delivery approach (predictive, adaptive, hybrid). Information is focused on those stakeholders who are:

- Experienced in project and program management
- Accountable for project outcomes, including project management offices (PMOs), sponsors, portfolio managers, and executive leadership
- Interested in furthering their project management knowledge with advanced concepts
- Preparing for advanced project certifications
- Involved in higher-level academic pursuits

Structure of This Practice Guide

There are five parts in this practice guide that lead the reader from understanding complexity, to working with it, and then to organizational applications.

Part 1 Introduction to Complexity

Part 1 provides introductory content on what project complexity is and types of complexity. These sections introduce key concepts and terminology that will be used throughout the book:

- **Section 1 Project Complexity Overview.** Sets the foundation for understanding project complexity and how it differs from related concepts.
- **Section 2 Types of Project Complexity.** Introduces six commonly encountered types of project complexity.

Part 2 Foundations for Navigating Complexity

Part 2 presents the foundational concepts needed to work effectively in a complex environment. It describes the importance of systems thinking and complexity theory, both of which are important mindsets when navigating complexity. This part also addresses the means for working with complexity using different development approaches.

- **Section 3 Systems Thinking and Complexity Theory.** Introduces concepts of systems thinking and complexity theory and how they relate to project complexity.
- **Section 4 Development Approaches for Complexity.** Introduces guidelines for selecting appropriate development approaches for different categories of project complexity.

Part 3 Human Factors in Complexity

Part 3 delves into the essential people skills needed to succeed in complex environments. These sections include essential competencies, communication and stakeholder engagement, decision-making tactics, and leadership strategies for complex project environments:

- **Section 5 Competencies for Managing Complexity.** Provides an overview of key competencies that are needed for complex project environments.
- **Section 6 Communication and Stakeholder Engagement.** Explores the role of communication in influencing how people make sense of complexity.

- **Section 7 Decision-Making in Complex Environments.** Presents decision-making models and options for complex projects.
- **Section 8 Leadership Strategies for Complexity.** Examines leadership strategies that empower project practitioners to navigate complexity.

Part 4 Assets for Working with Complexity

Part 4 assists project practitioners in applying the information from earlier parts of the practice guide by providing tools, techniques, frameworks, and case studies associated with project complexity.

- **Section 9 Tools and Frameworks.** Presents tools, frameworks, and other assets to aid in managing complex projects.
- **Section 10 Case Studies.** Provides case studies and analysis to link content in the practice guide to real projects.

Part 5 Organizational Enablers for Project Complexity

Part 5 provides strategies for thriving in complexity at the organizational level. The following sections discuss organizational agility, continuous organizational learning and adaptation, and developing a playbook for project complexity:

- **Section 11 Enterprise Agility in Navigating Complexity.** Presents enterprise agility as an integrated capability in navigating complexity.
- **Section 12 Organizational Learning and Adaptation.** Describes strategies for organization-wide learning, readiness, and building a resilient culture.
- **Section 13 Complexity Playbooks.** Discusses playbooks for complex projects, with a focus on complexity assessments.

Part 1

Introduction to Complexity

Part 1 of *Navigating Complexity: A Practice Guide*—Second Edition provides introductory content. It establishes a common understanding of project complexity and types of complexity. There are two sections in Part 1:

- **Section 1 Project Complexity Overview.** Section 1 identifies the key characteristics of complexity. It differentiates complex projects from complicated projects and explores the relationship among complexity, uncertainty, and ambiguity. This section also describes the historical roots of complexity theory and common misconceptions.
- **Section 2 Types of Project Complexity.** Section 2 introduces a consistent framework for project complexity by identifying six types of project complexity, establishing a shared vocabulary across the profession. The types of complexity are referenced throughout this practice guide.

Together these sections introduce key concepts for project complexity and equip project practitioners with the perspective and context for the topics addressed in the remaining sections.

Section 1

Project Complexity Overview

1.1 Introduction

In today's fast-paced, globally connected world, project professionals often encounter projects where traditional, linear planning falls short. Challenges such as COVID-19 pandemic-era supply chain disruptions, quickly evolving artificial intelligence (AI) technologies, and unclear regulatory environments introduce high levels of complexity into modern projects. Although complexity is increasingly common in project work, it is often misunderstood and underestimated. This section introduces the concept and study of project complexity, covering:

- Introduction to Project Complexity
- Project Characteristics That Cause Complexity
- Distinguishing Among Complexity, Complication, Uncertainty, and Ambiguity
- Common Myths About Complexity
- Developing a Complexity-Aware Mindset

Studying project complexity helps project practitioners anticipate challenges, engage stakeholders meaningfully, and apply adaptive strategies that drive successful outcomes. Although complexity and risk are related, they are not the same. Complexity reflects the structure and behavior of the system itself, whereas risk represents the potential consequences that emerge when complex interactions produce unpredictable outcomes. This section builds the foundation for studying complexity.

1.2 Introduction to Project Complexity

Complexity is a characteristic of a program, project, or its environment that is difficult to manage due to human behavior, system behavior, and ambiguity. It is an inherent quality in certain project environments that arises when many interdependent elements, such as tasks, stakeholders, technologies, and external influences, interact in dynamic and often unpredictable ways.

1.2.1 The Study of Complexity Theory in Project Management

The understanding of project complexity has evolved over the course of decades. The study of complexity theory in project management can be traced back to mid-20th century research that was motivated by large-scale, complex projects like the Manhattan Project, which famously led to the development of the atomic bomb. These studies demonstrated the significance of complexity within project environments. The studies highlighted the impact of complexity on project goals and objectives, project structure and organization, and the capabilities needed for managers at different levels.

The studies conducted in the mid-20th century established complexity theory as a necessary field of research and they expanded the perspective of project professionals. A number of theoretical approaches to managing complexity have emerged from the study of complexity. The field has become so prevalent that many project management information systems (PMIS) have integrated these theoretical approaches into modules that support their application to projects.

1.2.2 Benefits of Understanding Complexity

Identifying, defining, and studying complexity as an aspect of projects allows project practitioners to reframe how they engage with uncertainty and change. Rather than treating unpredictability as a barrier, complexity-aware professionals embrace it as a challenge that demands adaptive thinking, systems-level awareness, and collaborative problem-solving. Recognizing complexity allows teams to respond more effectively to change, design more resilient strategies, and position their projects for long-term value creation.

1.3 Project Characteristics That Cause Complexity

While project professionals often associate complexity with project size, duration, technical difficulty, and interconnectedness, these factors alone do not make a project complex. Complexity is not simply about how big or challenging a project is. Rather, complexity concerns how unpredictable and dynamic a project becomes.

Projects are complex when straightforward, cause-and-effect thinking no longer consistently applies. In a complex project, actions taken in one area may ripple unpredictably through others. Solutions might give rise to new problems, and outcomes cannot be reliably forecasted.

This section introduces the characteristics that contribute to complexity: emergence, nonlinear causality, and adaptive systems. These characteristics are what make complex projects uniquely difficult to manage using traditional, linear approaches. These characteristics are summarized here and discussed in more detail in Section 3.

1.3.1 Emergence

Emergence refers to the appearance of new patterns, properties, or behaviors that arise from interactions within a system but cannot be explained by the parts in isolation. Emergent dynamics resist traditional forecasting and control methods. Project leaders dealing with emergence should be prepared to adapt plans in real time and enable systems to evolve through feedback rather than rigid adherence to scope or schedule.

Example scenario

During a pandemic-response project, a simple community feedback channel unexpectedly became the central mechanism for prioritizing resource distribution, fundamentally shifting stakeholder engagement models.

1.3.2 Nonlinear Causality

Nonlinear causality is a relationship in which cause and effect are not directly proportional, where small changes can produce disproportionately large effects. This relationship between cause and effect raises the stakes for decision-makers and introduces unpredictable elements.

Example scenario

A minor, late-stage change to accommodate AI-driven surgical equipment triggered changes to structural load-bearing assumptions, substantially affecting timelines and contractor agreements.

1.3.3 Adaptive Systems

Complex projects often include elements that cross multiple domains such as technical, organizational, political, and cultural concerns. These elements interact with one another in unpredictable ways, creating an adaptive system, or a system whose behavior evolves due to interactions within a dynamic environment.

Working within an adaptive system requires cross-functional insight, flexible leadership, and the ability to hold multiple perspectives at once. It challenges project professionals to move beyond role-based thinking and become integrative problem-solvers.

Example scenario

A regional healthcare provider launched a US$500 million hospital construction project aimed at modernizing its infrastructure, expanding capacity, and integrating state-of-the-art medical technologies. The facility was to be built adjacent to an operational hospital campus, with overlapping utilities, patient services, and shared staff.

The project team navigated challenges such as:

- **Patient safety and live environment.** Construction had to occur without disrupting critical healthcare services. Infection control, noise levels, and material handling required close coordination with medical staff, which created management challenges.
- **Regulatory and government oversight.** Evolving healthcare compliance standards, environmental impact assessments, and multiple jurisdictional inspections led to regulatory shifts midproject (e.g., building code updates), which required redesigning and replanning.
- **Technological integration.** New imaging and diagnostic technologies were introduced during construction, requiring late-stage architectural changes, specialized electrical and HVAC systems, and cross-disciplinary vendor coordination.

1.4 Distinguishing Among Complexity, Complication, Uncertainty, and Ambiguity

As established in the previous sections, complexity is the result of project elements interacting in dynamic and unpredictable ways. The presence of complexity makes project management more challenging. However, it is not the only factor that can introduce challenges to projects. To further examine complexity, this section compares complexity with other factors that make projects challenging: complication, uncertainty, and ambiguity.

1.4.1 Complicated Versus Complex

A complication in a project refers to the addition of external parts or component—usually related to mechanical or structural intricacy— to a system. A project becomes complicated when it has many complications, meaning it consists of multiple parts and components. Although the words "complicated" and "complex" are often used interchangeably in casual conversation, a complicated project is not necessarily complex.

The number of components involved in a complicated project may create challenges for project managers. However, a complicated project is not complex if:

- Those components are largely independent from one another (lacking interconnectedness),
- The broader context of the project is stable (lacking emergence),
- Actions typically have predictable outcomes (lacking nonlinear causality), and
- Project elements are contained within individual domains (lacking multidimensionality).

Complicated systems and projects have challenges that can be systemically solved using established procedures. By contrast, complex projects may have challenges with no fixed solutions at all, requiring trial and error and creative problem-solving (see Table 1-1).

Table 1-1. Comparison Between Complicated and Complex Project Examples

	Complicated Project	Complex Project
Example	**Building a large commercial airplane**	**Developing a novel cancer treatment**
Characteristics	**Multicomponent:** An airplane consists of numerous systems (engine, fuselage, wings, avionics, etc.), each with its own set of subsystems and components. **Knowable:** Scientists and engineers on the development team possess the necessary knowledge to manage tasks. **Defined processes:** The manufacturing and assembly of these components follow well-established processes. **Predictable outcomes:** Given sufficient information about the design, materials, and manufacturing processes, it is possible to predict the performance and safety of the aircraft. **Technical expertise:** The project requires specialized engineering and manufacturing expertise, with a well-established knowledge base.	**Adaptive systems:** Cancer treatment involves intricate biological processes within the body. A change in one area can have unforeseen consequences in other areas. **Unpredictable:** Patient responses to new treatments vary significantly. What works for one person may not work for another, and side effects can be unpredictable. **Innovation:** Developing a novel treatment often requires exploring new avenues of research and technology, which carry inherent risks and uncertainties. **Dynamic environment:** The field of cancer research is constantly evolving, with discoveries and technologies emerging regularly. This evolution requires a flexible and adaptive approach.
Cause-and-effect connection	Determining connections between cause and effect requires expert analysis.	Nonlinear dynamics, feedback loops, and sensitivity to initial conditions can make connections between cause and effect challenging to determine.
What works well	Careful application of practices can work well.	Novel and experimental approaches can work well.

1.4.2 Uncertain Versus Complex

Uncertainty is a lack of understanding and awareness of issues, events, paths to follow, or solutions to pursue. An uncertain environment is another factor that creates challenges within projects but does not by itself indicate complexity. In project environments, uncertainty often appears as unpredictable variables that impact scope, schedule, cost, or quality.

Because complexity and uncertainty are both associated with unpredictability, these two characteristics are easily conflated. However, uncertainty can exist within projects that are not complex. Uncertainty alone does not cause complexity.

1.4.3 Ambiguous Versus Complex

Ambiguity is a state of being unclear, having difficulty in identifying the cause of events, or having multiple options from which to choose. When the approach to a project is ambiguous, teams often struggle to determine the appropriate meaning or implications of the information they have.

Ambiguous situations allow multiple interpretations of events and instructions. This lack of clarity may result in misaligned stakeholder perspectives, conflicting objectives, and decision paralysis. In project execution, ambiguity undermines the development of a shared understanding, hinders the creation of requirements, and complicates governance and change control processes.

The interconnectedness and multidimensionality of complex projects may often lead to ambiguity. Overlap among teams, project elements, and domains may cause a range of perspectives on the same information. However, ambiguity is a frequent effect of complexity, not a cause, and ambiguity exists in projects that are not complex.

1.4.4 Examples of Complicated, Uncertain, Ambiguous, and Complex Projects

The differences among complicated, uncertain, ambiguous, and complex projects are illustrated by the following examples:

- **Complicated.** A rail company is implementing its first high-speed rail line. The company navigates many different components such as railway track maintenance, coordination with existing rail services, and governmental safety regulations. Cause and effect are connected, but it requires expertise and effort to determine and understand those connections.
- **Uncertain.** A novice market analyst at an aircraft manufacturing company is uncertain about whether the commercial jet market will rise or fall over the next 5 years. This uncertainty stems from the lack of crucial information regarding future market trends and the company's potential performance.
- **Ambiguous.** A contract clause in a legal agreement between the aircraft manufacturer and a client is open to multiple interpretations. This situation exemplifies ambiguity, which may lead to disputes, scope creep, or compliance issues if not clarified through stakeholder engagement or legal review.
- **Complex.** Fulfilling a large-scale order for an advanced semiconductor factory in a remote country with limited infrastructure involves multiple subcontractors, international suppliers, and interdependent workstreams. Shifting geopolitical dynamics, cross-border regulations, and supply chain volatility further complicate the project, demonstrating high systemic complexity.

1.4.5 Project Type Summary

Effective project management requires identifying and handling a wide range of challenges, regardless of cause. Complexity, complications, uncertainty, and ambiguity all create challenges for project professionals. These four characteristics can coexist in projects; therefore, employing tailored approaches to handle each challenge according to its cause can significantly enhance project resilience and success. Although complicated, uncertain, and ambiguous projects are not necessarily complex, complex projects are often (but not always) complicated, uncertain, and ambiguous. Distinguishing among these project features helps project professionals identify optimal solutions.

1.5 Common Myths About Complexity

Complexity is increasingly recognized as a critical dimension in project work. However, there are common myths—or misunderstandings—about complexity that persist in the project management field. These myths can lead to oversights in planning, underinvestment in adaptive approaches, and misplaced confidence in traditional tools and processes. This section highlights and counters three of the most common myths about complexity.

1.5.1 Myth: Complexity Only Affects Large Projects

It is a common assumption that complexity scales with size. According to this incorrect assumption, the larger the project, the more complex it becomes. While large projects often contain more moving parts, size alone does not create complexity. As established in this section, complexity emerges when many interdependent project elements interact in a dynamic and often unpredictable way.

Reality: A large scope or budget does not guarantee complexity. Large projects may be complicated without being complex. By contrast, small projects can be highly complex if they involve multiple jurisdictions, emerging technologies, or rapidly shifting stakeholder expectations. For example, a short-duration policy implementation project may be highly complex due to political sensitivities, tight feedback loops, and conflicting stakeholder agendas—despite having few deliverables. Recognizing this distinction helps organizations better anticipate complexity, even in smaller initiatives.

1.5.2 Myth: Complexity Can Be Controlled

In predictive project environments, project practitioners may attempt to engineer their way through complexity through tighter controls or detailed plans. This mindset is more reflective of working on a complicated project rather than a complex project. Difficult problems are assumed to be solvable with the right expertise or system design.

Reality: Complexity is inherent in some projects. It can be navigated but not eliminated. Because it stems from dynamic interactions, human behavior, and emergent conditions, complexity should be approached with adaptive strategies rather than engineered solutions. Efforts to control complexity often backfire, creating brittle systems that lack flexibility when change inevitably occurs. Instead, high-performing teams embrace iterative planning, open communication channels, and decision-making frameworks designed for uncertain environments.

1.5.3 Myth: Complexity and Risk Are the Same

Complexity and risk are often discussed together, which leads to the common misperception that they are interchangeable terms. However, they are distinct issues. Risk involves known or identifiable (known-unknown) events with probabilities and impacts. Complexity, by contrast, deals with dynamic, interconnected, and multidimensional situations where predictability breaks down.

Reality: Complexity is not the same as risk; complexity is a source of risk. A highly complex project may contain predictable risks, such as delays due to permit approvals, as well as unforeseeable disruptions such as stakeholder coalitions forming around a previously uncontroversial issue. While risks can be mitigated, complexity should be understood, identified, and responded to. Confusing complexity and risk may lead project practitioners to apply inappropriate tools. For example, they may over-rely on risk matrices instead of using complexity-appropriate tools such as system mapping, scenario planning, or reflective decision forums.

1.6 Developing a Complexity-Aware Mindset

In project environments where complexity is inherent and unavoidable, project practitioners benefit from a fundamental shift in mindset. Rather than attempting to eliminate or bypass complexity, they learn to navigate the impact of complexity effectively. This section discusses pathways for adopting a complexity-aware mindset.

1.6.1 From Control to Adaptation

Many project professionals approach their work with the assumption of structure and predictability. Success is defined by precise planning, diligent monitoring, and tight control. Standard project phases, such as planning, development, and testing, feel like part of a well-rehearsed script. This controlled approach to project management is effective for predictable, low-complexity environments. Complex projects are unpredictable in ways that resist executing a controlled plan.

When project environments are less predictable, previously effective project management methods are no longer sufficient. In complex environments, project professionals find greater success through adaptability. This is a significant shift for the project manager. The role transforms its focus from establishing control to guiding and enabling teams. Success depends on iterating, listening to feedback, and being willing to adjust the course.

1.6.2 From Expert to Sensemaker

Every project leader eventually experiences a situation that tests their expertise. Today's project environments contain new challenges and increased uncertainty. Even well-researched, time-tested approaches may not be effective. In situations like these, project practitioners may find new direction by shifting from the mindset of an expert, relying on experience and knowledge to guide decisions, to that of a sensemaker. *Sensemaking* is the process of interpreting complex or ambiguous situations to build shared understanding and guide effective action. Project teams that are guided by sensemaking learn to let go of rigid assumptions, stay alert to new signals, and navigate challenges by interpreting evidence.

A sensemaking approach provides direction during challenging times; however, it does not guarantee success. Crises like the 2011 Tōhoku, Japan, earthquake and tsunami or the COVID-19 pandemic demonstrate that decisions may often be made with incomplete information and under immense pressure. In these circumstances, mistakes are inevitable. However, each misstep deepens a team's ability to adapt, respond, and build resilience for the road ahead.

Sensemaking project leaders are decisive when needed, while also taking time to reflect and adjust. Leadership under these circumstances requires fostering trust, encouraging diverse voices, and embracing a rhythm of inquiry and iteration. Developing comfort with a sensemaking approach supports leaders and teams experiencing the unpredictability that is a core feature of complexity.

1.6.3 Building Complexity Awareness

For many professionals, embarking on careers in program and project management begins with a desire for structure. In those early stages, complexity may feel like a concern for specialists in high-risk industries or technical domains. However, in reality, even the most carefully planned initiatives are rarely straightforward. Unexpected interdependencies emerge. Stakeholders pull in different directions. Technology shifts midstream, and assumptions unravel.

Successfully navigating complex projects requires developing an awareness of complexity as an inherent part of certain environments and projects. This awareness is necessary not just at the individual level, but also throughout the organization. Complexity-aware organizations recognize that complexity is a shared reality to be understood and navigated as a team. Across sectors and scales, managing complexity has become a core competency for all who shape programs and projects.

1.7 Summary

Complexity is increasingly common in modern project environments. Project practitioners and organizations benefit from understanding the characteristics of complexity so that they can recognize its presence within projects and initiatives.

This section established motivation and a foundation for the study of complexity in project management by:

- Defining complexity as a characteristic of a program or project or its environment that is difficult to manage due to human behavior, system behavior, and ambiguity;
- Describing the origins and purpose of complexity theory in project management;
- Identifying the project characteristics that cause complexity—interconnectedness, emergence, nonlinear causality, and multidimensionality;
- Distinguishing between complexity and other sources of challenges within projects—complication, uncertainty, and ambiguity;
- Listing and correcting common myths about complexity; and
- Explaining the mindset shifts necessary to develop a complexity-aware mindset.

The next section builds on this fundamental understanding of complexity by characterizing six commonly encountered types of complexity.

Types of Project Complexity

2.1 Introduction

Complex projects often exhibit dynamic circumstances and unpredictable outcomes. Beyond this common tendency, complex projects vary widely, necessitating different approaches depending on the features of the project. Complex projects have distinct patterns and features that project practitioners can recognize. This section provides a framework for identifying and categorizing common types of project complexity. After identifying the types of project complexity involved in an initiative, teams can implement strategies tailored toward the specific types of complexity involved.

This section introduces six commonly encountered types of project complexity:

- Structural Complexity
- Dynamic Complexity
- Human and Sociopolitical Complexity
- Environmental Complexity
- Technological Complexity
- Organizational Complexity

Each section includes the characteristics of that complexity type, the likely impact of that complexity type on a program or project, and an overview of relevant strategies. Identifying the types of complexity present in a project is essential for identifying the appropriate competencies, decision-making approaches, and leadership strategies needed to navigate that project. These complexity types will be referenced throughout subsequent sections.

2.2 Structural Complexity

Structural complexity refers to the degree to which a project contains numerous, interrelated components. A project becomes structurally complex when that project has a large quantity and variety of elements that should be coordinated to achieve project outcomes. This type of complexity is common in large-scale, multiphase, or multistakeholder initiatives.

A project with a moderate number of components that are largely independent from one another likely has little to no structural complexity. A project with many components that are interconnected has a high degree of structural complexity. Even smaller projects can exhibit high structural complexity if they involve dense interdependencies, complex regulatory requirements, or diverse stakeholder expectations.

2.2.1 Characteristics of Structural Complexity

There are several characteristics that typically signal the presence of structural complexity:

- **Numerous interdependent components.** Projects containing high numbers of activities, deliverables, disciplines, or technologies that should be coordinated.
- **Multilayered stakeholder ecosystems.** Projects involving multiple business units, jurisdictions, vendors, or regulatory bodies.
- **Interface density.** Projects with a high number of handoffs, integrations, or dependencies among teams, phases, or systems.
- **Geographical dispersion.** Teams, suppliers, or assets that are spread across regions or time zones.
- **Governance and approval structures.** Projects with layered decision-making processes and hierarchical oversight that can complicate coordination efforts.
- **Contractual arrangements and delivery models.** Projects with joint ventures, alliances, or multivendor environments that can create structural layers requiring alignment.

Characteristics of structural complexity can often be identified by reviewing project artifacts such as the work breakdown structure (WBS), organizational charts, communication management plans, RACI (responsible, accountable, consulted, informed) matrices, and interface control documents. If any of these project artifacts are extensive or intricately detailed, it may indicate structural complexity.

2.2.2 Impact of Structural Complexity

The large number of interconnected elements involved in a structurally complex project introduces risk, communication overhead, and a greater likelihood of misalignment, often creating inefficiency. When overlooked, structural complexity can lead to:

- **Delays and rework.** Missed handoffs, miscommunication, or unclear ownership across interfaces.
- **Conflicting objectives.** Differing priorities among functional groups, contractors, or stakeholders.

- **Decision-making bottlenecks.** Overly hierarchical or unclear governance, which slows down response times.
- **Fragmentation.** Dispersed or overlapping responsibilities.
- **Scope creep.** Expanded deliverables and tasks due to uncoordinated changes or unclear component ownership.

2.2.3 Strategies for Structural Complexity

Identifying and mapping structural complexity early in the project help project managers identify where tailored strategies and interventions will be needed. Some approaches that can help address the impact of structural complexity include:

- Integration planning,
- Interface controls,
- Streamlined governance structures,
- Modularization,
- Boundary management, and
- Colocated teams.

Implementing these approaches at the beginning of the project life cycle helps mitigate the negative effects of structural complexity. However, the presence of structural complexity makes unpredictable changes likely during the project. Any efforts to address structural complexity should be maintained and revisited throughout the project to be effective.

An example of structural complexity in a transit expansion project demonstrates how many of the key aspects of structural complexity (see Figure 2-1) combine, leading to schedule and budget overruns.

Example scenario

A metropolitan transit authority launched a multiyear subway expansion involving new stations, track upgrades, and system-wide signaling modernization. The project required coordination among multiple contractors, city departments, technology vendors, regulatory agencies, and community groups. While each project component had its own technical scope, structural complexity emerged from how the systems and stakeholders overlapped:

- Multiple subcontractors had to integrate designs using shared interface points, creating rework when changes were not communicated across teams.
- The governance structure involved both municipal oversight and federal transportation approvals, slowing key decisions.
- Teams were geographically dispersed, with engineering in one city, fabrication in another, and oversight in yet another, introducing time zone and coordination challenges.
- Despite being well-scoped, the project suffered delays and budget overruns that were not due to technical failures but to coordination gaps across structural interfaces—a hallmark of unmanaged structural complexity.

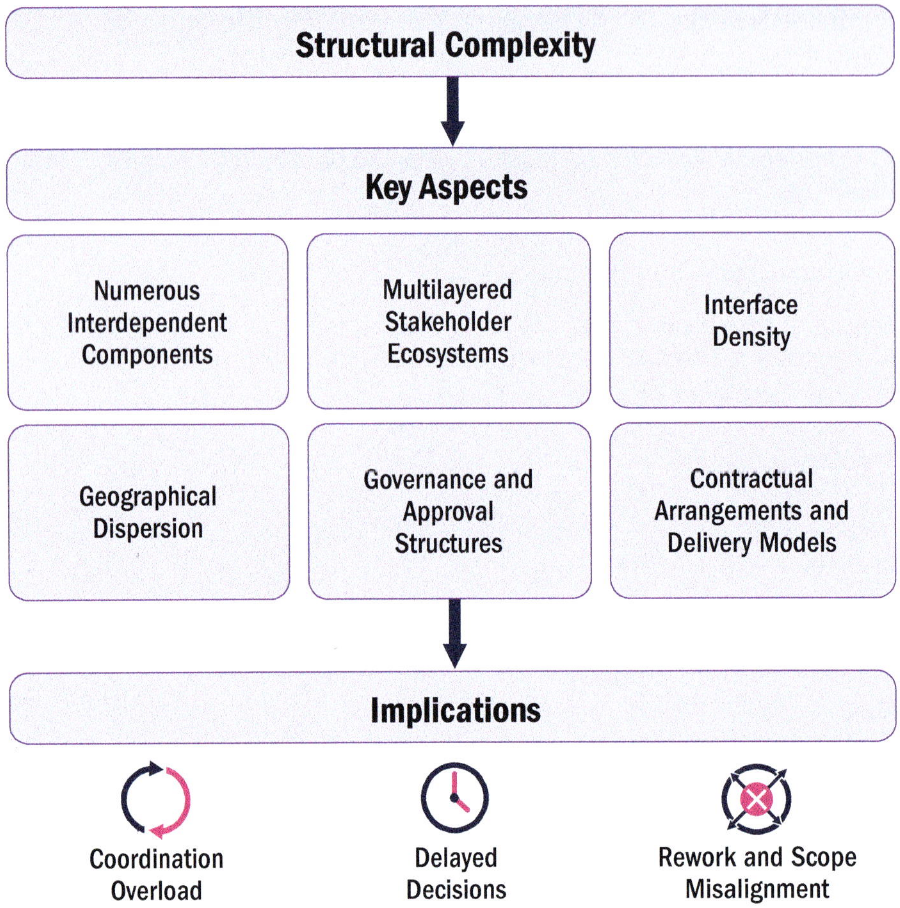

Figure 2-1. Structural Complexity Model

2.3 Dynamic Complexity

Dynamic complexity refers to the challenges arising from changing interdependencies, emergent behaviors, and nonlinear cause-and-effect relationships that evolve throughout project life cycles. It stems from temporal variations, feedback loops, and emergent properties that cannot be predicted from initial project conditions.

Dynamically complex projects are not static. These projects continuously evolve through stakeholder interactions, environmental changes, and system adaptations that create unpredictable project trajectories.

2.3.1 Characteristics of Dynamic Complexity

Projects with dynamic complexity exhibit one or more of the following characteristics:

- **Temporal evolution.** Project relationships and dependencies shift over time as stakeholder priorities change, environmental conditions evolve, and system interactions produce unexpected outcomes.
- **Feedback loops.** Actions and decisions create effects that impact the system, influencing future outcomes. For example, schedule pressure could lead to shortcuts that cause rework and further delay.

- **Emergent properties.** Interactions among project components may lead to unexpected outcomes or patterns.
- **Nonlinear cause and effect.** Small changes produce disproportionately large impacts due to the interaction of multiple variables.

Temporal complexity is a particularly significant dimension of dynamic complexity. It arises from changes to regulatory environments, market dynamics, and stakeholder expectations during project execution. Changes that cause temporal complexity include:

- Regulatory changes that result in midproject design modifications.
- Evolving compliance standards.
- Updates to approval requirements.
- Market volatility that reduces resource availability.

Successfully navigating temporal complexity requires continuous environmental scanning, flexible governance structures, and adaptive planning. These approaches accommodate emerging conditions, rather than attempting to predict all changes at project initiation.

The dynamic complexity model in Figure 2-2 illustrates how stakeholders, technology, processes, and the environment influence and are influenced by project objectives.

The model illustrates the following interconnected layers of dynamic complexity:

- The solid inner circles show bidirectional relationships among evolving project objectives and stakeholders, environment, technology, and processes.
- The dashed outer circle shows how relationships within the inner circles generate emergent effects that may manifest as misaligned outcomes, decision latency, emergent risks, and rework. These challenges arise from system interactions rather than individual component failures.
- The dynamic complexity management box includes adaptive planning, incremental delivery, rapid decision frameworks, frequent stakeholder feedback, and continuous learning loops that enable teams to navigate rather than eliminate dynamic complexity.

Managing dynamic complexity requires recognizing the evolution of cause-and-effect relationships during project execution, as small changes in one area may create cascading impacts across the entire system.

2.3.2 Impact of Dynamic Complexity

Dynamic complexity may impact projects in a variety of ways, including:

- **Scope evolution through learning.** Requirements change, not from poor initial analysis but from evolving project dynamics and environments.
- **Cascading schedule adjustments.** Delays that result from interdependency changes, where adjustments in one area trigger adaptations throughout the project system.

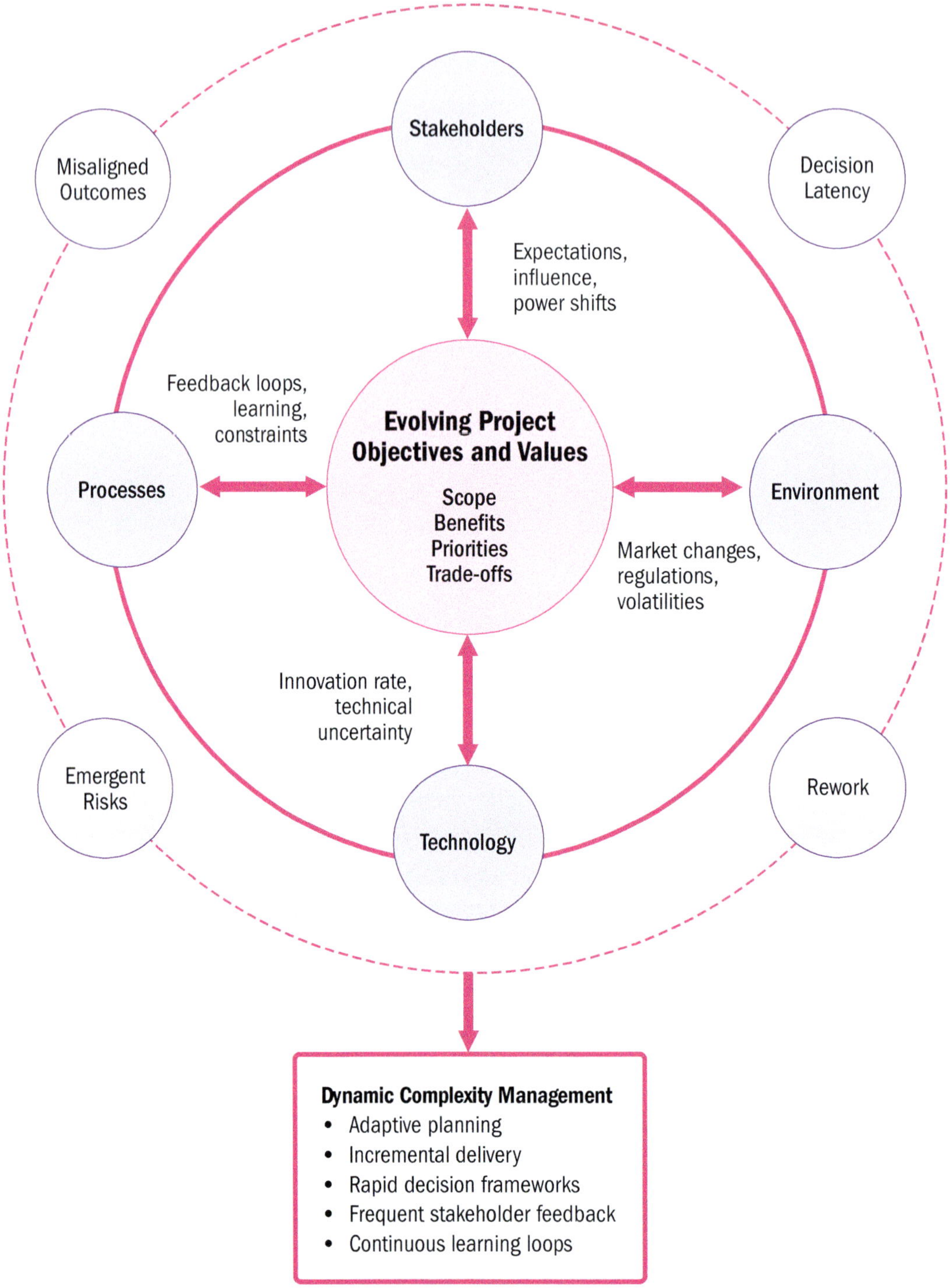

Figure 2-2. Dynamic Complexity Model

- **Emergent stakeholder resistance.** Opposition that develops through project evolution rather than initial disagreement, often emerging from unforeseen consequences of project decisions.
- **Technology integration surprises.** Challenges that emerge from system interactions rather than component failures, where integration reveals behaviors not present in individual elements.

2.3.3 Strategies for Dynamic Complexity

To navigate the unpredictable changes that dynamic complexity causes, project practitioners benefit from developing competencies in systems thinking, pattern recognition, and adaptive planning. These skills enable leaders to navigate uncertainty while maintaining project momentum. Projects characterized by high dynamic complexity often benefit from:

- Using iterative approaches that accommodate continuous adjustments;
- Maintaining continuous stakeholder engagement to manage emerging expectations;
- Establishing flexible governance structures that can respond to changing conditions;
- Applying rolling wave planning rather than detailed, up-front planning; and
- Employing probe-sense-respond approaches in uncertain environments.

Although the unpredictability of dynamically complex projects creates challenges, project practitioners who recognize and address this complexity can implement strategies tailored to unstable environments. Proactively managing dynamic complexity allows project teams to respond to emerging conditions while delivering successful project outcomes.

Example scenario

The Port of Melbourne Channel Deepening Project exhibited dynamic complexity because of evolving temporal interdependencies across its 6-year development timeline. The project involved dredging shipping channels to accommodate larger vessels. Regulatory conditions and environmental standards evolved substantially during the development and execution phases, causing uncertainty and challenges. [1][1]

To address the challenges caused by changing regulations and standards, the project team implemented the following adaptive management strategies:

- Iterative business case development allowed for systematic updates based on changing conditions.
- Flexible planning approaches enabled rapid responses to environmental and regulatory changes.
- Comprehensive stakeholder engagement addressed both planned and emergent stakeholder concerns.
- Continuous environmental assessment supported adaptive approval approaches.

This approach enabled the project to successfully navigate regulatory changes that created cascading effects throughout project planning and execution. The case shows how temporal interdependency evolution in infrastructure projects can be addressed by governance structures that accommodate uncertainty and change rather than attempt to eliminate them.

[1] The numbers in brackets refer to the list of references at the end of this practice guide.

2.4 Human and Sociopolitical Complexity

Human and sociopolitical complexity results from the intricate web of people dynamics that emerge when diverse stakeholders, team members, and external partners interact throughout a project. This complexity type operates on three levels, each warranting separate consideration:

- **Social complexity.** Individual and group dynamics, including personal biases, cultural differences, communication preferences, and team formation patterns, that influence collaboration effectiveness.
- **Political complexity.** Power structures, decision-making authority, resource allocation approaches, and competing organizational interests that shape project governance and support.
- **Sociopolitical complexity.** The intersection of social and political complexity factors, where stakeholder behaviors and coalition dynamics emerge unpredictably, exceeding beyond what social or political analysis alone can explain.

Figure 2-3 shows how features of social complexity interact with features of political complexity to create emergent behaviors that cannot be predicted from understanding either social or political factors alone.

2.4.1 Characteristics of Human and Sociopolitical Complexity

The complex dynamics that comprise human and sociopolitical complexity can be organized into the following characteristics:

- **Individual and group social dynamics.** Diverse teams comprised of individuals with varying backgrounds, communication styles, experience levels, and cultural perspectives.
- **Organizational and institutional political structures.** Political environments with formal authority structures, informal influence networks, resource allocation approaches, and competing organizational priorities.
- **Cultural and contextual integration factors.** Projects spanning multiple cultural contexts, including organizational cultures, national cultures, professional cultures, and industry-specific cultural norms.
- **Power dynamics and influence networks.** Formal and informal power structures that exist within and across organizations, leading to coalition shifts, changing alliances, and competing group interests.
- **Stakeholder interest alignment and conflict resolution.** Multiple stakeholders with diverse and often competing interests that require ongoing negotiation, compromise, and conflict resolution throughout the project life cycle.

Cultural differences are a significant source of human and sociopolitical complexity. Hofstede's Cultural Dimensions Framework provides a widely used lens for understanding how cultural contexts shape stakeholder behavior and project dynamics. [2] In the context of project work, the following dimensions are particularly influential:

- **Power distance.** The degree to which hierarchical authority and unequal power distribution are accepted.
- **Individualism versus collectivism.** Emphasis on individual goals versus group or collective priorities.

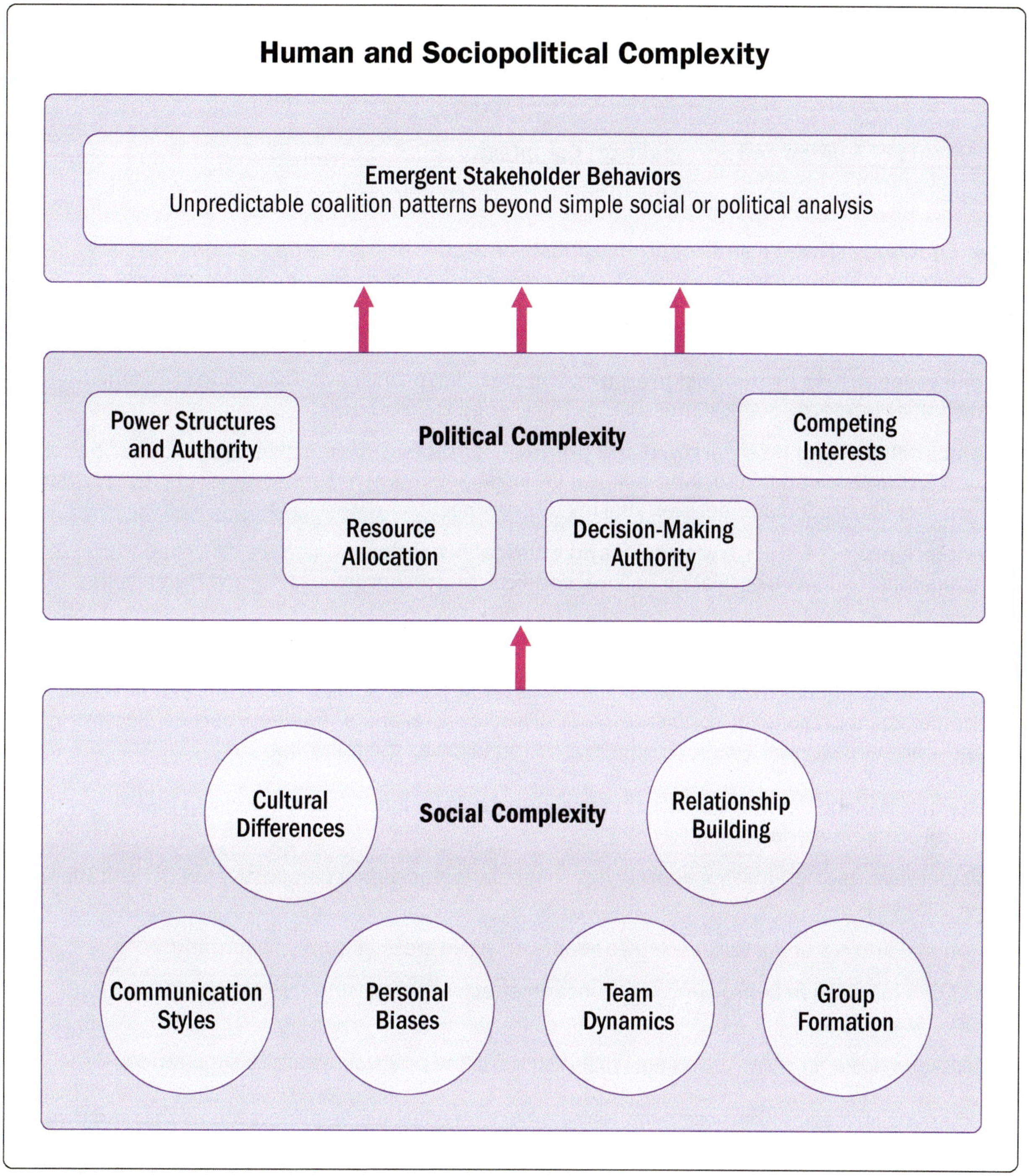

Figure 2-3. Human and Sociopolitical Complexity Model

- **Uncertainty avoidance.** Tolerance for ambiguity, risk, and unstructured situations.
- **Long-term versus short-term orientation.** Focus on future-oriented outcomes versus immediate results.

Project practitioners leading projects that span multiple cultural contexts will benefit from explicitly assessing these dimensions during stakeholder analysis. Then, they can tailor communication, decision-making, and governance approaches according to the cultural norms involved.

2.4.2 Impact of Human and Sociopolitical Complexity

Without careful management, human and sociopolitical complexity may lead to the following:

- **Stakeholder resistance and coalition opposition.** Active or passive opposition to project objectives driven by unaddressed social concerns, political interests, or cultural conflicts that undermine project support and resource availability through systematic stakeholder disengagement.
- **Scope creep driven by political pressure.** Uncontrolled project expansion due to competing stakeholder interests, political pressure, or misaligned stakeholders.
- **Project delays from interpersonal and political conflicts.** Timeline extensions caused by unresolved interpersonal tensions, political gridlock, or cultural misunderstandings that prevent effective collaboration and decision-making approaches.
- **Complete project failure from social and political breakdown.** Initiative cancellation due to loss of stakeholder support, escalating political conflicts, or irreconcilable cultural differences.

2.4.3 Strategies for Human and Sociopolitical Complexity

Projects with well-managed sociopolitical dynamics show higher success rates through effective stakeholder coalition building, conflict resolution, and cultural adaptation approaches. Success in managing human and sociopolitical complexity often involves the following:

- Sustained stakeholder engagement that accounts for both individual relationship building and political coalition management,
- Collaborative decision-making approaches that balance individual perspectives with institutional interests,
- Emotional and cultural intelligence that enable effective cross-cultural collaboration,
- Clear communication approaches that function effectively across diverse social and political contexts, and
- Adaptive leadership styles that can navigate cultural and political dynamics simultaneously.

Implementing strategies like these helps leaders build strong, diverse project teams that can thrive within complex political structures and power dynamics.

Example scenario

A multimillion-dollar program to construct several large stadiums in the Middle East faced significant human and sociopolitical complexity. The program required coordination among multiple international contractors, local subcontractors, and a national government client with a complex, fragmented authority structure.

The project team addressed human and sociopolitical complexity through the following:

- **Aligning strategic stakeholders.** The project reconciled the varied agendas of international partners, local communities, and government officials by forming a unified working group. This effort led to a key achievement: the first stadium in the region to achieve full International Federation of Association Football (FIFA) compliance.
- **Navigating power dynamics.** The project team navigated a complex landscape of formal and informal power networks. In one instance, they converted a former competitor into a cooperative, supervised subcontractor, turning a potential obstacle into a strategic asset.
- **Building trust and cohesion.** Leadership focused on building trust and maintaining operations despite external pressures and competing interests. They implemented culturally sensitive communication strategies and leveraged local expertise to foster a cohesive project environment.
- **Implementing innovative project governance.** Project leadership addressed challenges through adaptive governance and innovation. They maintained critical technical specifications, such as an epoxy specification for the stadium, despite significant cost pressures.

This example demonstrates how projects with human and sociopolitical complexity benefit from approaches that extend beyond technical solutions, focusing on relationship dynamics and trust.

2.5 Environmental Complexity

Environmental complexity refers to the external forces and contextual conditions that influence a project's ability to plan, execute, and deliver successfully. These forces are beyond the project team's control. Examples include regulatory shifts, economic cycles, market fluctuations, sociopolitical instability, and environmental regulations.

Because environmental complexity is caused by factors that are external to the project, managing it requires continuous awareness of changes outside the project's boundaries. Projects are especially vulnerable to environmental complexity when they are operating in volatile regulatory environments, cross-border jurisdictions, or politically sensitive sectors. This type of complexity requires project teams to be adaptive, vigilant, and responsive to external signals.

2.5.1 Characteristics of Environmental Complexity

Environmental complexity is caused by one or more of the following characteristics:

- **Regulatory and legal uncertainty.** Unanticipated regulatory or legal changes can delay approvals, require redesigns, or increase costs.
- **Economic volatility.** Shifting interest rates, inflation, commodity prices, and exchange rates can decrease project viability and stakeholder confidence.
- **Sociopolitical dynamics.** Elections, labor disputes, social movements, and community resistance may delay project timelines and diminish public support.

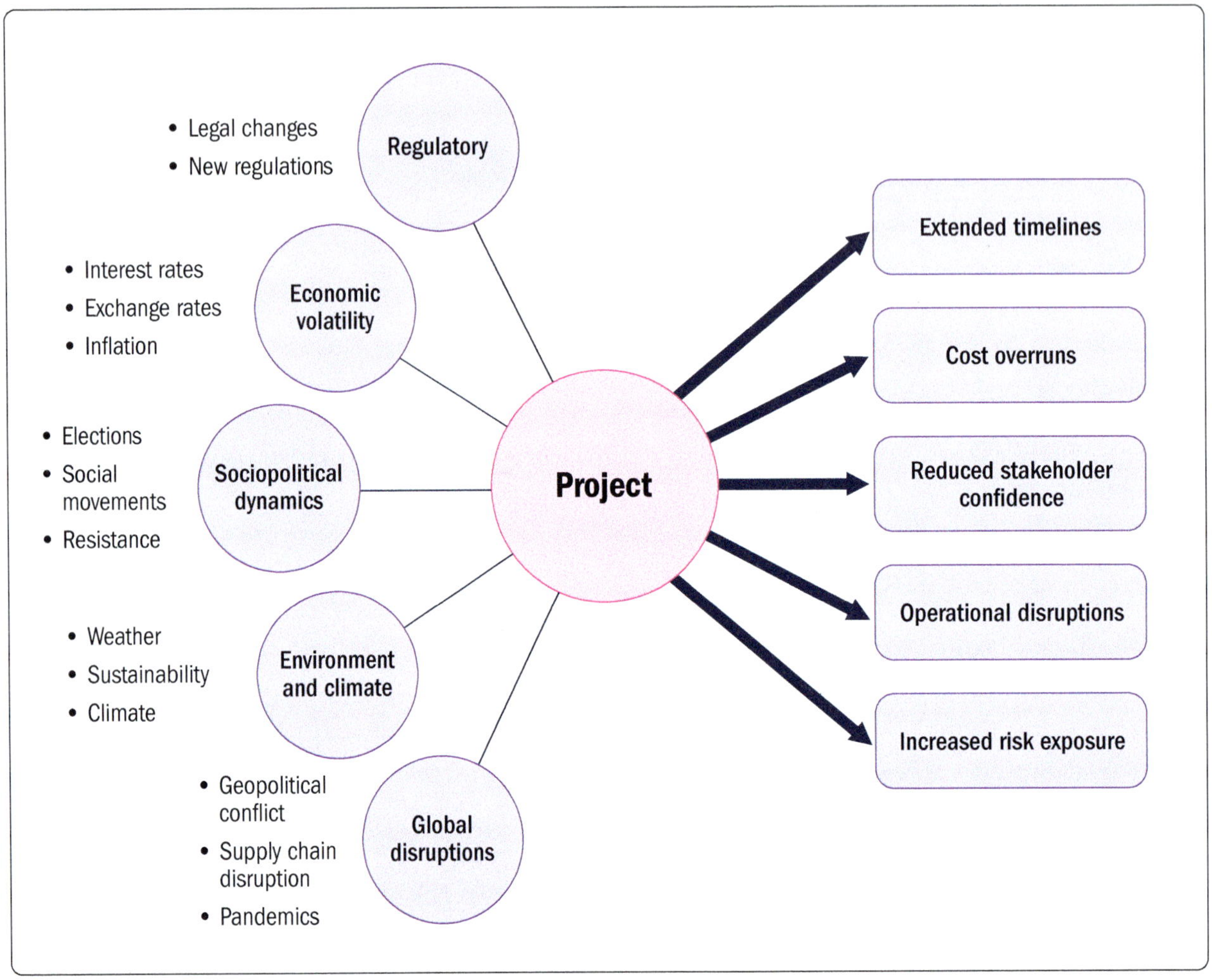

Figure 2-4. Environmental Complexity Model

- **Environmental and climate factors.** Extreme weather, climate regulations, and sustainability mandates can slow or halt project progress.
- **Global disruptions.** Events such as pandemics, geopolitical conflicts, and supply chain disruptions might suddenly impact access to resources, labor, and capital.

Figure 2-4 shows how characteristics of environmental complexity can impact a project, leading to unfavorable results if left unaddressed.

2.5.2 Impact of Environmental Complexity

Environmental complexity introduces risk and uncertainty that can undermine even well-planned projects. The potential impact of environmental complexity may include:

- **Extended timelines.** Regulatory changes, sociopolitical disruptions, or environmental events can delay approvals, permitting, or project execution.

- **Cost overruns.** Economic volatility, supply chain disruptions, and unplanned compliance measures may increase project budgets.
- **Reduced stakeholder confidence.** Shifting political, social, or economic conditions can erode trust and support among investors, regulators, or communities.
- **Operational disruption.** Extreme weather, global events, or sudden regulatory mandates may interrupt project activities or limit access to resources.
- **Increased risk exposure.** Unpredictable external events amplify the likelihood of cascading impacts across project systems.

2.5.3 Strategies for Environmental Complexity

Strategies for managing environmental complexity emphasize anticipation, adaptability, and resilience rather than control. Projects with environmental complexity benefit from the following approaches:

- **Scenario planning and flexibility.** Integrate scenario-based planning and contingency strategies to anticipate and respond to external shifts.
- **Stakeholder and regulatory engagement.** Proactively engage regulators, communities, and advocacy groups to build trust and reduce resistance.
- **Adaptive governance.** Incorporate mechanisms for reviewing and adjusting project plans as new environmental data emerges.
- **Resilience and sustainability focus.** Prioritize environmental responsibility and community impact to gain long-term support and withstand external pressures.
- **Environmental scanning and assessment.** Regularly assess external factors using tools such as PESTLE (political, economic, sociocultural, technological, legal, environmental) analysis and systematic environmental scanning.

Environmental complexity cannot be eliminated, but awareness, proactive engagement, and adaptive planning help project teams navigate uncertainty and reduce negative outcomes.

Example scenario

A multinational company launched a US$1.2 billion offshore wind farm project. The project had a viable business case and was financially backed by global investors. However, several political, economic, and environmental issues created an increasingly complex situation:

- An election in one of the supporting nations resulted in an administration change that suspended subsidies for foreign-owned projects.
- Local fishing communities organized protests about the perceived ecological disruption, leading to additional environmental impact assessments.
- Geopolitical tensions led to fluctuating steel processing rates, which delayed turbine shipments.

2.6 Technological Complexity

Technological complexity refers to the degree of difficulty involved in selecting, integrating, and maintaining technology solutions that align with a project's goals and organizational capabilities. This complexity arises from the rapid pace of technological innovation; the need to integrate new systems with legacy infrastructure; and the requirement to manage data security, interoperability, and technical uncertainty.

It frequently occurs in digital transformation initiatives; smart infrastructure development; automation projects; and technical initiatives related to AI, cloud platforms, or cybersecurity. Technological complexity may also arise due to engineering-intensive technologies, where physical systems, operational constraints, and life cycle considerations play a central role.

2.6.1 Characteristics of Technological Complexity

Technological complexity may be influenced by the following factors:

- **Rapid technological evolution.** Emerging technologies, such as AI, machine learning (ML), blockchain, or quantum computing, evolve quickly, outpacing an organization's ability to adopt or fully understand their implications.
- **Legacy system integration.** Outdated and modern systems coexist, creating interoperability issues, data incompatibility, and unforeseen integration failures.
- **Cybersecurity and data protection.** Projects shall manage cybersecurity risks, comply with data privacy laws, and protect against evolving digital threats.
- **Unproven tools and methods.** Adoption of immature platforms with limited documentation, vendor support, or performance benchmarks increases risk.
- **Skill gaps and expertise.** Teams may lack in-house expertise in new technologies, increasing reliance on specialized consultants or training.
- **Vendor and supplier dependency.** Dependence on vendors or suppliers may introduce additional coordination, risk, or cost considerations, while also creating opportunities to access specialized expertise, accelerate delivery, or enhance innovation.

Figure 2-5 shows various types of technological complexity. Effective management requires cross-functional collaboration, technical assessments, and early alignment among project, IT, and security teams.

2.6.2 Impact of Technological Complexity

Technological complexity can affect project outcomes in several ways:

- **Increased risk of delays and rework.** Technical uncertainties and integration failures can cause delays, rework, or scope changes.
- **Higher implementation costs.** Specialized tools, cybersecurity protocols, or system upgrades often require unplanned investments.
- **Change resistance.** Teams unfamiliar with new technologies may resist adoption, creating barriers to implementation.

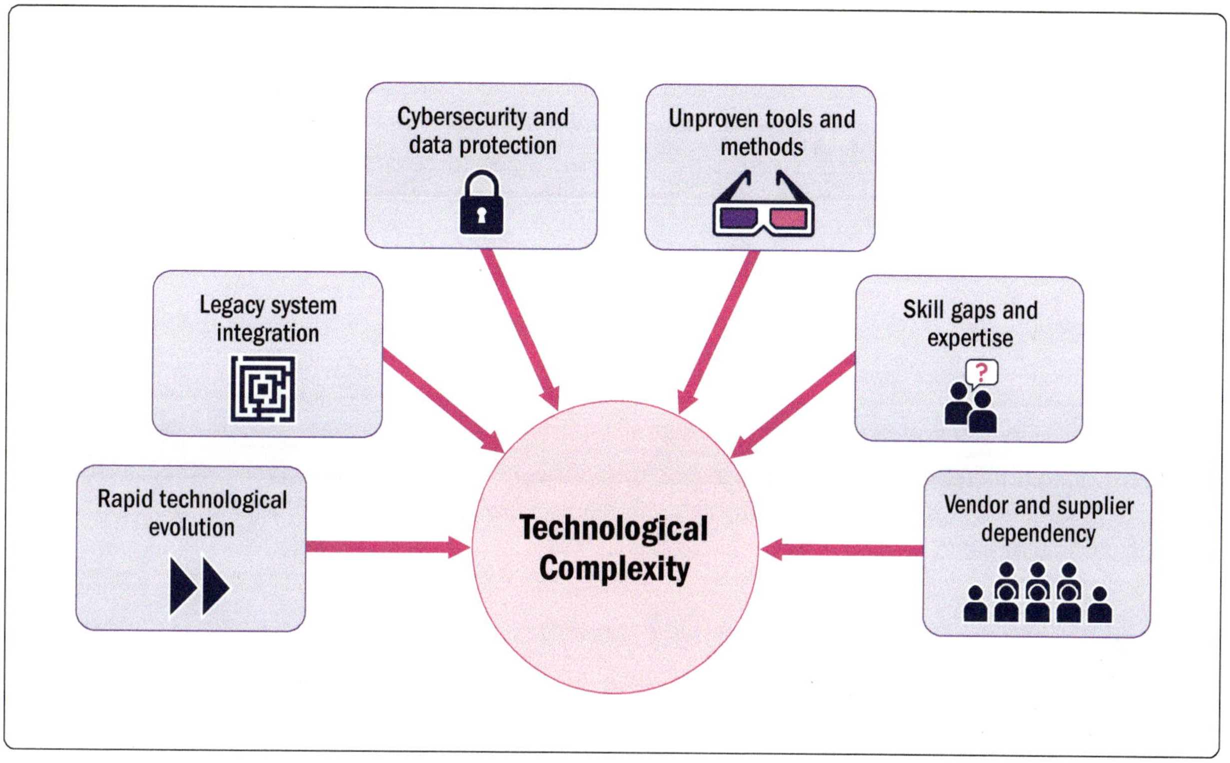

Figure 2-5. Technological Complexity Model

- **Need for agile and iterative delivery models.** High-tech projects benefit from methods that allow continuous testing, learning, and course correction.
- **Importance of early technical readiness reviews.** Assessments and pilot testing before full-scale deployment help clarify feasibility and mitigate risk.
- **Innovation opportunity.** Technological complexity can create opportunities for differentiation, improved performance, and innovation if managed proactively.

2.6.3 Strategies for Technological Complexity

To navigate technological complexity, project practitioners may benefit from the following strategies:

- **Cross-functional collaboration.** Involve IT, security, engineering, operations, and project teams early in the process.
- **Iterative approaches.** Use short cycles to test, learn, and adapt technologies.
- **Technology readiness assessments.** Conduct pilot tests and feasibility studies before full deployment.
- **Skills development and knowledge transfer.** Invest in training and knowledge sharing to reduce reliance on external experts.
- **Vendor management and contract controls.** Establish clear expectations, service level agreements (SLAs), and contingency plans with technology suppliers.

Example scenario

A national healthcare network undertakes a digital transformation initiative to unify patient records across 200 hospitals, clinics, and urgent care facilities. The healthcare network is integrating different systems, some that are decades old, into a new AI-driven health information platform. Elements that introduce technological complexity include:

- AI systems require real-time, secure access to patient data;
- Rapid evolution of AI tools often leads to component upgrades midimplementation;
- Lack of internal expertise, which requires contracting with multiple external vendors; and
- Inexperience with AI governance in the organization.

Coordinating the architectures and schedules from different vendors, mapping the new system, and testing data integrity while maintaining uninterrupted clinical operations challenge the team's agility and resilience.

2.7 Organizational Complexity

Organizational complexity refers to the intricate and multifaceted nature of modern organizations. Complex organizations contain many interconnected elements, specialized roles, extensive communication channels, and often have diverse goals and unclear project boundaries, requiring careful coordination and management.

Projects that involve complex organizations experience complexity that stems from task division, cross-unit coordination, technology use, organizational scale, and stakeholder diversity.

2.7.1 Characteristics of Organizational Complexity

Organizational complexity results from multiple, interacting factors. These factors can be categorized into the following three dimensions:

- **Structural factors.** How the organization is designed and configured.
- **Behavioral/cultural factors.** How people interact and collaborate.
- **Contextual factors**. External factors such as globalization and market volatility.

These factors interact, creating emergent challenges that cannot be managed in isolation.

Characteristics of organizational complexity caused by structural factors may include:

- **Interdependence and interrelations.** Changes in one area of the organization can unexpectedly affect others, creating cascading effects that require coordination, communication, and oversight. This effect is heightened in matrix organizations, where resources are shared across functional boundaries.
- **Division of labor and specialized roles**. Breaking work into specialized activities improves efficiency but creates coordination challenges, especially across locations. Functional silos can develop when specialized teams operate independently without sufficient oversight and coordination.

Characteristics of organizational complexity caused by behavioral and cultural factors may include:

- **Stakeholder diversity and competing interests.** Complex organizations involve many stakeholders with differing priorities and agendas. These differences span hierarchical levels, functional disciplines, geographic locations, and external partners. When stakeholder incentives and goals are misaligned, organizational complexity increases.
- **Management practices and cultural patterns.** Management approaches, contractor relationships, supplier dependencies, and overlapping methodologies can add layers of complexity. Trust deficits, competing group interests, and informal power dynamics can override formal organizational structures, complicating decision-making. Cultural variation across units and disciplines can further hinder collaboration, particularly when psychological safety is low and information sharing is constrained.

Characteristics of organizational complexity caused by contextual factors may include:

- **Globalization and context dependence.** International projects operate within diverse legal, cultural, and business environments. Each location may have different labor practices, regulatory compliance requirements, and market dynamics. Even within a single country, different business units may encounter distinct regulatory or market contexts.
- **Ambiguity and uncertainty**. Unclear project scope, resource constraints, shifting organizational priorities, evolving technologies, and changing market conditions can introduce uncertainty and ambiguity. When organizational direction is unclear or frequently shifts, maintaining focus and alignment becomes difficult.

2.7.2 Impact of Organizational Complexity

Without careful management, organizational complexity can substantially impact projects, causing different types of challenges depending on the factors that are driving the complexity.

Organizational complexity caused by structural factors may lead to:

- **Coordination challenges.** When integration points are not clearly defined or monitored, projects with interdependent tasks and diverse teams may experience miscommunications, missed handoffs, and rework.
- **Scope and schedule uncertainty.** Ambiguous roles, unclear objectives, and evolving priorities can lead to scope creep and timeline extensions.
- **Decision-making bottlenecks.** Complex reporting structures, layered governance, and unclear decision rights may delay approvals and responses, slowing progress.

Organizational complexity caused by behavioral and cultural factors may lead to:

- **Collaboration breakdowns.** Low trust, psychological safety deficits, or unresolved interpersonal conflicts negatively impact information flow and coordination efforts, slowing progress and preventing innovation.
- **Stakeholder misalignment.** Competing group interests and differing agendas may lead to passive resistance, scope creep driven by political pressure, or coalitions that work against project objectives.

- **Informal power dynamics overriding formal structures.** When informal influence networks dominate, formal governance structures become ineffective. Decisions made in unofficial channels may contradict official guidance, creating confusion and rework.

Organizational complexity caused by contextual factors may lead to:

- **Resource strain.** Managing diverse stakeholders, overlapping responsibilities, and multiple processes can stretch resources, time, and budgets beyond initial estimates.
- **Cultural and contextual conflicts.** Global or multiunit projects may face misalignment due to differing norms, regulations, or organizational priorities, or market conditions.
- **Governance and accountability ambiguity**. When organizational structures span multiple contexts or jurisdictions, decision-making authority, escalation processes, and work accountability may be unclear or ambiguous.

2.7.3 Strategies for Organizational Complexity

To avoid or mitigate negative impacts from organizational complexity, project practitioners can employ targeted strategies based on the specific driving factors within their projects.

To address structural factors that cause organizational complexity, project practitioners should clarify how work is organized and coordinated by:

- Establishing clear decision rights and authority;
- Streamlining reporting processes;
- Simplifying governance and clarifying roles;
- Mapping dependencies and managing interfaces; and
- Coordinating planning and scheduling.

To address behavioral and cultural factors that cause organizational complexity, project practitioners should foster trust, alignment, and effective collaboration by:

- Focusing on stakeholder engagement and coalition building;
- Building trust and psychological safety across teams;
- Supporting cross-functional collaboration and team integration efforts; and
- Using adaptive leadership approaches and sensemaking strategies.

To address contextual factors that cause organizational complexity, project practitioners should analyze the environment and adapt to local conditions by:

- Surveying the environment for regulatory, market, and geopolitical shifts;
- Localizing processes while maintaining strategic alignment across teams;
- Enabling flexible governance and planning approaches to accommodate changes; and
- Optimizing resources and building team capabilities.

The effectiveness of these strategies depends on the quality of leadership and governance. Successful navigation of organizational complexity is supported by:

- Strong executive sponsorship and alignment;
- Adaptive governance structures;
- Mature project and program management practices; and
- Continuous organizational learning.

Organizations that employ these strategies will be better able to maintain alignment, respond to uncertainty, and achieve project objectives despite complex structures.

Figure 2-6 depicts the three categories of factors that drive organizational complexity. The outer ring represents leadership, governance, and organizational capability. This moderating factor may amplify or mitigate organizational complexity, depending on how well-aligned and adaptive leadership practices are.

Example scenario

A global consumer goods enterprise initiates a sustainability program aimed at achieving net-zero emissions by 2035. The initiative includes 20 countries on four continents and spans marketing, procurement, manufacturing, logistics, and research and development.

Structural complexity factors arise from interdependencies across functions and geographies, compounded by the introduction of carbon accounting. Manufacturing decisions affect procurement and supplier relationships, whereas logistics choices directly influence emissions outcomes. Operating across 20 countries with different supply chains, capabilities, and regulations creates numerous coordination points. Unclear decision rights, particularly between corporate sustainability leaders and regional executives, further increased complexity.

Behavioral and cultural complexity factors include diverse stakeholder priorities and local contexts. Business units operate under different regulatory, cultural, and market conditions, which requires local adaptation while maintaining alignment with global strategy. Regional leaders oppose mandates they perceive as disconnected from local realities; procurement teams raise cost concerns; and manufacturing teams resist changes that threaten production stability.

Contextual complexity factors include uncertainty and change in the external environment. Carbon accounting regulations vary by country and evolve over time, whereas supply chain disruptions affect schedules and emissions targets. Shifting market conditions influence customer willingness to absorb higher costs associated with sustainable products, increasing ambiguity in planning and execution.

To address the challenges caused by structural factors, the project team establishes a global steering committee with regional representation to clarify decision rights for strategic and operational choices and strengthen coordination between procurement and manufacturing. To address behavioral and cultural challenges, they engage regional leaders in designing targets, supported by cross-regional working groups and transparent communication about trade-offs. Contextual factors are addressed by regular reviews of regulatory trends, flexible timelines and targets, and regional tailoring supported by a shared strategic framework. Executive sponsorship from the CEO, adaptive governance, and investment in sustainability and carbon accounting capabilities support ongoing alignment as conditions change.

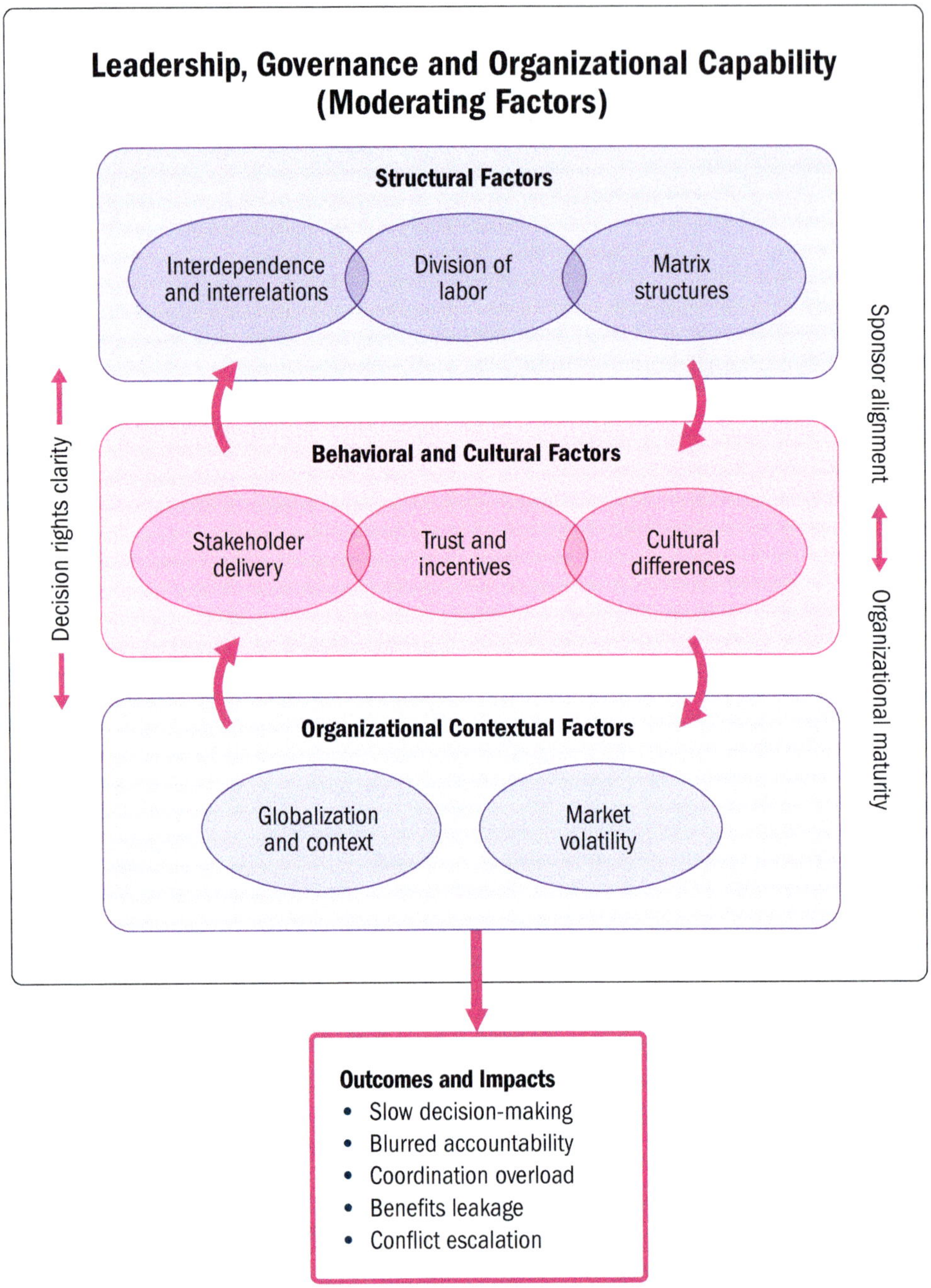

Figure 2-6. Organizational Complexity Model

2.8 Summary

This section established an approach for recognizing and categorizing six primary types of project complexity. Each complexity type presents distinct characteristics and management considerations, yet projects often encounter multiple types simultaneously, creating compound effects. The complexity types discussed include the following:

- **Structural complexity.** Numerous interrelated components require coordination.
- **Dynamic complexity.** Temporal variations, feedback loops, and emergent properties.

- **Human and sociopolitical complexity.** Interpersonal, cultural, and political dynamics.
- **Environmental complexity.** External forces beyond project control.
- **Technological complexity.** Challenges related to technological solutions.
- **Organizational complexity.** Intricate organizational structures, approaches, and stakeholder networks.

Understanding and recognizing complexity types enables project practitioners to anticipate challenges and apply context-specific strategies. This approach supports movement from complexity recognition to complexity navigation, enabling project practitioners to transform complexity challenges into competitive advantages.

Part 2

Foundations for Navigating Complexity

Part 2 of this practice guide provides foundational content. It provides a basis for thinking about how to work with complex projects. It provides an overview of systems thinking and considerations for selecting development approaches for complex projects. There are two sections in Part 2:

- **Section 3 Systems Thinking and Complexity Theory.** Section 3 provides an overview of systems thinking and complexity theory. Using systems thinking as a lens to view complex projects helps project practitioners navigate and make sense of interdependencies.
- **Section 4 Development Approaches for Complexity.** Section 4 introduces guidelines for selecting appropriate approaches to address different levels and types of complexity.

These sections lay the groundwork for navigating complexity by providing structured ways to think about and organize complex projects.

Section 3

Systems Thinking and Complexity Theory

3.1 Introduction

Complex projects require two complementary ways of thinking: systems thinking and complexity theory. Systems thinking focuses on understanding a system and its component parts, and complexity theory centers on strategies for adapting to dynamic and unpredictable project environments. When systems thinking and complexity theory are both incorporated into ways of working, they provide a balance of structure with agility. These ideas support the design of resilient and adaptable systems that can withstand the challenges that complexity brings.

This section details the aspects of systems thinking and complexity theory that support project practitioners as they navigate complex projects. The section includes the following subsections:

- Fundamentals of Systems Thinking
- Fundamentals of Complexity Theory
- Purposeful Systems
- Leverage Points
- System Dynamics Theory

Exploring these theories and ideas provides theoretical support for the practical approaches that are discussed in subsequent sections.

3.2 Fundamentals of Systems Thinking

Systems thinking is a holistic approach that views projects as interconnected systems, recognizing how people, processes, technology, and the working environment interact; and how feedback loops, time delays, and interdependencies shape patterns and outcomes over time.

A systems thinking mindset views projects as interconnected wholes, rather than as a collection of parts. This mindset focuses on examining relationships between system parts to see how they work together to produce an outcome.

Figure 3-1 shows two interconnected systems that are part of a larger system that includes people, processes, technology, and the organization.

3.2.1 Holism

Holism states that a system should be analyzed as a whole, not just as a collection of parts. The concept is often contrasted with reductionism, which attempts to understand systems by analyzing their individual components. Holism suggests that the whole is greater than the sum of its parts.

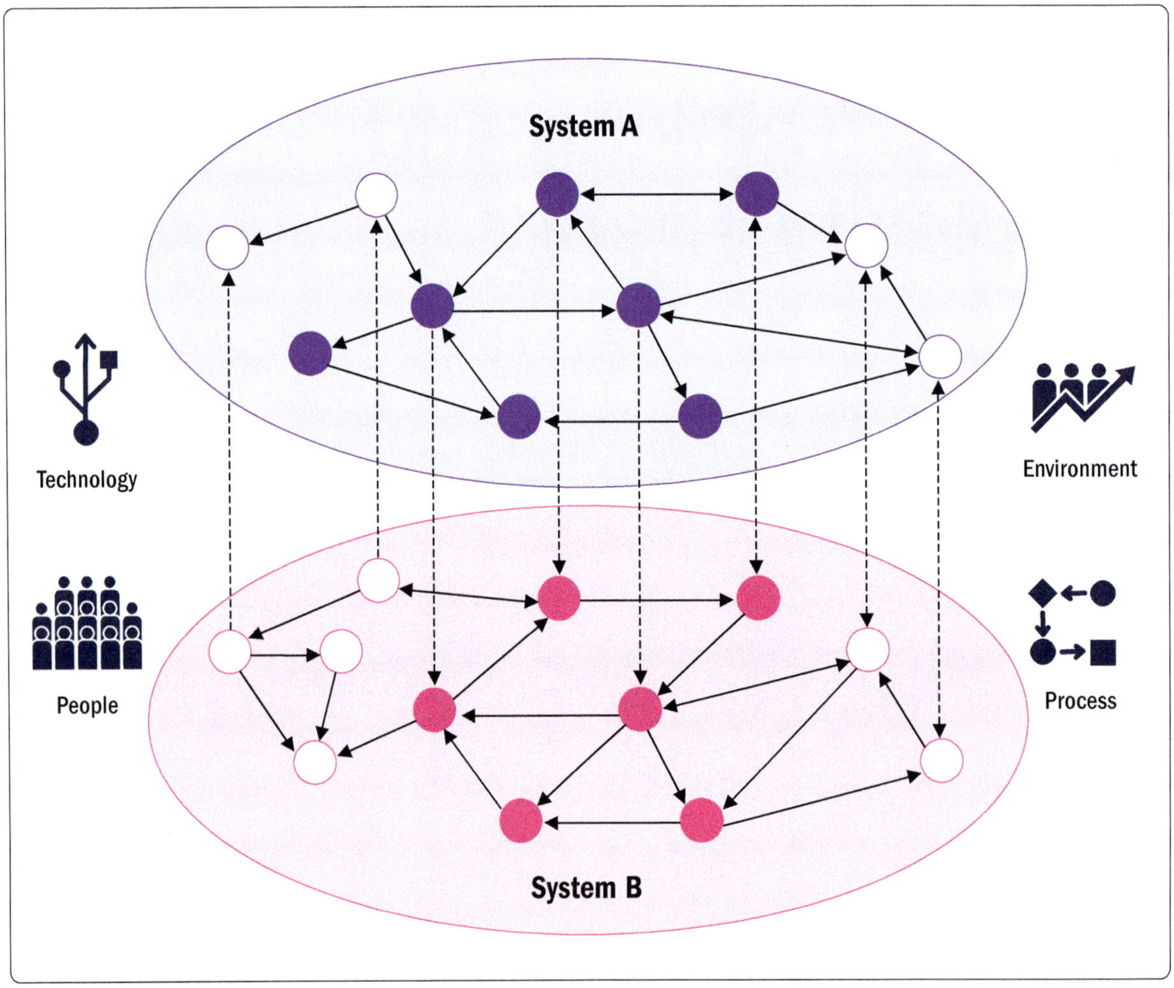

Figure 3-1. Systems Thinking

Understanding a system and predicting its behavior requires examining both the system components and how they interact with one another. Interactions between parts introduce dynamics and outcomes that cannot be predicted from the parts alone.

Example scenario

In a project team, individual competencies are important, but the team dynamics, culture, and collaboration patterns determine the project outcome. A team made up of high-performing individuals will be successful only if the team members are able to collaborate effectively.

Holistic thinking insists that context matters. Systems should be understood within their environment, because environmental factors influence how the system behaves. Project managers who think holistically consider all enterprise environmental factors (EEFs) in designing systems. This holistic approach results in systems that are more effective and resilient than those designed to consider independent variables alone.

3.2.2 Interconnectedness

Interconnectedness is the condition in which elements of a system are linked, with changes in one part influencing other parts of the system overall. In a holistic system, each part affects—and is affected by—other parts; no component functions in complete isolation. As the parts of a system influence one another, they create feedback loops that impact future system behavior.

Due to interconnectedness, a decision or change in one area can create a chain reaction across the system, and predicting outcomes in complex systems is difficult. As such, a small decision might trigger cascading effects in planning cycles, delivery rhythms, user satisfaction, and even team morale. The more interconnected a system is, the more vulnerable it is to systemic risk.

Example scenario

In global supply chain management, an event in a single location, such as a port strike, factory closure, or force majeure, can have widespread effects.

3.2.3 Applications in Project Management

Systems thinking is particularly relevant in project management. In project management, optimizing specific tasks, timelines, or performance in isolation from the broader project can inadvertently result in adverse outcomes, diminishing overall project success. By understanding projects holistically, project professionals can more effectively plan for risks and interactions. A system-based approach equips project professionals with the ability to anticipate and manage interconnectedness more efficiently than an approach that focuses on optimizing individual components.

Systems thinking also helps project practitioners prioritize long-term impact over short-term fixes. This aspect of systems thinking is especially helpful in large-scale infrastructure projects. The absence of systems thinking in such projects frequently results in costly rework, incomplete or suboptimal functionalities, and insufficient capacity for future enhancements.

Example scenario

A metropolitan transit system designed with a projected life cycle exceeding a century demands a forward-looking, systems-oriented perspective to help ensure long-term viability, adaptability, and value.

3.3 Fundamentals of Complexity Theory

Complexity theory is the study of how complex systems, composed of many interacting components, exhibit unpredictable emergent and nonlinear behavior. The theory focuses on understanding how patterns and behaviors emerge from interactions in dynamic and adaptive systems. This theory also adds the concept of uncertainty to systems thinking. Whereas systems thinking reflects a system that is structured and can be mapped and understood, complexity theory reflects evolving and unpredictable systems.

As shown in Figure 3-2, complexity theory builds on systems thinking by considering emergence, nonlinear causality, and complex adaptive systems (CAS).

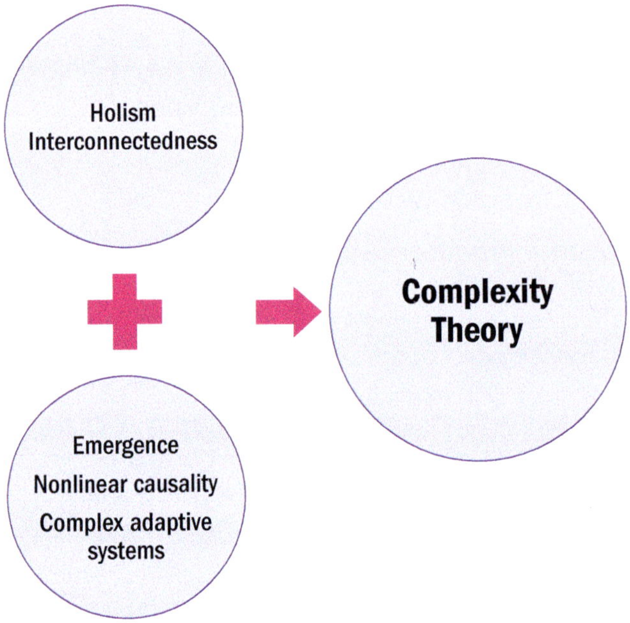

Figure 3-2. Complexity Theory

3.3.1 Emergence

Emergence describes the development of novel patterns, characteristics, or behaviors that result from interactions among system elements and cannot be understood by examining individual components on their own. Emergence often happens during project execution, when unanticipated risks and demands are introduced by interactions among people, processes, technology, and the environment.

Example scenario

An organization implemented an AI program to analyze customer behavior in various markets. During testing, it became apparent that the program was introducing bias into its results. This risk was not accounted for during planning. It emerged based on the specific data that was being analyzed and the way the AI program interacted with that data.

3.3.2 Nonlinear Causality

Nonlinear causality is a relationship in which cause and effect are not directly proportional, where small changes can produce disproportionately large effects. Due to nonlinear causality, in complex systems, the effect of a change or intervention is not predictable.

In contrast to linear causality, where an action or input causes a predictable outcome, nonlinear causality introduces loops, delays, and interactions that make the effect emergent, amplified, delayed, or diffused.

Example scenario

A consumer healthcare company developed a new mobile app. During development, a minor tweak to a planned feature caused cascading effects to processes, including testing, documentation, and compliance reviews. This small change led to a disproportionately large impact, causing months of delay.

3.3.3 Complex Adaptive Systems

A complex adaptive system (CAS) is an interdependent system (not independent) composed of interconnected people, processes, and systems (agents) whose behavior evolves through feedback, learning, and interaction with a dynamic environment. The components within a CAS continuously adapt to internal and external changes, thus exhibiting emergent behavior.

A CAS self-organizes and evolves, especially when facing change or uncertainty. A CAS learns to evolve over time through feedback and interaction.

Example scenario

Agile software development teams include members who have different skills with high interconnectedness. Team members adapt their behavior based on retrospectives, stakeholder feedback, and changing priorities.

Figure 3-3 illustrates how the CAS receives information from the environment and disseminates information to the environment. Based on this information, the components of the system (interconnected people, processes, and systems) receive positive or negative feedback. The components also receive information from the environment and disseminate information to the environment. The combination of feedback from the system and information in the environment contributes to emergent behavior, which becomes an input to the CAS; this cycle is continuous.

3.3.4 Applications in Project Management

Many modern projects are not predictable, linear, or controllable. Assuming these projects function as a CAS, they can enable better implementation by building in the expectation of change and evolution. Managing a CAS requires a leadership paradigm of facilitation rather than control. For

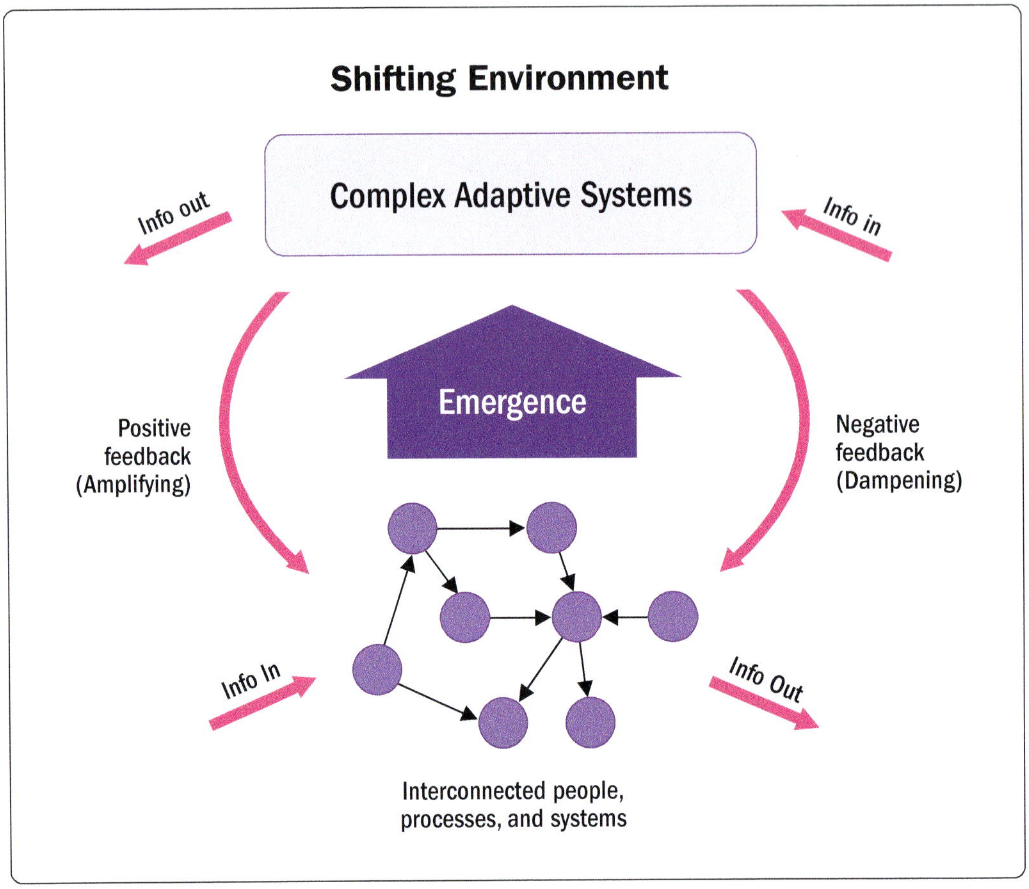

Figure 3-3. Complex Adaptive Systems

these projects, planning is adaptive, teams are trained to expect emergence, and frequent feedback encourages reflection and learning.

Adaptive thinking refers to the capacity to modify one's perspectives, strategies, and actions in response to evolving circumstances, newly emerging information, or unforeseen challenges. In the context of project management, this cognitive flexibility is essential for navigating a CAS, which involves dynamic environments, evolving stakeholder needs, and changes in scope, risk, or resources. This type of thinking reflects an openness to continuous learning and a readiness to realign project approaches as conditions shift.

Adaptive thinking enables project practitioners to do the following:

- **Navigate uncertainty** by responding effectively to disruptions, unforeseen risks, and shifting project parameters;
- **Enhance decision-making** by incorporating diverse perspectives and integrating new data to refine plans and strategies;
- **Address complexity** by developing innovative and context-sensitive solutions to multidimensional project challenges;

- **Promote continuous improvement** by fostering a learning-oriented culture that embraces experimentation and iterative refinement; and
- **Help ensure long-term relevance** by aligning project outcomes with emerging technologies, evolving stakeholder needs, and broader organizational objectives.

By using adaptive thinking, teams are able to align immediate actions with a broader, long-term strategic vision, helping ensure short-term execution contributes meaningfully to sustained project success. In response to increasing complexity, many industries have assumed adaptive practices such as role flexibility, decentralized decision-making, and rapid feedback mechanisms. These approaches support a mindset well-suited to complex project environments, where the ability to adapt to emerging conditions and strategic changes is critical.

3.4 Purposeful Systems

A purposeful system is a system in which individual elements, such as people or organizations, work together to achieve a shared goal or objective. When a CAS has a clear objective and its components are capable of making purposeful decisions, it is a purposeful system.

Purposeful systems encourage alignment of individual and organizational goals. Figure 3-4 differentiates a purposeful system from a self-organizing system—a system that develops order and structure without centralized control. The shared goals and objectives that define a purposeful system help organizations become more intelligent, adaptive, and effective in a complex world.

Purposeful systems are goal-oriented adaptive systems that are designed to achieve specific outcomes. Human behavior is an integral part of a purposeful system that determines if a purposeful system will achieve its desired outcomes.

People are active agents who have their own goals, make decisions, and adapt based on feedback from the environment. Their actions are shaped by both personal goals and systemic constraints such as policies and culture. The performance of a system depends on how the people within it interpret information, respond to incentives, and interact with one another.

Because of this individual agency, purposeful systems benefit from aligning explicit goals with implicit goals. Explicit goals directly communicate desired behavior and outcomes. For example, a company

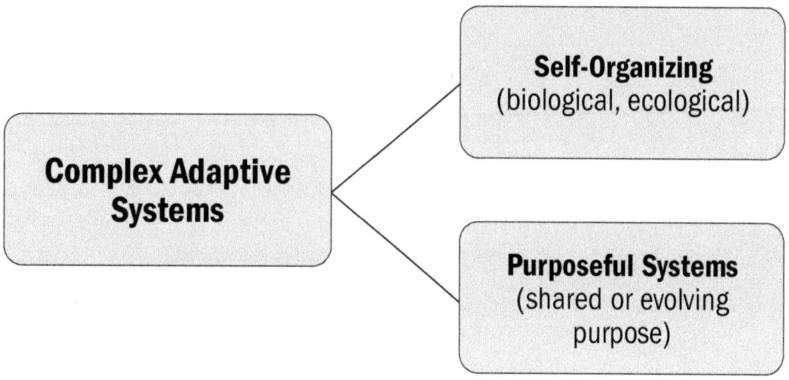

Figure 3-4. Purposeful Systems

handbook is a source of explicit goals. Implicit goals communicate desired behavior and outcomes indirectly, through rewards and punishments and encouragement and discouragement. A manager's praise, critical feedback, or promotion decisions are all sources of implicit goals.

Contradictions between implicit and explicit goals create tension that undermines organizational purpose. For example, a company that explicitly promotes collaboration but determines employee raises on individual performance alone may be implicitly rewarding competitive rather than collaborative behavior. Moreover, people adjust their behavior based on feedback loops. For example, if a team is rewarded for speed over quality, members will prioritize faster delivery, even at the cost of defects. This demonstrates how the system's structure drives behavior.

Human behavior is influenced by deep beliefs and assumptions that are part of the system. By acknowledging human behavior as an important and dynamic system component, leaders can build environments that align individual and organizational purposes, leading to more effective and sustainable outcomes.

3.5 Leverage Points

Leverage points are places within a complex system where a small shift in one element can produce significant changes in the larger system. Leverage points can be thought of as "pressure points" within a system. Placing effort on a targeted area creates a greater impact than distributing that effort across the entire system.

Leverage points illustrate the principle of nonlinear causality: Small, well-placed changes can create disproportionately large effects. A common mistake leaders make in complex systems is to focus on fixing isolated problems without addressing the deeper structures that generate those problems. Leverage points help project practitioners focus their effort where it will have the most impact.

This section introduces common types of leverage points, as well as guidance on how to identify leverage points in context.

3.5.1 Meadows' 12 Leverage Points

Donella Meadows' paper, "Leverage Points: Places to Intervene in a System," introduces 12 types of leverage points that can be used to impact a complex system. [3] Figure 3-5 lists Meadows' 12 leverage points.

These leverage points, in the order of least possible impact on a project to the largest possible impact on a project, are as follows:

- **Constants, parameters, numbers.** Changing values like budgets, taxes, or performance standards can be a common way to intervene in systems. These adjustments usually only fine-tune outcomes rather than fundamentally alter how the system behaves.
- **Buffers.** The term buffer refers to the size of a reserve compared to the flow moving through it. Inventory in a supply chain and savings within a budget are both examples of buffers. Increasing the size of buffers can make systems more stable, but systems with excess buffers may be slower to adapt to change.

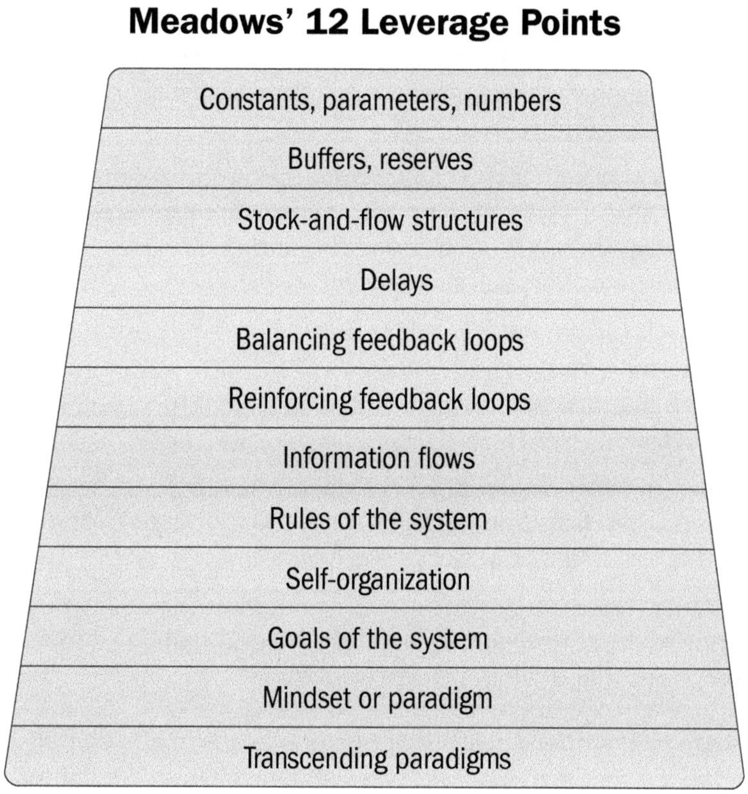

Figure 3-5. Meadows' 12 Leverage Points

- **Stock-and-flow structures.** The physical or organizational structure of resources or people in a system shapes how that system functions. Changes to these structures can have a big impact. However, once they are in place, they can be difficult and expensive to redesign. Some structures may be easier to change than others. For example, teams are easier to reorganize than road networks.
- **Delays.** A delay is the time between an action and its effect. When delays are long, systems can become unstable or overreact. Shorter delays usually make systems more responsive. For example, a software change that makes project performance data accessible daily rather than monthly will allow leaders to adapt their approach more readily in response to feedback.
- **Balancing feedback loops.** Balancing feedback loops can help keep a system stable by counteracting change. These loops are critical for regulating systems over time. For example, on a project that is running over budget, more oversight or tighter spend controls may counteract the overages.
- **Reinforcing feedback loops.** Reinforcing feedback loops can amplify change in either a positive or negative direction. For example, recognizing and rewarding excellent work reinforces that behavior. Once a reinforcing feedback loop is implemented, it can drive rapid growth or decline.
- **Information flows.** The flow of information determines who has access to information and at what time. Changes to information flow can dramatically impact behavior and decision-making across a system. For example, increasing access to financial results can help team leaders set effective performance goals.

- **Rules of the system.** Rules define what actions are possible or rewarded within a system. System rules, such as incentives, penalties, and organizational policies, can create the boundaries within which people operate. Implementing changes to rules can powerfully impact individual behavior, which in turn impacts system performance.
- **Self-organization.** Self-organization is the capacity of a system to adapt, learn, and create new structures on its own. Systems that are able to self-organize are more resilient and have a higher chance of long-term survival. Shifting from a command-and-control mindset to a facilitative mindset encourages teams to self-organize.
- **Goals of the system.** Every system has a purpose, even if that purpose is implicit or hidden. Shifting goals can change the direction and outcomes of the entire system. For example, changing the explicit purpose of an organization from profit maximization to sustainability maximization can have a substantial impact.
- **Mindset or paradigm.** A mindset or paradigm is a deeply held belief or assumption that shapes how people see the world. Mindsets and paradigms are the foundation for goals, rules, and structures. Changing them is difficult but can powerfully transform system behavior.
- **Transcending paradigms.** The most powerful leverage point is the ability to step outside of—and change—the underlying mindset from which a system arises. Changing a mindset or paradigm transforms the assumptions that drive the entire system.

These 12 types of leverage points offer powerful opportunities to change complex systems. The first step toward making those changes is to identify leverage points within the context of a system.

3.5.2 Identifying Leverage Points by System Type

Different types of systems have different types of leverage points. For example, holistic systems that are not complex will respond to structural leverage points such as changing a feedback loop or adjusting a delay. Complex adaptive systems can respond to different types of leverage points depending on how the system evolves. A team within a CAS might conduct experiments or adjust interactions to respond to a change in the system. Purposeful systems benefit from leverage points that shift the intent or goal of the system such as reframing the shared purpose.

Table 3-1 describes which leverage points are effective within different types of systems. These systems are organized from the least complex to the most complex.

Because leverage points can create a disproportionate impact, small, safe-to-fail experiments are a practical way to test interventions before scaling them. This approach allows project practitioners to explore options, learn from outcomes, and adjust without causing harm to the wider system.

3.6 System Dynamics Theory

The next level of systems thinking to explore in this section *is system dynamics theory*. Systems dynamics is the quantitative aspect of systems thinking. Where systems thinking provides a qualitative, holistic, and interconnected conceptual framework, systems dynamics theory operationalizes systems thinking by using models and simulations.

Table 3-1. Comparing Leverage Point Types

System Type	Leverage Point Type	Description	Example
Predictable system	Structural	Change a feedback loop.	Add real-time inventory tracking to reduce stockouts (strengthens balancing feedback).
Predictable system	Structural	Adjust a delay.	Reduce customer response time to improve the satisfaction feedback loop.
Complex adaptive system	Conditional	Enable experimentation.	Allow safe-to-fail trials to test new workflows before scaling up.
Complex adaptive system	Conditional	Adjust interactions.	Alter communication patterns to create cross-functional learning to improve innovation.
Purposeful system	Intentional	Reframe shared purpose.	Refine the goals such as move from maximizing profit to creating sustainable value.
Purposeful system	Intentional	Build psychological safety.	Enable open dialogue and discuss dissent to surface smaller issues before they escalate.

System dynamics theory allows project practitioners to determine root causes of problems, visualize interactions over time, and identify leverage points for improvement, thus identifying problems before they are operationalized. There are four methods that are commonly used in system dynamics:

- Feedback, delay, and change;
- Stock-and-flow models;
- Causal loop diagrams; and
- Simulation models.

Although only simulation models are effective when complexity is present, all of the methods support the application of systems thinking principles to project components. The following sections provide additional details about each method.

3.6.1 Feedback, Delay, and Change

In systems thinking, *feedback* refers to a process where a system's output is looped back as an input, influencing future behavior. Feedback helps a system regulate, adapt, or amplify desired behavior. There are two types of feedback: negative, which reduces change to moderate system behavior, and positive, which amplifies change and accelerates system behavior. Positive feedback can lead to exponential growth or collapse.

Example scenario

Agile teams use reviews to receive feedback from the customer and retrospective reviews to reflect on iteration performance and the need for process changes.

Delay is the time gap between an action (the cause) and its observable result (the effect). Long delays mask cause-and-effect relationships, making systems harder to manage. For example, stakeholders might not notice declining team morale until employee turnover increases. This is a perceptual delay. Process or decision delays can occur when approvals, escalations, or governance steps slow project execution.

Unrecognized delays can lead to overreaction, underreaction, or misdiagnosis. For example, people may assume a decision or intervention is unsuccessful because there have been no measurable results. However, the system may need more time to respond before showing results. Delayed feedback may cause systems to behave nonlinearly, with outcomes appearing suddenly or disproportionately after a lag.

Change refers to any shift in the state, structure, behavior, or environment of a system. Changes in complex systems are often unpredictable and nonlinear. This lack of predictability creates tension in the system, which may trigger balancing or reinforcing loops. For example, introducing a new process changes workflow, communication patterns, and possibly team culture.

3.6.2 Stock-and-Flow Models

A stock-and-flow model is used to represent how quantities accumulate and change over time in dynamic systems. Essentially, this model shows how the input into a system (stock) relates to the output of a system (flow). Stock-and-flow models help project practitioners visualize and understand how resources, people, information, money, or effort accumulate or deplete over time. Understanding these processes is crucial for analyzing project systems, organizations, or social dynamics.

As shown in Figure 3-6, the key components of the model are stock, inflow, outflow, and the feedback loop:

- *Stock* is the accumulated level of a resource at any given time.
- *Inflow* refers to resources that are added to the stock.
- *Outflow* refers to processes that reduce the stock.
- *Feedback loop* refers to how the stock level affects the flow.

For example, in adaptive projects, stock is the total number of user stories in the product backlog, new stories added by stakeholders provide inflow, and stories completed by the team are the source of outflow. This model allows the inference that if inflow exceeds outflow, the backlog of user stories grows.

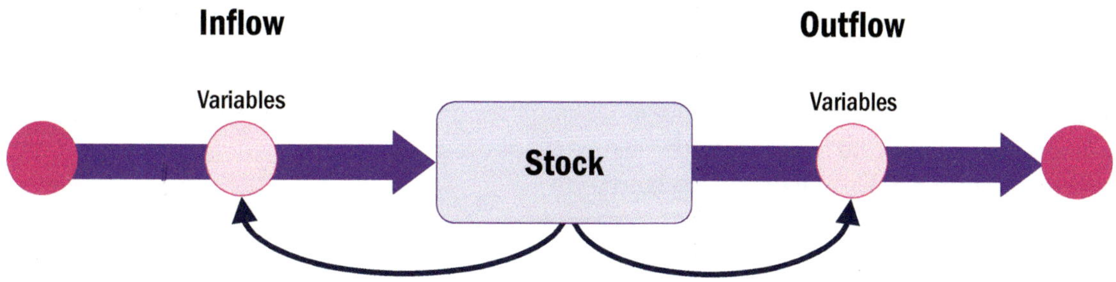

Figure 3-6. Stock-and-Flow Model

Stocks change gradually over time, and systems may react to change slowly. This situation can hide problems until they become severe. These models also visualize feedback loops, which are essential in complex project environments. There are two types of feedback loops:

- **Reinforcing loop.** An automated process leads to success, which leads to increased resources, which leads to more success.
- **Balancing loop.** A request to accelerate work production leads to more bugs, which causes more rework, leading to slower progress, which keeps the work production rate steady.

3.6.3 Causal Loop Diagrams

Causal loop diagrams are visual tools used to represent the feedback structures within a system. These diagrams illustrate the cause-and-effect relationships of variables in a system, helping to identify feedback loops that influence system behavior over time.

Figure 3-7 is an example of a causal loop diagram. The figure shows variables, such as morale, workload, and productivity, with arrows showing causal links as follows:

- A positive symbol "+" indicates a direct causal relationship.
- A "–" indicates an inverse causal relationship.

This diagram shows that a team that starts with good morale accomplishes the workload. But as the workload increases (the "+" sign), the productivity decreases (the "–" sign). Lower productivity adds

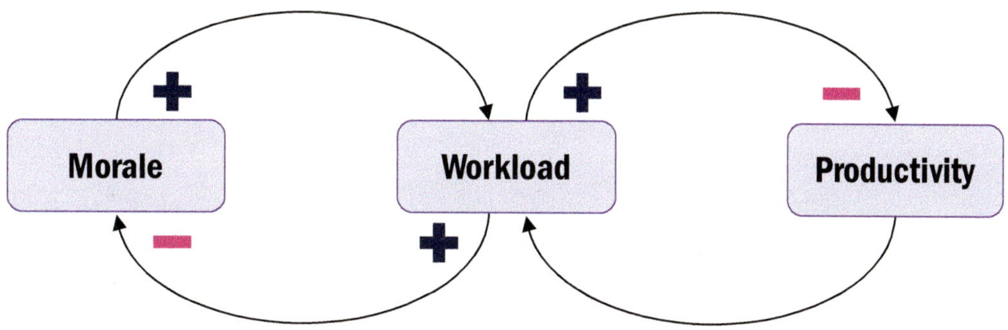

Figure 3-7. Causal Loop Diagram

to the workload, and the increased workload lowers morale. The diagram also shows the feedback loops that can either amplify or stabilize the system's behavior.

Causal loop diagrams are often used in the early stages of problem analysis. Creating and analyzing these diagrams can provide insight into the structure of the problem and help uncover dynamic complexities that may be impacting the system.

3.6.4 Simulation Models

Simulation models use quantitative methods and graphical software to test and analyze how a system behaves over time under various scenarios. The purpose of simulation models is to use mathematical equations that capture the relationships between variables over time.

Simulation models enable decision-makers to test different strategies, forecast outcomes, and better understand long-term consequences in a risk-free environment. The models are particularly useful for policy testing, capacity planning, and scenario analysis.

3.7 Summary

This section examined how systems thinking and complexity theory support project practitioners in navigating complex projects and environments. By embracing holistic perspectives, feedback dynamics, and adaptive learning, project professionals can enhance decision-making, mitigate risks, and improve project outcomes in complex and uncertain conditions.

The section established the relevance of systems thinking and complexity theory to complex projects by discussing:

- The fundamentals of systems thinking, including holism, interconnectedness, and applications to project management;
- The fundamentals of complexity theory, including emergence, nonlinear causality, complex adaptive systems, and applications to project management;
- Purposeful systems and the way that human behavior impacts their success or failure;
- Leverage points, including Meadows' 12 Leverage Points; and
- System dynamics theory, including feedback, delay, change, stock-and-flow models, causal loop diagrams, and simulation models.

These theories, ideas, and models provide the foundation for the complexity management strategies that will be introduced in subsequent sections.

Section 4

Development Approaches for Complexity

4.1 Introduction

Development approaches can be classified on a spectrum or continuum from more predictive or traditional approaches to more adaptive or agile approaches. Predictive approaches tend to work best in stable environments, whereas adaptive approaches are designed to withstand unpredictability. However, all approaches have benefits and drawbacks, and projects benefit from tailoring the methods used to the specific details of the project.

This section explains the main features of commonly used approaches and provides guidance on selecting the optimal approach based on a project's needs and complexity types. The section includes the following subsections:

- Predictive Approaches for Managing Complexity
- Adaptive Approaches for Managing Complexity
- Tailoring Project Approaches
- Adaptive Governance

Understanding these well-established approaches and exploring their relationships to complexity supports project practitioners who are seeking the optimal approach for their projects.

4.2 Predictive Approaches for Managing Complexity

Predictive approaches, also known as waterfall or traditional approaches, are used when scope, schedule, and cost are known, relatively stable, and can be accurately planned. Predictive approaches are effective when the product or result is well-defined, or when regulatory, contractual, or technical requirements necessitate structured planning, monitoring, and controlling.

Typical elements of predictive approaches include the following:

- **Phase-based structure.** Projects progress through defined phases, often with phase gates.
- **Detailed up-front planning.** Scope, schedule, budget, and quality requirements are established before work begins.
- **Change control.** Changes are managed through formal processes and discouraged once baselines are established.
- **Centralized decision-making.** Governance relies on structured hierarchies with formal roles and responsibilities.
- **Documentation-centric delivery.** Plans, requirements, contracts, and progress are documented and audited throughout the project life cycle.

These approaches are suited for complex projects where integration, compliance, and predictability outweigh the need for flexibility.

4.2.1 Benefits of Predictive Approaches

Predictive approaches have significant benefits, including up-front planning and forecasting, monitoring and controlling methods, and risk management.

4.2.1.1 Comprehensive Planning and Forecasting

Projects using predictive approaches complete a comprehensive planning process at the outset of the project. This process includes the development of detailed project management plans, schedules, risk registers, and stakeholder communication strategies. Forecasting in predictive environments often leverages historical data, expert judgment, and deterministic scheduling models. A detailed forecasting process helps stakeholders align expectations, secure funding approvals, and identify potential risks early.

Frequently used planning and forecasting tools include the following:

- Work breakdown structures (WBS),
- Gantt charts,
- Critical path method,
- Resource histograms and cost curves, and
- Monte Carlo simulations (for probabilistic forecasting).

4.2.1.2 Monitoring and Control Mechanisms

Monitoring and control mechanisms are central to predictive approaches. Once the initial plan has been established, project leaders monitor performance using quantitative metrics such as:

- Schedule variance (SV) and cost variance (CV),
- Earned value management (EVM),
- Key performance indicators (KPIs), and
- Change request logs and issue trackers.

Collecting and reviewing this data enables early issue detection, allowing project leaders to take corrective actions. This degree of monitoring and control is critical to managing interdependencies and helping ensure contract compliance for complicated initiatives such as engineering, defense, or infrastructure projects.

4.2.1.3 Risk Identification and Mitigation

Predictive risk management processes are rigorous, involving risk identification, qualitative and quantitative analyses, response planning, and monitoring.

Risk tools often used in predictive projects include the following:

- Risk breakdown structures,
- Risk registers with ownership and response plans;
- Decision trees, modeling, simulation, and sensitivity analysis; and
- Reserve analysis (management and contingency reserves).

Predictive risk management is particularly valuable in projects where legal, safety, or environmental risks should be systematically documented and controlled.

4.2.2 Predictive Approaches for Complex Projects

Projects that take place in a low-volatility environment but require high technical intricacy can benefit from the rigor and foresight that predictive approaches provide. Such projects may involve interconnected systems, advanced technical implementations, or many component parts.

Examples of complex projects that may benefit from predictive approaches include the following:

- Capital infrastructure projects, such as highways, bridges, and rail systems;
- Aerospace and defense initiatives, aircraft design, and satellite launches;
- Pharmaceutical development under strict regulatory oversight; and
- Public sector projects with multiyear procurement and stakeholder engagement requirements.

Example scenario

On the Green Line Light Rail Transit project in Calgary, Alberta, Canada, predictive approaches were employed during the early phases of procurement and civil construction. Extensive baseline planning helped the project team align various city departments, coordinate with external utilities, and comply with public reporting standards. While elements of the project evolved, the delivery strategy benefited from the stability and accountability of predictive practices.

4.2.3 Limitations of Predictive Approaches

Although predictive approaches offer strengths in control and documentation, they often lack the flexibility needed to navigate highly volatile or emergent contexts. Frequently encountered limitations of predictive approaches include the following:

- Resistance to late-stage change,
- Overreliance on up-front assumptions, and
- Difficulty responding to innovation-driven complexity.

To address these limitations, many organizations introduce buffering strategies within predictive frameworks such as the following:

- Allowing for progressive elaboration during design stages,
- Embedding contingency reserve for scope and cost uncertainties, and
- Using rolling wave planning to periodically refresh future tasks.

Complex projects taking place in unpredictable environments may also benefit from a tailored approach, combining some predictive approaches with more flexible approaches. Tailored approaches are further discussed in Section 4.4.

4.3 Adaptive Approaches for Managing Complexity

An adaptive approach is a development approach in which the requirements are subject to high levels of uncertainty and volatility and are likely to change throughout the project. Adaptive approaches emphasize flexibility, rapid decision-making, and continuous learning, reframing change as an opportunity for innovation and improvement.

Typical elements of adaptive approaches include the following:

- **Iterative and incremental development.** Work is broken down into small, manageable increments, enabling stakeholder involvement through early value delivery and feedback.
- **Continuous learning and adaptation.** Project teams are encouraged to learn through ongoing feedback, experimentation, and reflection, and plans and processes are adapted as new insights emerge.
- **Team empowerment.** Teams are self-organizing and empowered to make decisions at the operational level, which increases responsiveness and accelerates problem-solving.

- **Visual management and transparency.** Visual tools, such as kanban boards, burndown charts, and value stream maps, allow teams to monitor progress and bottlenecks, enhancing situational awareness and aligning team efforts.
- **Elimination of waste.** Any activities that do not add value are identified and removed from processes, simplifying workflows and reducing unnecessary complexity.
- **Sustainable pace and team empowerment.** Work is paced consistently to avoid team fatigue and burnout.

These elements are shared by most adaptive approaches. There are two prominent, well-defined adaptive approaches with distinct features that warrant further exploration: Lean and agile.

4.3.1 Lean Management

Lean management is a systematic approach to optimizing operations by eliminating waste, streamlining processes, and maximizing value. This streamlining is achieved through continuous improvement initiatives, empowering employees, and adopting a customer-centric approach to value delivery. A lean approach prioritizes eliminating unnecessary steps, time, and resources, without negatively impacting quality.

There are five principles of lean management:

1. **Identifying value from the customer's perspective.** Determine the outcomes and deliverables that bring value.
2. **Mapping the value stream.** Analyze the project delivery process to identify activities that do not bring value, known as waste.
3. **Creating flow.** Optimize processes so that work moves smoothly and continuously through each stage of the project, without bottlenecks or delays.
4. **Establishing pull systems.** Determine production needs based on demand rather than forecasts or assumptions; activities are "pulled" by real needs, rather than "pushed" by plans.
5. **Pursuing perfection.** Learn from feedback and incorporate process improvements that drive better project outcomes over time.

When applied to projects, these principles help teams improve flow and efficiency. Project practitioners should use the following tools to implement lean principles:

- **Value stream mapping.** Visualize and analyze processes to eliminate waste and increase transparency and situational awareness.
- **Last Planner System® (LPS®).** Use collaborative planning to help ensure reliable task execution.
- **Five whys analysis.** Apply root cause analysis for problems by repeatedly asking "why" to go beyond symptoms and get to the root cause of the problem.
- **Kanban board.** Visualize workflows and manage progress.
- **Daily coordination meetings.** Daily coordination meetings can keep teams aligned and on track.
- **Kaizen event.** Conduct focused improvement workshops to solve specific issues.

Lean principles provide a foundation for agile, which extends them to team-level empowerment and iterative delivery methods.

4.3.2 Agile Approaches

Agile is a term used to describe a mindset of values and principles as set forth in the *Manifesto for Agile Software Development*. Agile values and principles focus on people, communication, and collaboration, rather than rigid processes. The mindset promotes an iterative and incremental approach to project work. Although agile originated in software development, it has been widely adopted across industries such as marketing, product development, and education.

A core tenet of agile approaches is team empowerment. Self-organizing teams decide how to accomplish their work, are accountable for the outcomes, and pursue continuous learning. This effort leads to higher motivation, innovation, and productivity.

Agile teams encourage open communication and risk taking. Regular feedback loops create short cycles of reflection and adjustment that can drive continuous improvement. Common feedback loops include the following:

- **Daily coordination meetings.** Hold short, frequent meetings focused on coordinating work and identifying obstacles.
- **Sprint reviews.** Use dedicated time to review feedback from stakeholders and demonstrate sprint progress.
- **Retrospectives.** Conduct a review of team performance, lessons learned, and opportunities for process improvement.
- **Backlog refinement.** Implement a process of revisiting, reprioritizing, and adjusting remaining tasks or backlog items.

These feedback loops reduce risk, improve quality, and help ensure the product meets real customer needs. Empowered agile teams respond faster to change and solve problems more creatively in complex and changing environments.

4.3.3 Application to High-Uncertainty and Rapidly Changing Contexts

Adaptive approaches, such as lean and agile, are best used in volatile, rapidly changing environments marked by evolving customer needs, technological disruption, and regulatory or geopolitical instability. Success in high-uncertainty environments depends on how quickly a team can adapt and learn.

Adaptive approaches, which embrace iterative learning, collaborative leadership, and continuous feedback mechanisms, help organizations remain competitive and deliver sustained value even in the most unpredictable circumstances.

Example scenario

A tech startup developing innovative digital products has unpredictable requirements, which makes long-term planning less effective. Self-organizing, empowered agile teams that use iterative development cycles can be more effective.

4.4 Tailoring Project Approaches

Most organizations do not rely on purely predictive or adaptive approaches. Projects, especially complex ones, demand flexibility, structure, and adaptability simultaneously. In such cases, project approaches may be tailored to meet the needs of stakeholders and the project environment. A tailored approach includes elements from a continuum of both predictive and adaptive approaches, used in tandem.

Common reasons for tailoring the project approach include the following:

- **Established organizational culture and legacy systems.** Many organizations have established governance frameworks, hierarchical structures, and regulatory requirements that align with predictive approaches. However, they are also under pressure to be more adaptive to rapidly changing environments.
- **Stakeholder expectations.** Executives and sponsors often want the predictability, detailed plans, and cost control of predictive approaches. However, other stakeholders, such as clients, customers, or product users, expect the fast feedback, iterative improvements, and flexibility provided by adaptive approaches.
- **Compliance and risk management.** Regulatory, legal, or safety requirements may necessitate detailed documentation, traceability, and formal controls, which are inherent in predictive approaches. However, teams may want to manage uncertainty, evolving technology, or emerging risks using adaptive tools.
- **Challenges of scaling adaptive approaches.** Scaling adaptive approaches across large programs or enterprises often requires some predictive elements such as roadmaps, stage gates, and coordination structures. Hence, organizations should combine approaches to create a realistic and scalable framework.
- **Transition and maturity.** Many organizations have begun to incorporate adaptive approaches but have yet to fully embed adaptive mindsets and tools into their culture and workflows.

Tailoring is an effective way to balance the tension between control and flexibility. Successfully executing a tailored approach requires careful consideration to determine how to meet project needs. Table 4-1 shows several options for tailoring approaches for different needs.

The tailoring options outlined in Table 4-1 assume a flexible approach for tailoring various project aspects as needed. However, there are options that present a structured approach for blending approaches. The following sections describe two such frameworks: Water-scrum-fall and Scrumban.

Insight

Hybrid project management is often used to describe means for blending predictive and adaptive approaches and techniques on a project. As the information in this section shows, this is a key component to success. However, the term *hybrid* is often used to avoid planning, instead stating that a project is using a hybrid approach, therefore there is no need to plan. In complex projects, nothing can be further from the truth. Therefore, project practitioners should focus on tailoring project approaches to fit the need. Tailoring is a deliberate act of considering multiple variables to arrive at an individualized approach for the project.

Table 4-1. Tailoring Options

Feature	Tailoring Approach
Blended planning	Combine detailed, up-front planning (predictive) with iterative planning (agile) for the project's evolving aspects.
Flexible structure	Maintain structured governance and scope control while allowing agility where needed.
Dual life cycle	Use different delivery models for various components; for example, a waterfall approach for infrastructure and an agile approach for software.
Stakeholder engagement	Balance formal stakeholder approvals with ongoing collaboration and feedback loops.
Team composition	Include both traditional (functional) roles and agile (cross-functional) teams working in parallel.
Change management	Provide structured change control for fixed elements and flexible adaptation for evolving features.
Documentation	Create "fit-for-purpose" documentation that provides just enough information.

4.4.1 Water-Scrum-Fall

Water-scrum-fall is a project management approach that combines elements of the traditional waterfall approach with the iterative and flexible nature of Scrum. Waterfall approach is another way to refer to a predictive approach. Scrum is a lightweight, agile project management framework used primarily for iterative and incremental product development, especially in software. Because this approach combines predictive and adaptive approaches, it is beneficial in environments that require both formal controls and agility.

As shown in Figure 4-1, the water-scrum-fall approach typically includes the following phases:

- **Water phase—initiation and planning.** The project commences with detailed planning, scope definition, and documentation of requirements. This phase may involve establishing budgets, timelines, and governance structures that align with predictive project management practices.
- **Scrum phase—iterative development.** During the core execution phase, the project adopts adaptive approaches. Work is divided into short, timeboxed sprints, with iterative development supported by practices such as daily coordination meetings, sprint planning, reviews, and retrospectives. This approach allows adaptability and continuous improvement based on stakeholder feedback.
- **Fall phase—deployment and maintenance.** In the final stages, the project reverts to a predictive approach for deployment, quality assurance, documentation, and ongoing support. This effort is often necessary for organizations with strict regulatory, compliance, or release cycle requirements.

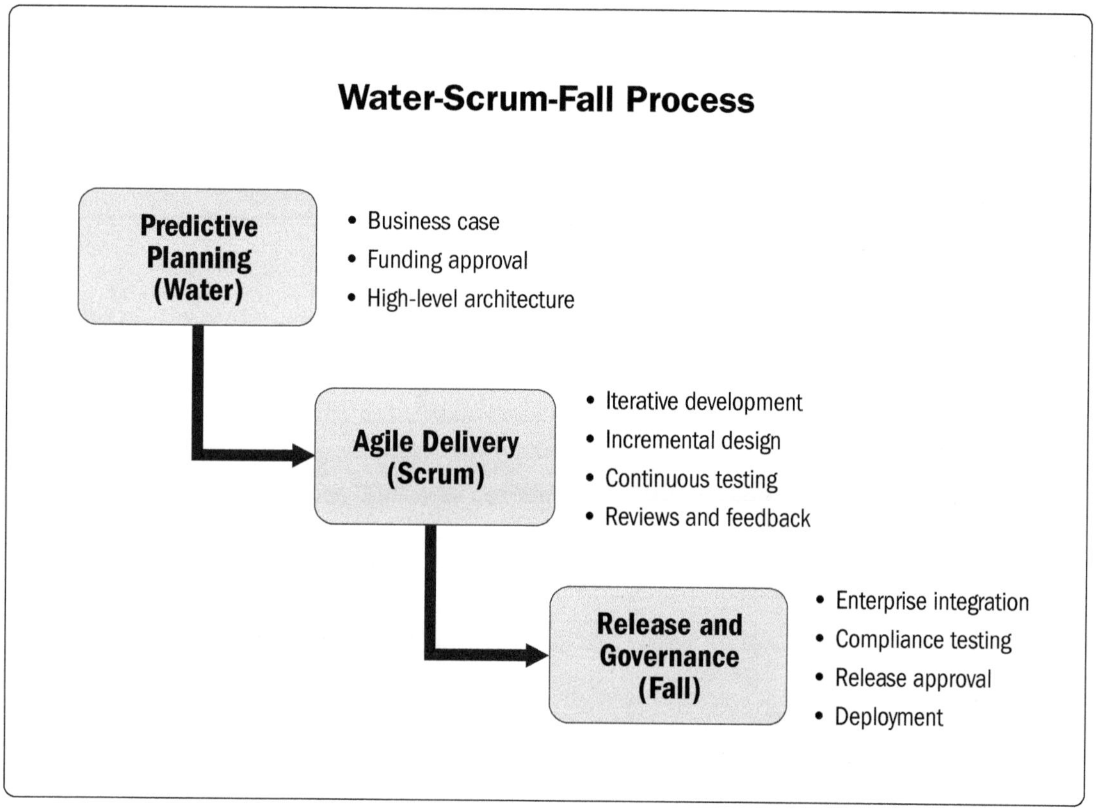

Figure 4-1. Water-Scrum-Fall Process

Water-scrum-fall offers a pragmatic approach for managing projects that require both rigorous, up-front planning and iterative development cycles. The benefits of using this approach include the following:

- **Balanced flexibility and control.** The structured planning of the initial phase helps ensure project alignment with organizational objectives, whereas the Scrum phase introduces flexibility to accommodate evolving user needs and empower development teams.
- **Support for transitional environments.** Organizations undergoing transitions from predictive to adaptive practices may find that this offers a gradual and manageable integration of new approaches.
- **Accommodates regulatory constraints.** Projects in regulated industries may benefit from adaptive development cycles while still meeting the demands of formal documentation and validation procedures.

Water-scrum-fall can be a practical approach for a range of different organizations and projects, provided it is implemented with intention.

4.4.2 Scrumban

Scrumban is a project management approach that combines elements of both Scrum and Kanban. Kanban is a visual workflow management method that uses boards, cards, and continuous flow principles to help teams limit work in progress (WIP), increase efficiency, and deliver value

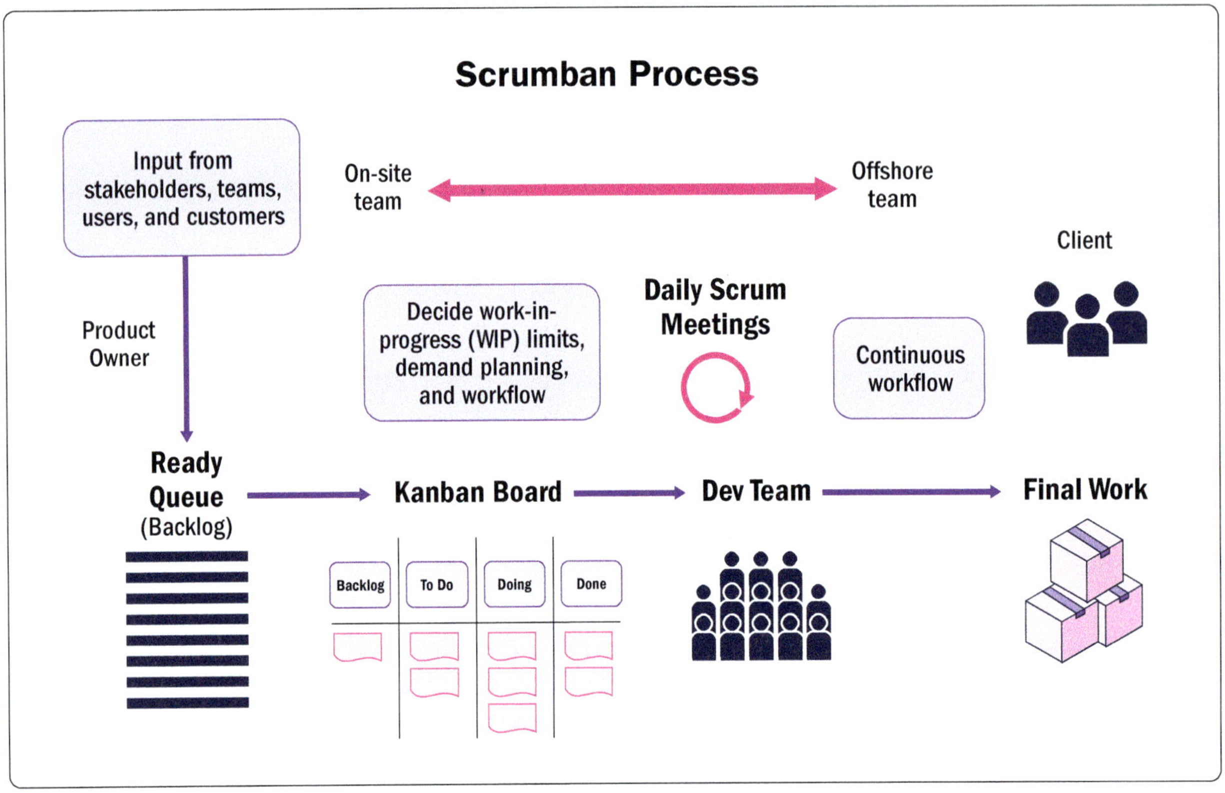

Figure 4-2. Scrumban Process

incrementally. Scrumban combines the structured cadence and defined roles of Scrum with the visual workflow management and continuous delivery principles of Kanban.

This approach is commonly used either as a transitional model for teams moving from Scrum to Kanban, or as a stand-alone framework for organizations seeking a more flexible and responsive method of project execution.

As shown in Figure 4-2, a Scrumban approach employs elements from Scrum, such as adaptive and iterative development approaches and structured events. In addition, it incorporates a visual process management approach that emphasizes workflow visualization, WIP limits, and continuous delivery.

Some of the benefits of a Scrumban approach include the following:

- **Structural integration.** Foundational Scrum approaches provide structure without the rigid timeboxes that Scrum approaches may have.
- **Workflow visualization.** Kanban boards and WIP limits support transparency.
- **Process flexibility.** Teams are able to customize workflows based on project contexts.
- **Evolutionary transition.** Scrumban supports teams seeking to gradually shift from a highly structured workflow to a more flexible option.

Scrumban merges the discipline and role clarity of Scrum with the flexibility and continuous improvement mindset of Kanban. It is a robust, adaptive framework for project teams operating in complex, fast-paced environments.

4.4.3 Tailoring Approaches for Complexity Types

Different types of complexity lend themselves to different types of tailoring. The following sections present tailoring considerations based on the type of complexity in the project.

4.4.3.1 Tailoring for Structural Complexity

Structurally complex projects have multiple components, diverse teams, and layered governance intersections. Such projects benefit from a tailored approach that integrates predictive and adaptive approaches. To tailor an approach for this variety of complexity, project practitioners may do the following:

- **Segment work based on stability and volatility.**
  - Apply a predictive approach to work packages in which scope, requirements, and deliverables are clearly defined and unlikely to change.
  - Apply an adaptive approach to components with evolving requirements, user-centric features, or exploratory development.
- **Synchronize adaptive iterations with predictive milestones.**
  - Align sprint cycles with predefined milestones or stage gates from the predictive plan.
  - Help ensure adaptive deliverables contribute to larger work packages with fixed timelines.
  - Define "integration sprints" in which adaptive outputs are consolidated for milestone reviews or handoffs to downstream teams.
- **Establish dual governance structures.**
  - Maintain a centralized governance model (e.g., project management office [PMO]) to oversee progress, budget, and risk across the entire project.
  - Enable decentralized adaptive governance within teams, allowing autonomy in how teams deliver their assigned outcomes.
- **Align roles and responsibilities.**
  - Assign a project manager to oversee the overall schedule, resource allocation, and risk management.
  - Appoint product owners or scrum masters to lead adaptive teams in value delivery and iteration management.
- **Collaborate consistently.**
  - Help ensure regular communication between project managers and product owners.
  - Reconcile changes in scope, schedule, or stakeholder feedback.

Example scenario

An innovative building project uses predictive planning for foundation and electrical systems while employing adaptive approaches for Internet of Things (IoT) integration and user dashboards.

4.4.3.2 Tailoring for Dynamic Complexity

Dynamic complexity arises when cause-and-effect relationships are unclear, stakeholder needs evolve, and decisions made early in a project have far-reaching, often unforeseen consequences. In such contexts, tailoring predictive and adaptive approaches enables project teams to maintain strategic direction and control while allowing flexibility for changing circumstances. To tailor an approach for this variety of complexity, project practitioners may do the following:

- **Phase the project using predictive milestones, executed via adaptive cycles.**
  - Break down the project into predictive phases (e.g., discovery, development, delivery).
  - Within each phase, apply adaptive iterations to deliver value incrementally and manage uncertainty.
- **Create cross-functional, role-aligned governance.**
  - Maintain a project manager role to monitor scope, time, and cost across the life cycle.
  - Empower product owners and scrum masters to manage delivery teams and iterative work.
  - Use a hybrid governance model to balance control and autonomy, helping ensure adaptive learning supports predictive accountability.
- **Allow adaptive budgeting and forecasting.**
  - Forecast at the program level using predictive techniques but allocate budgets in incremental tranches based on adaptive performance and learning.
  - Plan contingency buffers for rework or pivots driven by discovery.

Example scenario

In a healthcare technology project, a predictive timeline outlines three phases: compliance discovery, platform development, and clinical rollout. Each of these phases is executed using adaptive sprints.

4.4.3.3 Tailoring for Human and Sociopolitical Complexity

Human and sociopolitical complexity emerges in projects involving diverse stakeholder interests, conflicting priorities, cultural dynamics, organizational politics, and decision-making uncertainty. In such settings, authority and legitimacy should be in place to advance critical decisions, but rigid planning may alienate stakeholders.

A tailored approach that combines the clarity and control of predictive approaches with the adaptability and engagement strengths of adaptive practices offers a balanced solution. To tailor an approach for this variety of complexity, project practitioners may do the following:

- **Use predictive planning to establish shared expectations and governance.**
  - Develop a formal project charter, RACI (responsible, accountable, consulted, informed) matrix, and governance structure to help ensure stakeholder alignment and transparency.
  - Develop a comprehensive, high-level roadmap that informs sponsors and stakeholders about sensitive political interests.
- **Apply adaptive approaches to foster engagement and cocreation.**
  - Use adaptive events (e.g., workshops, sprint reviews, demonstrations) to engage stakeholders in iterative decision-making processes.
  - Employ frequent feedback loops to diffuse conflict early and build shared ownership.
- **Institutionalize iterative planning and conflict resolution.**
  - Establish timeboxed planning cycles to revisit stakeholder alignment, update risk registers, and review the impact of changes.
  - Use retrospectives and structured dialogue (e.g., facilitated workshops) to surface and address tensions or misalignments.

Example scenario

In a cross-departmental public sector project, predictive artifacts signal professionalism, legitimacy, and accountability.

4.4.3.4 Tailoring for Environmental Complexity

Environmental complexity refers to the challenges that arise from external factors such as market shifts, technological changes, regulatory updates, supply chain disruptions, climate events, or geopolitical instability. These factors are outside the project's control but directly impact its success.

In such situations, a tailored project approach that strategically integrates predictive and adaptive approaches can provide both the stability needed for long-term planning and the adaptability to respond to rapidly changing external factors. To tailor an approach for this variety of complexity, project practitioners may do the following:

- **Use predictive planning for regulatory, financial, and contractual anchors.**
  - Establish baseline plans for elements governed by compliance, contracts, or funding constraints.
  - Confirm predictive elements such as regulatory deadlines, budget ceilings or funding cycles, and high-level contractual obligations.
- **Apply agile approaches for rapid response to environmental signals.**
  - Use adaptive approaches in areas exposed to volatility such as technology development, user-facing features, and market-facing components.

- **Timebox predictive phases with agile checkpoints.**
  - Break the project into phased predictive cycles, each containing adaptive iterations.
  - Use adaptive feedback to validate assumptions before proceeding to the next predictive phase.

Example scenario

A project that sources components from multiple global partners uses predictive phase gates for the overarching project while remaining flexible to purchasing parts with volatile pricing or availability as needed.

4.4.3.5 Tailoring for Technological Complexity

Technological complexity arises when a project involves emerging technologies, high technical uncertainty, system integration challenges, or rapidly evolving technical requirements.

These conditions can create ambiguity around feasibility, architecture, and performance, posing risks to cost, schedule, and stakeholder confidence. To tailor an approach for this variety of complexity, project practitioners may do the following:

- **Use predictive approaches to define architecture, integration, and compliance boundaries.**
  - Establish technical baselines early (e.g., system architecture, interoperability standards, cybersecurity frameworks).
  - Define nonnegotiable constraints such as technical regulations, hardware-software integration milestones, and data security or platform requirements.
- **Apply agile approaches for prototyping, discovery, and validation.**
  - Use adaptive approaches (e.g., sprints, minimum viable products [MVPs], proofs of concept) to explore and validate emerging technologies, user interface options, algorithm performance, and technical feasibility.
  - Segment work based on technical uncertainty so that stable areas progress linearly and volatile components evolve iteratively.
- **Incorporate dual-layer technical planning.**
  - Establish a high-level system roadmap, release milestones, and technical reviews.
  - Enable cross-functional teams to iteratively design, test, and refine their work within each technical workstream.

Example scenario

A system integration project that incorporates out-of-the-box work, integration with legacy systems, and custom-built applications, uses predictive approaches for the out-of-the-box work, high-level milestone tracking for legacy system integration, and adaptive approaches for custom-built applications.

4.4.3.6 Tailoring for Organizational Complexity

Organizational complexity refers to the challenges arising from multiple business units, hierarchical structures, decision-making layers, divergent priorities, and competing stakeholder interests. Projects in such environments often face slow approvals, misaligned expectations, communication breakdowns, and challenges in cross-functional coordination. To tailor an approach for this variety of complexity, project practitioners may do the following:

- **Use predictive governance for alignment, oversight, and stakeholder engagement.**
  - Establish formal governance mechanisms such as stage gates and tollgates, progress reports and dashboards, and steering committees or executive sponsors.
  - Use predictive approaches to provide clear escalation paths and accountability in layered organizations.
- **Apply adaptive approaches at the execution level for cross-functional delivery.**
  - Enable speed and flexibility within teams while aligning outputs to organizational expectations.
  - Empower teams to operate with autonomy using iterations and backlog-driven planning, daily coordination meetings, retrospectives, and customer-centric iteration cycles.
- **Establish bridging roles to align adaptive teams with stakeholders.**
  - Appoint product owners, project coordinators, or delivery leads to serve as translators between adaptive teams and stakeholders.
  - Help ensure strategic objectives are translated into actionable backlogs.
  - Use blended roles to bridge communication gaps between sponsors and delivery teams.

Example scenario

An adaptive transformation project uses predictive governance during the transition from predictive to adaptive approaches to maintain high-level oversight while evolving workflows to adaptive approaches.

4.5 Adaptive Governance

When considering different project approaches, governance warrants special attention. Predictive models center on linear plans and static oversight that offer stability and accountability but often struggle with emergent risks, rapid stakeholder shifts, and evolving success criteria. Adaptive governance relies on continuous reassessment to guide decision-making in uncertain conditions.

Adaptive governance helps project teams detect changing conditions, reevaluate priorities, and pivot when necessary. These approaches replace rigid control with responsiveness and static oversight with dynamic learning.

4.5.1 Continuous Evaluation

An important aspect of an adaptive governance approach is continuously evaluating circumstances and responding to changes. Adaptive approaches that support continuous evaluation and response include:

- **Rolling wave planning.** Update the near-term plan in detail while allowing room for change in future plans.
- **Frequent scenario-based forecasting.** Use "what-if" models to understand the consequences of changes in scope, resourcing, or external conditions.
- **Integrated performance dashboards.** Review real-time dashboards that visualize schedule, cost, risk, and stakeholder sentiment across systems and teams.

Such tools allow teams to plan for the future while reacting to the present.

Example scenario

On complex infrastructure projects with evolving community needs and municipal oversight, teams hold quarterly adaptive reviews to evaluate project assumptions, risks, and external changes (e.g., policy shifts, market pricing).

4.5.2 Dynamic Replanning

Continuous evaluation supports the process of dynamic replanning, which involves ongoing prioritization of work based on updated inputs. This prioritization benefits projects facing technological uncertainty, regulatory fluidity, social or political concerns, and supply chain volatility. Tools and methods for dynamic replanning include the following:

- Change impact matrices to evaluate the impact of change on processes, technology, or budget.
- System dynamics models to predict system behavior.
- Regular backlog review to assess and reprioritize work as appropriate.
- Decision cadence calendars to drive rhythm for reevaluation.

The role of the project manager shifts from enforcing the baseline to facilitating ongoing alignment between project execution and strategic intent.

4.5.3 Adaptive Learning

Predictive governance supports single-loop learning, which involves analyzing actions and outcomes. Complex projects benefit from double-loop learning, which includes analyzing underlying assumptions and governance structures.

Double-loop learning involves the following:

- Reflecting on how decisions are made, not just what decisions are made;
- Challenging assumptions and mental models underlying project plans; and
- Shifting from blame to inquiry in governance culture.

Feedback loops enable learning by providing information about ongoing project work. Because complex systems generate a constant flow of signals, effective governance focuses on information that is:

- **Timely.** Close to the event.
- **Multidirectional.** Vertical and horizontal across teams and stakeholders.
- **Actionable.** Linked to changes in process or strategy.

Examples of adaptive learning mechanisms include the following:

- Retrospectives at sprint or phase ends;
- Stakeholder feedback tools, such as pulse surveys or sentiment analysis;
- Cross-disciplinary sensemaking workshops; and
- Learning reviews triggered by significant events (e.g., major scope change or risk realization).

Project governance structures that support adaptive learning benefit from regular feedback, leading to greater efficiency.

Example scenario

A major healthcare IT transformation project embedded "learning weeks" every quarter, where all governance committees paused approvals to reflect, analyze decision outcomes, and reprioritize based on lessons learned.

4.5.4 Decentralized Governance

In complex projects, centralized authority figures may not have the context or responsiveness needed to act quickly. Adaptive approaches encourage distributing decision-making toward lower-level leaders who have the most relevant information. This distribution is referred to as decentralized governance.

Decentralized governance offers the following:

- Empowers teams by delegating authority while providing clear boundaries;
- Provides real-time information access, which supports frontline decision-making; and
- Allows guiding values to replace rigid rules.

This leadership philosophy focuses on enabling conditions for success, rather than asserting control. It is intended to create a culture of intelligent risk taking to help ensure alignment without micromanagement.

Decentralized governance requires balance: Too little oversight can lead to fragmentation, whereas too much stifles innovation and responsiveness.

Effective adaptive leaders foster the following:

- Shared purpose and goals that guide decentralized action,
- Transparent information flows to synchronize understanding, and
- Light-touch oversight that encourages initiative while managing interdependencies.

Leaders can also use tools that support adaptive leadership, including the following:

- Decision rights matrices,
- Delegation boards (e.g., RACI models adapted for an adaptive approach), and
- Governance charters codeveloped with teams.

With sufficient communication, leaders can coordinate decision-making while empowering team members to be autonomous. Decentralized governance can even be incorporated within existing governance models. This decentralized governance may be implemented in the following ways:

- Hybrid stage-gate models that allow for conditional progress based on evolving insights,
- Dual-operating systems in which innovation teams operate by using adaptive approaches while core governance provides stability, and
- Tailored dashboards that integrate traditional KPIs with adaptive metrics (such as learning velocity, stakeholder resilience).

Example scenario

On a public infrastructure project with multiple contractors and government stakeholders, the steering committee adopts a hybrid governance model with formal monthly meetings supplemented by working groups empowered to make local decisions within their scope.

4.6 Summary

This section provides a comprehensive exploration of how development approaches can be leveraged and tailored to manage project complexity. The section emphasized that no single approach is universally superior. The selection and tailoring of approaches can be aligned with the specific nature of the project, its environment, and the stakeholders involved.

This section reviewed how development approaches apply to complexity by:

- Describing predictive approaches and their applications to complexity,
- Introducing different adaptive approaches and their characteristics,
- Discussing how project approaches can be tailored to include both predictive and adaptive approaches, and
- Detailing the elements and benefits of an adaptive governance approach.

The approaches described in this section support project practitioners as they determine how to navigate complex projects.

Part 3

Human Factors in Complexity

Part 3 explores the interpersonal skills needed to excel in complex projects. Information in these sections goes beyond the basic people skills needed to manage projects and focuses instead on the advanced competencies and skills needed in complex environments. There are four sections in Part 3.

- **Section 5 Competencies for Managing Complexity.** Section 5 describes how competencies and leadership interact. It provides an overview of eight key competencies needed to effectively lead complex projects and identifies strategies for developing and integrating those competencies.
- **Section 6 Communication and Stakeholder Engagement.** Section 6 explores communication, biases, and political dynamics. It continues by introducing more advanced stakeholder engagement topics such as framing effect and differentiating between perception and conception.
- **Section 7 Decision-Making in Complex Environments.** Section 7 presents the characteristics and types of decisions project practitioners face. It introduces a variety of decision-making models and guidance on when to apply them.
- **Section 8 Leadership Strategies for Complexity.** Section 8 examines leadership strategies that assist in navigating uncertainty, fostering innovation, and cultivating resilient teams. It then describes how various leadership styles interact with different complexity types.

Mastering the content in these sections helps project practitioners lead their teams successfully in uncertain and continually changing situations.

Section 5

Competencies for Navigating Complexity

5.1 Introduction

Navigating complex projects requires skills beyond the standard project practitioner's toolkit. These additional, more advanced skills are associated with project aspects such as strategy, systems, culture, and environmental awareness. Project practitioners who develop advanced competencies can apply them to a range of complex situations, employing thinking styles, problem-solving approaches, and culturally appropriate responses that are a best fit for emerging and changing project needs.

This section describes eight competencies that enable project practitioners to work with project complexity effectively. The section includes the following subsections:

- Competencies for Complex Projects
- Strategic Thinking and Organizational Alignment
- Value Creation and Motivational Leadership
- Systems Thinking and Integration
- Emotional Intelligence
- Cultural and Ethical Competencies

- Analytical Thinking and Bias Recognition
- Situational Awareness and Environmental Intelligence
- Technical Literacy
- Competency Development and Integration

Reviewing the characteristics and impact of these competencies can support project practitioners seeking to analyze their current skill sets and identify areas for growth. The competencies discussed in this section support individual development. The competencies also interact with and enable leadership approaches for complexity, which are discussed in Section 8.

5.2 Competencies for Complex Projects

A competency is the combination of conditions and characteristics of knowledge, skills, abilities, and behaviors that can enable superior performance. Successful project managers demonstrate competencies such as written and verbal communication, prioritization of competing demands, organization, and risk management. In addition to these fundamental skills, many project practitioners develop technical competencies specific to their domain such as aerospace, construction, or system integration.

Complex projects require advanced competencies such as those presented in this section. These competencies are relevant across all forms of project complexity. Because each project is unique, project practitioners should be able to employ, tailor, and combine these competencies depending on the context.

5.2.1 Relationship Between Competencies and Leadership

Individual competencies have a close relationship to leadership strategies, which will be discussed in Section 8. Leadership involves influencing, guiding, and enabling individuals and teams to achieve project objectives. Individuals demonstrate competencies such as analytical thinking and technical literacy through their work products and behavior.

Effective leaders use competencies to coordinate work efficiently. By regularly evaluating the competencies of team members, leaders are able to strategically assign work to the individuals and teams that are best equipped for success. Thoughtful leaders use competency levels to inform their decisions.

Project leaders can also work with individuals and teams to develop competencies, supporting growth and development for future needs, even as they assign work according to current strengths.

5.2.2 Competency Development

Environments in complex projects are subject to frequent change, and teams facing complexity benefit from proactive and continuous competency development. By developing relevant competencies that may not be currently needed, individuals and teams can equip themselves for unexpected change.

The abilities to learn, adapt, and tailor competencies in evolving and emerging contexts are important skills in themselves. Continuous learning enables project practitioners to recognize, interpret, and respond to complexity in coordinated, adaptive, and effective ways.

Competency development should incorporate structured experiential learning approaches, such as Kolb's Experiential Learning Cycle (Concrete Experience → Reflective Observation → Abstract Conceptualization → Active Experimentation) and deliberate practice techniques, supported by activities like simulations, case studies, mentoring, and reflective exercises.

5.3 Strategic Thinking and Organizational Alignment

The strategic thinking and organizational alignment competency focuses on applying strategic thinking skills to the project to maintain alignment between project execution and organizational objectives. Strategic thinking helps project practitioners analyze interconnected systems, anticipate emergent patterns, and adapt to changing contexts, helping ensure projects remain relevant amid shifting priorities.

The skills within this competency originate from systems thinking research, strategic management theory, and complexity science. The skills emphasize adaptive responsiveness rather than detailed prediction and control.

5.3.1 Strategic Thinking and Organizational Alignment Behaviors

Individuals who are adept at strategic thinking and organizational alignment demonstrate the following proficiencies:

- **Strategic goal integration.** Understand and realign project outcomes with organizational mission, vision, and objectives while adapting to evolving priorities.
- **Business case evolution.** Create and update value propositions as living documents that evolve with strategic contexts.
- **Organizational change navigation.** Support transitions while maintaining project momentum during organizational flux.
- **Portfolio awareness.** Optimize individual project decisions for broader portfolio value while maintaining project objectives.
- **Governance alignment.** Operate effectively within decision-making structures while adapting to changing governance models.

These proficiencies represent the application of strategic thinking to a dynamic environment while keeping organizational needs at the forefront.

5.3.2 Impact of Strategic Thinking and Organizational Alignment

Behaviors and actions associated with strategic thinking and organizational alignment enable project practitioners to position initiatives for continued organizational support. Project practitioners who develop these skills often experience:

- Enhanced stakeholder buy-in,
- Improved project sustainability beyond completion, and
- Greater resilience when organizational priorities shift.

Organizational support is particularly important during periods of strategic uncertainty, organizational change, or competing priorities.

Example scenario

A large-scale smart city development project demonstrated strategic thinking through flexible goal integration with national objectives. The project also incorporated a governance structure involving both public and private sector partners. The project's business case was treated as a living document that evolved with strategic contexts. This effort showcased how portfolio-level decisions can be optimized for broader value during a major national transformation initiative.

5.4 Value Creation and Motivational Leadership

The value creation and motivational leadership competency focuses on motivational resilience, which is the ability to maintain focus and commitment when goals shift or conditions change.

The skills within this competency originate from transformational leadership theory, complexity leadership, and motivational psychology. These skills help project practitioners maintain momentum and engagement in the face of complexity.

5.4.1 Value Creation and Motivational Leadership Behaviors

Project practitioners skilled in value creation and motivational leadership exhibit the following behaviors:

- **Stakeholder value identification.** Translate diverse needs into actionable outcomes with clear organizational benefit.
- **Benefits realization planning.** Connect deliverables to tangible benefits while adapting to evolving priorities.
- **Value communication.** Present benefits using audience-relevant language to build collective commitment.
- **Adaptive goal setting.** Adjust objectives while maintaining strategic direction and stakeholder confidence.
- **Motivational communication.** Enable rapid feedback incorporation while preserving project confidence.

These behaviors strengthen teams, allowing them to deliver results under challenging circumstances.

5.4.2 Impact of Value Creation and Motivational Leadership

Value creation and motivational leadership are stabilizing forces when projects encounter uncertainty, stakeholder pressure, resource constraints, or environmental changes. Project practitioners who develop this competency may be able to maintain team unity and stakeholder support during challenging periods.

This competency becomes particularly valuable in projects with technological or organizational complexity, as these skills are critical for maintaining stakeholder buy-in. Project practitioners who develop these skills often experience the following:

- Increased stakeholder trust through transparent communication of benefits,
- Improved team cohesion and morale during periods of ambiguity,
- Sustained project momentum and productivity despite changing conditions, and
- Greater alignment between project outcomes and long-term organizational value.

When project practitioners strengthen their ability to create value and motivate others, they foster a culture of shared purpose that enhances both project performance and organizational resilience.

Example scenario

During a software upgrade across multiple auto dealerships, new requirements force the team to redesign key reporting features just weeks before the launch. The project lead gathers the IT staff, dealership managers, and vendor representatives. The project lead acknowledges the setback and refocuses the team on the opportunity to improve sales tracking and customer service consistency across locations. After inviting input from each dealership about the process and schedule going forward, the project lead emphasizes the bigger goal of building a more connected customer experience.

5.5 Systems Thinking and Integration

The systems thinking and integration competency focuses on applying systems thinking to integrate interconnected elements within a project. As described in Section 3, systems thinking is a holistic approach that views projects as interconnected systems, recognizing how people, processes, technology, and the environment interact and how interdependencies shape patterns and outcomes over time. Applying this in practice often requires systems-architecture thinking, structuring projects as interacting with subsystems, and explicitly managing their interfaces to reduce emergent complexity.

This competency helps project practitioners recognize how project elements influence one another, enhancing decision quality and adaptability. By applying a systems perspective to project planning and problem-solving, project practitioners can better anticipate ripple effects, manage complexity, and deliver greater organizational value.

5.5.1 Systems Thinking and Integration Behaviors

Project practitioners who demonstrate systems thinking and integration exhibit the following behaviors:

- **Holistic understanding of interdependence.** Consider how different components of a project interact as a cohesive system.
- **Identification of systemic risks and delays.** Identify risks and delays that emerge from interdependencies among project elements.

- **Feedback loops and adaptive learning.** Use feedback mechanisms to monitor unintended effects, refine processes, and enhance project outcomes.
- **Root cause and system-level problem-solving.** Address the root causes of issues rather than treat surface-level symptoms.

These behaviors enhance operational efficiency across complex project environments by recognizing the ways that individual components interact to create larger effects.

5.5.2 Impact of Systems Thinking and Integration

Applying systems thinking to project management helps project practitioners anticipate challenges. This competency supports better decision-making, improving project progress, results, and organizational value. Project practitioners who develop these skills often experience the following:

- Improved decision quality through recognition of interdependencies and long-term effects,
- Greater risk anticipation by identifying ripple effects early in project planning,
- Enhanced collaboration and coordination across interconnected project teams, and
- Continuous organizational learning through embedded feedback and adaptation mechanisms.

Systems thinking applied to project management strengthens an organization's ability to manage complexity in projects, increasing successful outcomes.

Example scenario

A city's public transportation agency is overhauling its bus routes to reduce delays and congestion. Early in the planning process, the route planner points out that changes to the bus routes affect traffic patterns, pedestrian flow, and local business deliveries. As part of optimizing route selection, the team maps how the routes, schedules, traffic signals, parking restrictions, and commuter behavior all interact.

When initial simulations show delays at key intersections, the team investigates underlying causes rather than adding more buses. By adjusting signal timing, rerouting options, and coordinating with local business delivery schedules, they are able to address many of the root causes of congestion.

Continuous monitoring and feedback loops allow the team to refine schedules and routes as real-world usage data comes in, resulting in a smoother rollout, fewer delays, and a more efficient urban system.

5.6 Emotional Intelligence

Emotional intelligence is the ability to identify, assess, and manage the personal emotions of oneself and other people, as well as the collective emotions of groups of people. Complex projects require not only individual emotional intelligence but team-level emotional capacity as well. Collective emotional intelligence is the ability to share, collectively process, and constructively respond to emotions among team members. This directly impacts team psychological safety, collaboration quality, and stress tolerance.

Complex projects create unique pressures where team members need to act quickly, build relationships, and assess emotions under time constraints. Emotional intelligence allows team members and leaders to regulate their emotions in times of stress and tension, strengthening team cohesion, trust, and effectiveness.

5.6.1 Emotional Intelligence Behaviors

Project practitioners with emotional intelligence exhibit the following behaviors:

- **Empathetic relationship building.** Understand, as well as feel, the thoughts and emotions of others to build relationships that bridge disagreements.
- **Receptivity to change.** Be willing to consider and recognize the legitimacy of changes.
- **Mobilization toward goals.** Connect different segments of people to realize common goals.
- **Learning and growth.** Use feedback and outcomes to revise initial beliefs.

These behaviors help individuals and teams create positive and productive working environments.

Insight

Empathy is considered one of the foundational components of emotional intelligence. A study on open innovation projects highlights that empathetic skills play a central role when firms are unfamiliar with their partners and their organizational expectations. Encouraging collective empathy contributes to higher organizational flexibility, regardless of the habits or reliability of others. Empathy facilitates the collective transformation of ideas into concrete solutions. [4]

5.6.2 Impact of Emotional Intelligence

Developing stronger relationships through emotional intelligence supports teams through difficult times by anticipating stressors, managing conflict, and creating a positive emotional environment. Project practitioners who implement emotional intelligence skills may experience the following:

- Improved team resilience and performance through stronger relationships,
- Greater trust and collaboration resulting from empathetic communication,
- Enhanced decision-making that balances emotional regulation with situational awareness,
- Increased adaptability and engagement through leaders who model vulnerability and authenticity, and
- Positive transformation of negative emotions such as channeling fear into proactive action or anger into constructive advocacy.

These impacts enable project leaders to foster trust, maintain motivation, and guide teams effectively through uncertainty and complexity.

Example scenario

A merger between two financial management groups sparks concerns among the employees. The employees worry that their organizations' distinct identities and reputations will be lost in the merger. To address this, the project lead organizes a meeting between the merged leadership team and other team members to reaffirm company values. The project lead invites employees to share what they are proud of and what they fear losing, listening closely to create a shared vision for the future. As the conversation unfolds, tensions ease and employees begin to see themselves as part of something larger. In the weeks that follow, the project lead reinforces this vision in team meetings, linking the changes back to the mission of creating a client experience both teams can stand behind.

5.7 Cultural and Ethical Competency

Cultural competency is the ability to navigate diverse cultural contexts and organizational boundaries by confronting challenges, taking risks, and learning from mistakes. Ethical competency is the ability to protect an organization's reputation and build trust by applying ethical reasoning and articulating persuasive arguments within and beyond the organization.

Together, these skills combine to form cultural and ethical competency, which focuses on navigating different cultural environments with sensitivity while protecting organizational reputation through ethical reasoning. This competency helps navigate human and sociopolitical complexity; structural complexity, such as geography, oversight and coordination; environmental complexity arising from elections, labor disputes, or emergent regulations; and organizational complexity related to management practices or stakeholder diversity.

5.7.1 Cultural and Ethical Competency Behaviors

Project practitioners who develop the cultural and ethical competency exhibit the following behaviors:

- **Metacognitive awareness.** Plan for and reflect on cross-cultural interactions, monitoring assumptions and adapting behavior based on cultural feedback.
- **Motivational drive.** Sustain a commitment to learn from and engage across cultures.
- **Behavioral adaptability.** Demonstrate appropriate verbal and nonverbal behaviors across diverse cultural contexts to build trust and connection.
- **Ethical reasoning and integrity.** Evaluate actions and decisions through an ethical lens, balancing stakeholder interests and maintaining accountability in complex situations.

These behaviors enable project practitioners to navigate diverse environments with sensitivity, uphold ethical standards, and foster trust among global stakeholders.

5.7.2 Impact of Cultural and Ethical Competency

Applying cultural and ethical competency allows project practitioners to recognize and navigate the values, relationships, and unspoken rules that shape project environments. By building awareness of both organizational and cultural dynamics, project practitioners can alleviate potential sources of tension, strengthen collaboration, and protect stakeholder trust.

Typical impacts of cultural and ethical competency include the following:

- Improved collaboration across diverse and geographically distributed teams;
- Stronger stakeholder trust through consistent ethical decision-making;
- Increased sensitivity to organizational and cultural values that influence project outcomes;
- Greater ability to identify and manage ethical dilemmas in complex, high-stakes environments; and
- Enhanced organizational reputation through transparent, values-driven leadership.

These impacts help project practitioners sustain integrity, foster inclusivity, and align project decisions with the ethical and cultural expectations of their organizations and stakeholders.

Example scenario

An initiative focused on improving vaccination rates in multiple countries faces regional differences that impact strategy. To ease the rollout, the project team engages with local healthcare workers and community leaders to gather feedback and adopt communication materials, outreach strategies, and engagement approaches to respect cultural practices. Conflicts between local customs and data collection integrity are evaluated to balance stakeholder interests and transparency.

5.8 Analytical Thinking and Bias Recognition

The analytical thinking and bias recognition competency focuses on making informed, conscientious decisions despite uncertainty and cognitive biases. *Bias* is an inclination that influences judgment and perceptions in ways that may be unfair, unbalanced, or subjective. Developing the analytical thinking and bias recognition competency helps project practitioners evaluate information objectively, question assumptions, and make decisions despite cognitive biases in complex project environments.

The skills within this competency originate from behavioral economics research, complexity science, and evidence-based management practices. These skills enable project practitioners to maintain decision quality under uncertain circumstances, while recognizing the impact of mental shortcuts and systematic errors.

5.8.1 Behaviors of Analytical Thinking and Bias Recognition

The analytical thinking component of this competency improves information evaluation and integration processes through the following behaviors:

- **Multiple-source integration.** Triangulate diverse inputs while assessing source credibility.
- **Uncertainty acknowledgment.** Recognize and communicate information limitations while making necessary decisions.
- **Pattern recognition.** Identify recurring themes and systemic issues across project situations.
- **Evidence integration.** Combine quantitative analysis with experiential insights and stakeholder feedback.

The bias recognition aspect of this competency enhances decision quality through the following behaviors:

- **Optimism bias reduction.** Apply reference class forecasting and historical data analysis to counter estimation errors.
- **Anchoring bias awareness.** Incorporate new information to avoid overreliance on initial estimates.
- **Framing effect recognition.** Present options objectively without inadvertent manipulation.

5.8.2 Impact of Analytical Thinking and Bias Recognition

Thinking analytically and recognizing potential biases improves decision quality by reducing conscious or unconscious cognitive errors that contribute to project failures. Project practitioners who develop these skills often demonstrate the following:

- Improved risk identification,
- More accurate estimation,
- Enhanced stakeholder confidence in decision-making, and
- Greater adaptability when assumptions prove incorrect.

These skills are particularly valuable for projects involving significant uncertainty, multiple stakeholders, or high-stakes decisions.

Insight

An article published in *Project Management Journal*® [5] examined cost overruns in complex systems development projects, identifying five key drivers of risk:

- Schedule management,
- System performance/design stability,
- Technology maturity,
- Risk assessment accuracy, and
- Reliability factors.

Project practitioners who applied systematic analytical approaches, such as reference class forecasting, triangulating information, and bias recognition, demonstrated the following:

- Improved risk identification and early detection of potential overruns,
- More accurate cost and schedule estimates,
- Greater stakeholder confidence in decision-making, and
- Increased adaptability when project assumptions changed.

The study highlights how structured analytical thinking helps project teams recognize optimism bias, anticipate cascading effects, and develop predictive models that improve project predictability in complex technology-driven environments.

5.9 Situational Awareness and Environmental Intelligence

The situational awareness and environmental intelligence competency focuses on making informed decisions, proactively addressing challenges, and aligning projects with broader environmental factors to increase the likelihood of successful outcomes.

Situational awareness is the ability to interpret shifting conditions, anticipate their impact, and make informed decisions to mitigate issues and risks in dynamic environments. Environmental intelligence is the ability to detect, analyze, and strategically respond to external forces that influence the project context.

Together, situational awareness and environmental intelligence support project practitioners as they assess complexity, considering intangible but impactful factors such as organizational culture, political dynamics, economic conditions, and technological trends. This competency is particularly relevant when managing projects with dynamic, sociopolitical, or environmental complexity.

5.9.1 Situational Awareness and Environmental Intelligence Behaviors

Project practitioners who develop the situational awareness and environmental intelligence competency may exhibit the following behaviors:

- **Situational perception of elements.** Detect and recognize cues within the project environment.
- **Synthesis and comprehension.** Interpret observations to understand their meaning for the project.
- **Actionable insights.** Derive meaningful insights from information to inform decision-making and strategic planning.
- **Political astuteness.** Identify informal power structures and key influencers within the organization.
- **Cultural intelligence.** Understand organizational values and unspoken rules through empathy and observation.
- **Flexibility and adaptability.** Remain flexible and ready to adjust plans as new information emerges.

By combining observational, interpretive, and strategic skills, project practitioners can better recognize patterns and anticipate shifts within complex project environments.

5.9.2 Impact of Situational Awareness and Environmental Intelligence

Strong situational awareness and environmental intelligence skills contribute to project success by enabling the following:

- Improved decision-making via real-time awareness of internal and external conditions,
- Effective risk management and mitigation by proactively anticipating problems,
- Enhanced team performance through fostering trust and communication among stakeholders, and
- Increased stakeholder satisfaction by evaluating success beyond traditional metrics.

Example scenario

In a multiregional high-speed rail initiative, project specialists use situational awareness to manage intricate stakeholder relationships. Early indicators of community opposition, such as feedback at town hall meetings or on social media, prompt focused engagement initiatives before issues escalate.

Additionally, environmental intelligence enables the team to monitor and adapt to changing regulatory environments that impact the project. When a new ecological rule is initiated midproject, the team immediately evaluates its effect and makes design and resource distribution changes that prevent schedule delays. Integrating situational awareness and environmental intelligence helps the project team stay on track, reduce risk, and build stakeholder confidence.

5.10 Technical Literacy

The technical literacy competency focuses on building knowledge of technology needs and options associated with a project environment. This competency includes awareness of existing and emerging technologies, the risks and opportunities associated with them, and the ability to translate technical needs into business decisions. Technical literacy helps ensure that technology decisions support innovation, strategy, and stakeholders.

Technical literacy bridges the managerial and technological aspects of a project, enabling project practitioners to help ensure technological choices are contextually relevant and strategic.

5.10.1 Technical Literacy Behaviors

Project practitioners with technical literacy exhibit the following behaviors:

- **Learning agility.** Continually update understanding of the technological landscape to remain credible and effective in guiding innovation and anticipating disruption.
- **Technical credibility.** Establish trust with technical teams and stakeholders so they are considered credible partners capable of participating in technical discussions and decisions.
- **Strategic translation.** Translate engineering constraints into business trade-offs, helping ensure technical judgments are based on strategic outcomes and stakeholder priorities.
- **Systemic framing.** Preemptively manage risk within technical projects, considering timelines, cost budgets, and governance structures.
- **Technology governance.** Consider how adoption of new technologies may impact compliance, resilience, and long-term sustainability.

As these behaviors demonstrate, building technical literacy enables project practitioners to actively collaborate on technology initiatives.

5.10.2 Impact of Technical Literacy

Technical literacy skills contribute to project success by enabling the following:

- Better-informed decision-making on technical issues, particularly in fast-moving environments;
- Improved ability to extract value from project-generated data and use analytics to guide decision-making and anticipate risks; and
- Deeper understanding of the ethical, security, and compliance risks of adopting new technology.

Technology is no longer a supporting function; it is the strategic environment where projects occur. As technology expands and evolves, technical literacy is a beneficial competency for project practitioners in all fields.

Example scenario

In a multistakeholder transformation program, a project practitioner used generative AI (GenAI) tools to accelerate essential project work—automating meeting minutes, reporting, and action planning. Intelligent assistants produced structured minutes in real time, while analytics platforms summarized team progress data, forecasting financial trends and delivery risks. AI-driven task assignment improved execution quality by matching responsibilities to team strengths.

To help ensure quality outputs and the appropriate use and protection of sensitive data, project practitioners selected mature technologies, avoiding tools with security risks or potential ethical issues.

5.11 Competency Development and Integration

Teams are most effective when they combine the skills of specialists from different disciplines to address shared challenges. The process of combining individual skills to create a necessary collective capability is called competency integration. Effective competency integration turns a group of specialists into a cohesive system, creating an environment that fosters innovation, accelerates problem-solving, and helps organizations adapt more quickly.

The role of the project practitioner in identifying the competencies needed for a project is critical. This can be achieved in various ways depending on the organizational context:

- In some organizations, competencies are planned and developed in advance;
- For skill gaps, the project practitioner may collaborate with human resources (HR) for talent acquisition, engage procurement for external suppliers, or leverage centers of excellence (CoE) and resource managers.

In more mature organizations, these practices are often institutionalized through joint planning with HR and other support functions. The quality of talent acquisition plays a vital role in determining project success.

Integrated projects that connect technical systems (e.g., cybersecurity, AI), organizational structures (e.g., governance, regulatory), and human dimensions (e.g., ethics, stakeholder engagement) create a foundation for collective success. This section discusses approaches for implementing competency integration.

5.11.1 Dimensions of Integration

A competency integration process begins with a shared understanding of the project's purpose and goals, which are often represented in system maps, operating models, or structured frameworks. Integration can then be analyzed through structural, behavioral, process, and strategic dimensions such as the following:

- **Structural integration.** Deliberate mechanisms, like integrated PMOs, agile release trains, and cross-functional teams, are designed to enable the flow of skills and knowledge, helping ensure that expertise is utilized where it adds the most value.
- **Behavioral integration.** Norms around supportive behaviors, such as reciprocity, mutual trust, and constructive conflict, are established to facilitate collaboration and synergy, even under pressure.
- **Process integration.** Embed competency frameworks into core project and organizational processes (e.g., governance, resource allocation, performance management) to help ensure consistent application throughout the project life cycle.
- **Strategic integration.** Leadership develops a shared strategy to help ensure all competencies are directed toward a common purpose and adaptive approach, remaining focused on business outcomes while staying flexible as changes occur.

5.11.2 Practices That Support Integration

The following practices support competency integration:

- **Competency mapping.** Competency maps identify strengths, uncover hidden capabilities, and bridge gaps, serving as living documents that inform team building and development.
- **Facilitated workshops.** Facilitated workshops simulate complex scenarios, helping pressure-test decisions. Examples include dry runs of crisis simulations, peer role-playing to address stakeholder conflict, and walkthroughs to avoid technological disruption.
- **Communities of practice (CoPs).** CoPs shift the focus from static, role-based positions, as documented in RACI charts, toward adaptive roles that evolve with project demands. These communities are knowledge hubs that capture lessons and help grow capabilities.
- **Technology support systems.** Tools such as AI-driven knowledge graphs, digital twins, and collaborative dashboards make expertise visible and accessible in real time.
- **Cross-domain teaming.** Teams that blend technical depth with cultural and strategic awareness address both system and human dimensions of complexity. For example, teams can pair engineers with communication specialists or data scientists with policy experts.

The practice of integration should be tailored to the specific project, choosing appropriate integration methods based on complexity type, stakeholder needs, and the strategic intent of the project.

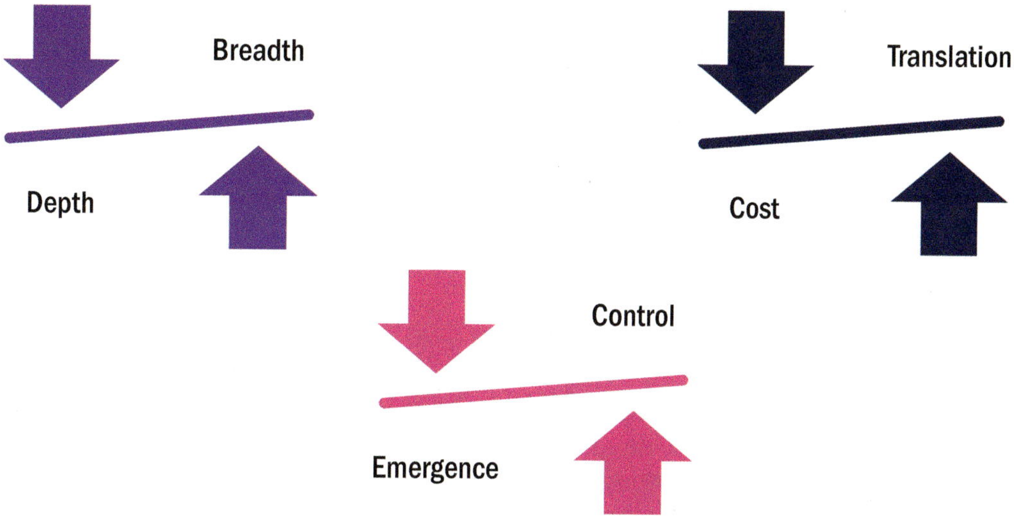

Figure 5-1. Tensions and Trade-Offs

5.11.3 Tensions and Trade-Offs of Competency Integration

Despite the many benefits of competency integration, there can be tensions and trade-offs such as the following:

- **Breadth versus depth.** Deep expertise is essential but risks tunnel vision. Project practitioners benefit from moving between depth and breadth, changing perspectives depending on the need of the project.
- **Control versus emergence.** Too much structure stifles innovation; too little can lead to fragmentation and drift. Project practitioners should aim to build frameworks that are robust but flexible, emphasizing the capacity to guide but not constrain.
- **Translation versus costs.** Bridging disciplines, cultures, and perspectives takes time, effort, and emotional intelligence. These costs are especially high in complex, emerging domains such as AI ethics; environmental, social, and governance (ESG) initiatives; and data governance. However, these costs lead to benefits in the forms of integration and alignment.

Figure 5-1 shows the balancing act that may help to successfully integrate the competencies needed for complex projects.

5.11.4 Indicators of Success

Successful competency integration is focused on coordinating skills in real time to meet objectives. Integration-fluent project practitioners should be able to identify where the competencies are out of alignment, anticipate ripple effects, and intervene before small problems become major failures. This anticipatory ability is particularly beneficial in complex, interconnected systems where decisions have wide-ranging impact.

Project practitioners are responsible for assessing and building competencies for project success. For example, coaching/mentoring approaches can significantly improve team members' competencies and project performance.

Project practitioners can monitor the success of integration efforts by using tools such as integration frameworks, adaptive RACI matrices, cross-functional governance mechanisms, and knowledge integration hubs. Such tools not only support integration efforts but also sustain learning beyond a single project.

Competency integration plays an important role within organizations. These project practitioners practice leadership by applying systems thinking and communication skills while helping ensure alignment with organizational goals and vision.

5.12 Summary

The competencies discussed in this section combine with foundational project management skills to support project practitioners in a wide range of complex settings. Skills such as strategic thinking, organizational alignment, systems thinking and integration, and cultural and ethical competence can provide project practitioners with a comprehensive framework for professional growth.

This section established competencies for complex project environments, including the following:

- Exploring the idea of competencies and how they relate to complexity;
- Defining eight competencies that are beneficial in complex environments and discussing their associated behavior and impact; and
- Establishing the importance of competency integration for connecting different areas of expertise to work toward a shared goal.

The competencies in this section provide a strong foundation for project practitioners seeking to build a complexity toolkit. The following sections will build on these competencies, exploring how they relate to leading projects in complex environments.

Section 6

Communication and Stakeholder Engagement

6.1 Introduction

Communication is often the decisive factor among alignment and confusion, momentum, and delay. The way messages are delivered, received, and interpreted can be critical to making progress, particularly in complex projects. The unpredictable, dynamic, and multifaceted nature of complexity often creates high-stress environments that impact how communication is received by stakeholders. Even experienced project practitioners with strong communication skills may face challenges as they communicate within a complex environment.

This section explores communication as a factor that influences how people understand complexity. The section considers how cognitive biases, political dynamics, social norms, and emotional triggers shape message interpretation and engagement levels. The following subsections are included:

- How Stakeholders Process Communication
- Factors That Impact Project Communication
- Practical Applications for Stakeholder Engagement

This section offers tools and strategies for simplifying ambiguity, engaging diverse stakeholders, navigating political and social influences, and managing perceptions in times of change. Topics such as empathy mapping, power mapping, storytelling, feedback loops, and communication are presented as practical mechanisms that improve understanding and accelerate alignment.

6.2 How Stakeholders Process Communication

Communication and stakeholder engagement occur within environmental and organizational contexts. Examples of environmental context include global, marketplace, and business-centric conditions, whereas examples of organizational context include strategy, culture, and processes.

All communication is subject to the contextual interpretation of its audience. When people receive information, they rely on both emotional and cognitive processes to make sense of it. Understanding is created as information filters through an individual's experiences, mental models, and emotional state. Interpretations are influenced by the following:

- The information that was shared;
- What the person already knows or believes;
- Their emotional state and level of stress; and
- Their assumptions, biases, and prior experiences.

Because interpretation involves more than the message itself, two people may understand the same message in entirely different ways. Even the same person may react differently to the same information depending on context or mood. In complex project environments, where uncertainty, interdependence, and change are key features, these variations can have significant consequences.

Ultimately, stakeholder reactions and decisions depend less on the original message than on how that message was perceived and internalized. This section examines the factors that influence communication in complex environments and introduces practical tools for understanding stakeholder perspectives.

6.2.1 Emotional and Cognitive Interpretation

Organizational pressures and environmental issues are filtered through individual perceptions and conceptions. Perception refers to the sensory information a person receives. Information is processed through social norms and emotional and cognitive filters. These filters transform data into meaning. The filters mold what the stakeholder believes is happening and why it matters. Figure 6-1 illustrates how information, social norms, and emotional and cognitive filters interact to create perceptions.

Conception is the mental model that is the result of the meaning-making process; it is how people organize perceived information to create a subjective understanding. Conception is shaped by experience, emotions, culture, and prior knowledge. Thus, people perceive through their senses and emotions and conceive a personal version of perceived reality.

Stakeholders in complex projects—executives, technical specialists, end users, and regulators—have diverse backgrounds and interests. How information is framed significantly affects how it's received

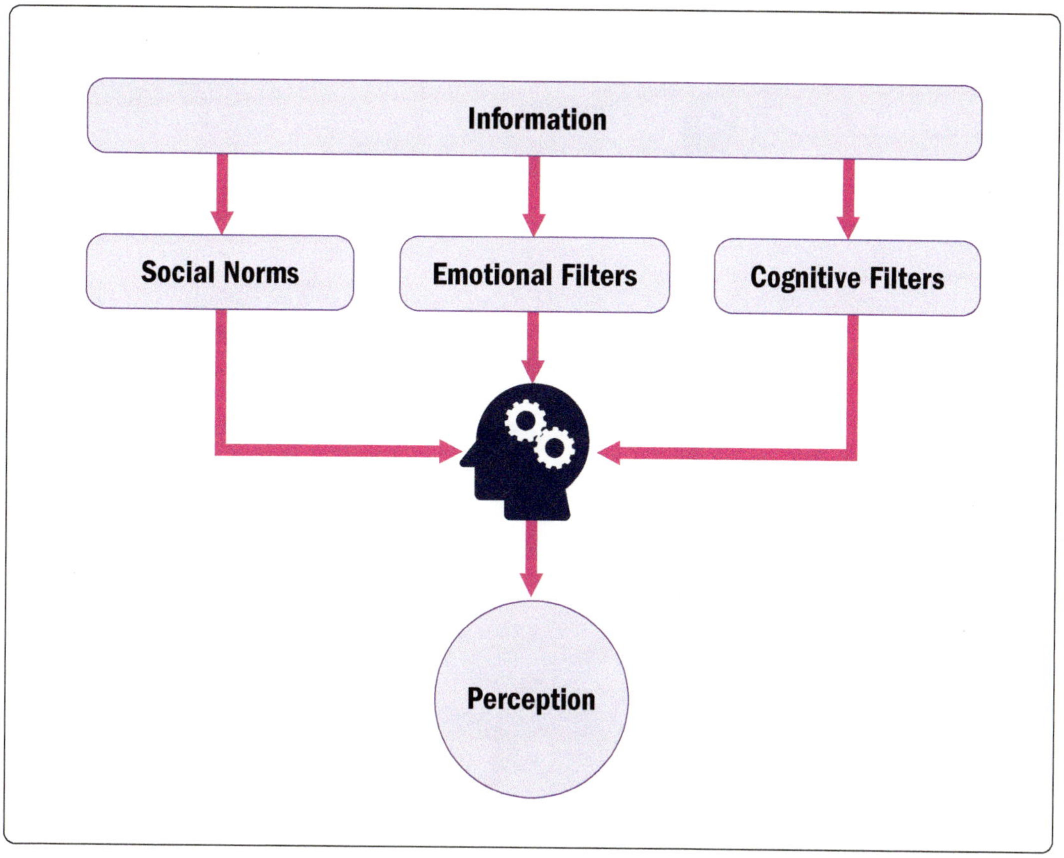

Figure 6-1. Stakeholder Perceptions

and acted upon. Effective project managers should be "information translators" who can speak each stakeholder's language. Stakeholders, therefore, interpret project communication not only through logic, but also through emotion, intuition, and personal history. These filters influence how messages are understood, how risks are judged, and how decisions are made.

Human cognition operates through two interacting systems:

- **Reflexive processing.** Fast, automatic, and emotionally driven, including implicit assumptions, stereotypes, and gut reactions that often shape perception before conscious reasoning begins.
- **Reflective processing.** Slower, analytical, and more deliberate, this type of processing allows people to evaluate evidence, plan actions, and consider multiple perspectives.

By understanding these two processing modes and recognizing which system is likely dominant, project leaders can adjust their communication strategies. [6]

Within stressful, high-pressure, or fast-paced environments, quick reflexive responses may preempt the rational decision-making that reflective processing can bring. Calm, clear, deliberate communication fosters reflective thought, whereas stress or threat cues trigger reflexive reactions such as defensiveness or avoidance. Strategic communication choices can impact which processing mode dominates.

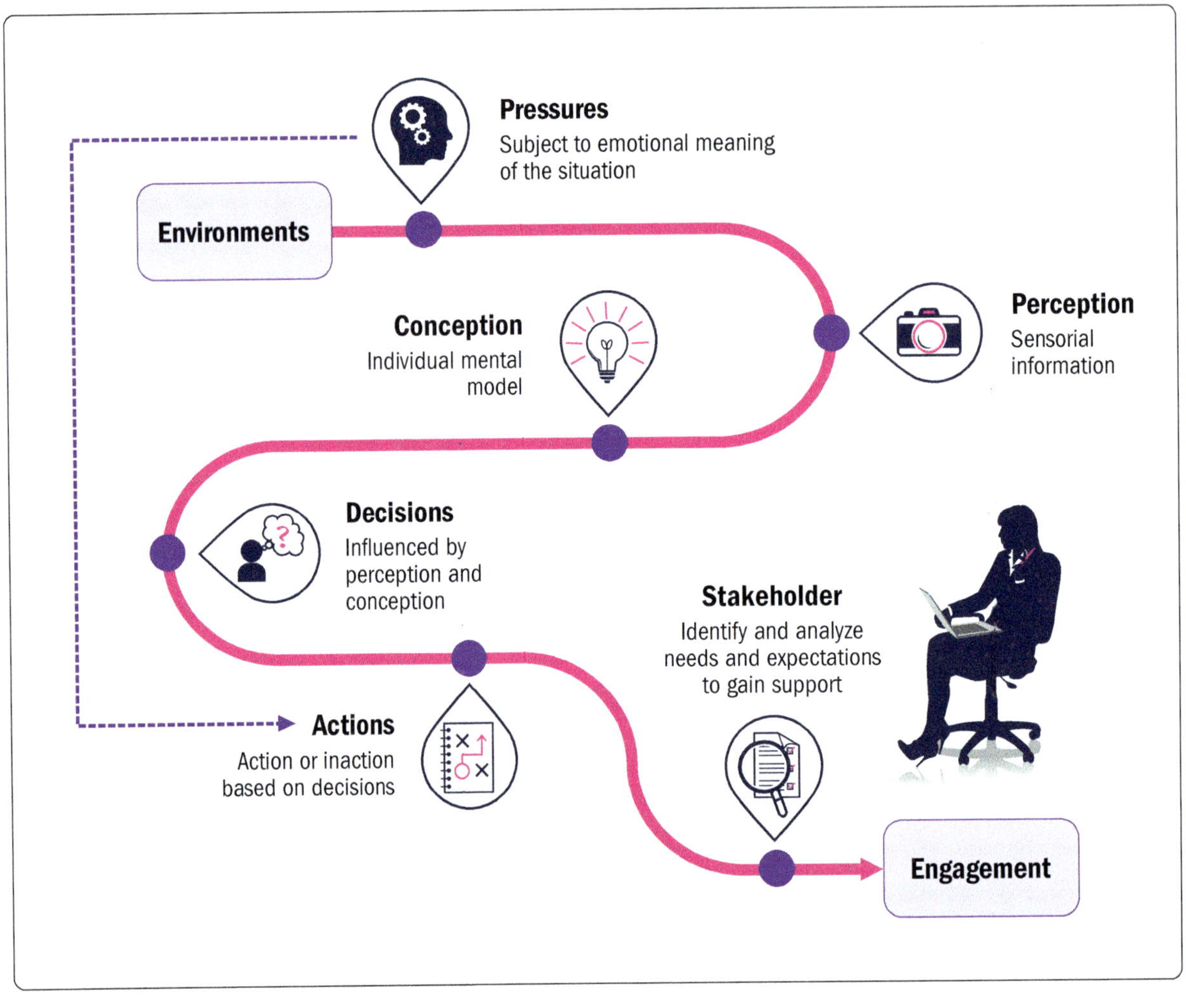

Figure 6-2. Stakeholder Engagement Path

Intuition also plays a role in the way information is processed. Intuition allows people to act despite uncertainty or ambiguity, drawing from tacit experience rather than explicit reasoning. However, intuition can lead to incorrect assumptions or misguided actions. Encouraging stakeholders to articulate the reasoning behind their intuitive judgments and actions can reveal assumptions, align interpretations, and prevent misunderstandings.

Figure 6-2 illustrates how stakeholder engagement evolves. The process starts with emotional reactions to the environment and organizational pressures. These reactions influence stakeholders' perceptions as well as the mental models or conceptions they create. Conceptions then influence decisions, which determine actions. To engage with stakeholders effectively, project professionals should understand how different variables influence stakeholders' emotions, thoughts, decisions, and actions.

6.2.2 Cognitive Adaptation and Meaning Making

When new information contradicts existing beliefs or expectations, individuals should reconcile the difference. This process, known as cognitive adaptation or meaning making, is central to how stakeholders learn and adjust within complex systems.

The result of cognitive adaptation or meaning making will differ depending on whether people experience conflict as a threat or a challenge:

- **Threat framing.** Narrows perception, prompting defensive reasoning or dismissal of new information.
- **Opportunity framing.** Broadens perspective, enabling curiosity, learning, and collaborative problem-solving.

Framing changes as challenges, rather than threats, support productivity in dynamic environments. Effective communication supports adaptation through the following:

- Clarifying uncertainty without oversimplifying it,
- Framing change as purposeful rather than chaotic, and
- Reinforcing shared goals and values to maintain psychological safety.

Complex environments frequently generate ambiguity, requiring individuals and organizations to interpret incomplete or conflicting data, which could be perceived as threats to project success. Clear communication and purposeful framing help stakeholders integrate new information, treating updates and changes as challenges rather than threats.

Figure 6-3 illustrates how adaptation occurs. A message causes dissatisfaction or cognitive dissonance when reality differs from expectations. Reflexive thinking is reevaluated, then reflective thinking uses learning loops to reconcile differences between initial assumptions and later reconsideration. Expectation includes social norms, filters, and perceptions that were formed (see Figure 6-1). Learning can generate adjusted expectations and new decisions or actions.

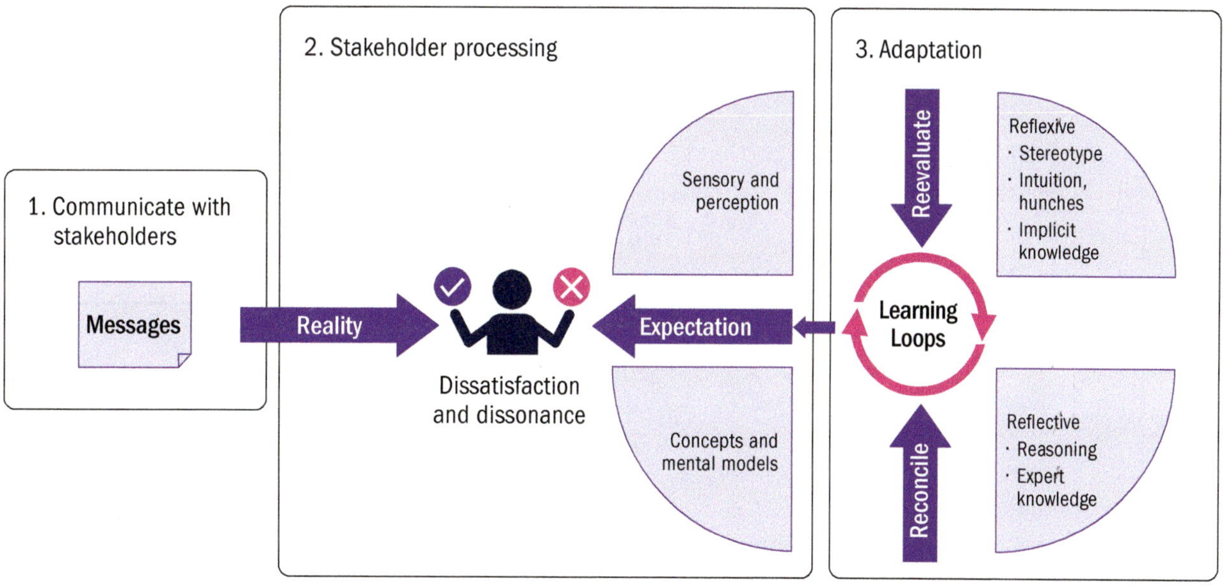

Figure 6-3. Dissonance and Adaptation

6.2.3 Tools and Practices for Understanding Stakeholders

Because interpretation is subjective, project success often hinges on understanding how different stakeholders experience and interpret the same situation. Structured tools can clarify diverse perspectives, allowing project leaders to engage more effectively with stakeholders.

Relevant diagnostic and sensemaking tools include the following:

- **Empathy mapping.** Captures what stakeholders think, feel, see, say, and do to reveal emotional drivers, pain points, and desired outcomes. Figure 6-4 shows a sample empathy map.
- **Power and interest mapping.** Visualizes influence, motivation, and interdependencies across stakeholders to inform engagement strategies. Figure 6-5 shows a sample power and interest map.
- **Stakeholder doubt analysis.** Surfaces latent skepticism or hesitation that could undermine alignment, often through reflection sessions, anonymous input, or scenario testing.
- **Storytelling.** Uses narrative to connect facts to emotions, making complex or abstract information relatable and memorable.
- **Scenario planning.** Compares current assumptions of strategy and operations for initiatives and/or business models against alternative futures to identify gaps in perception and readiness.

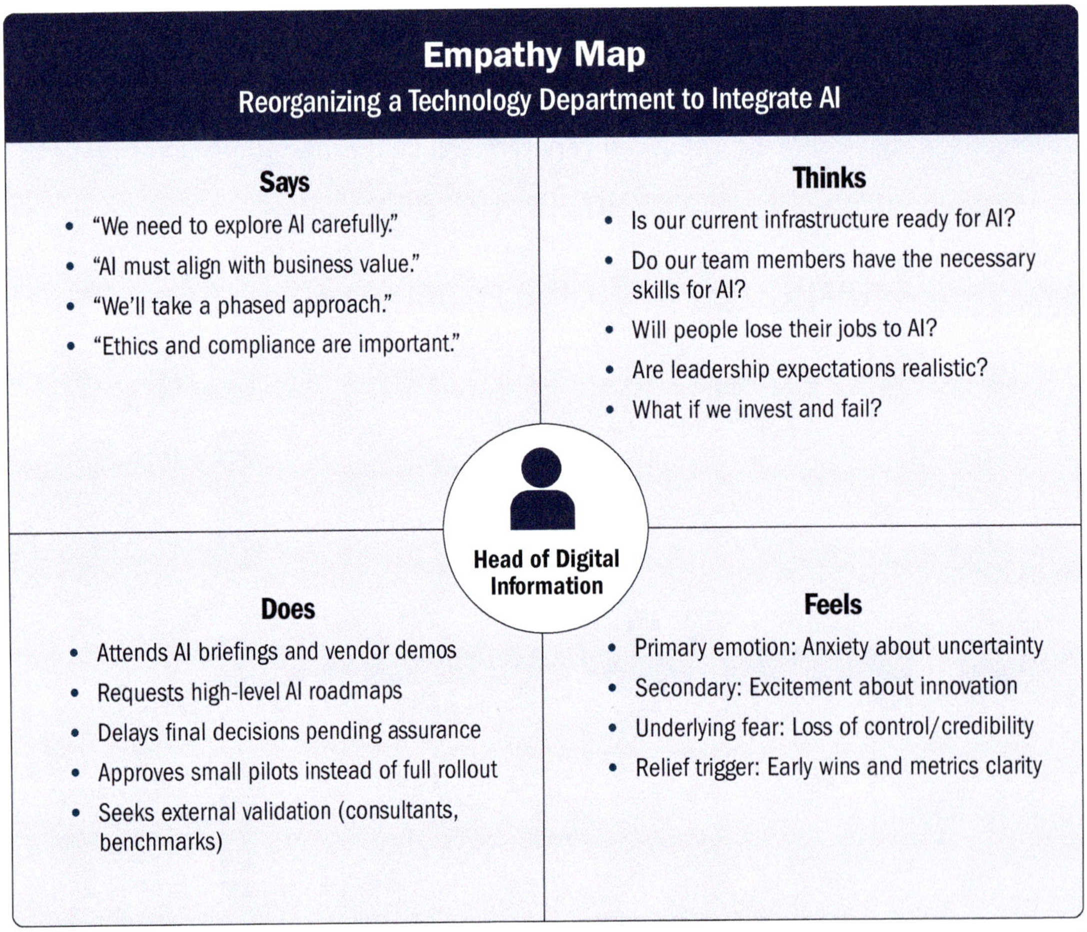

Figure 6-4. Empathy Map

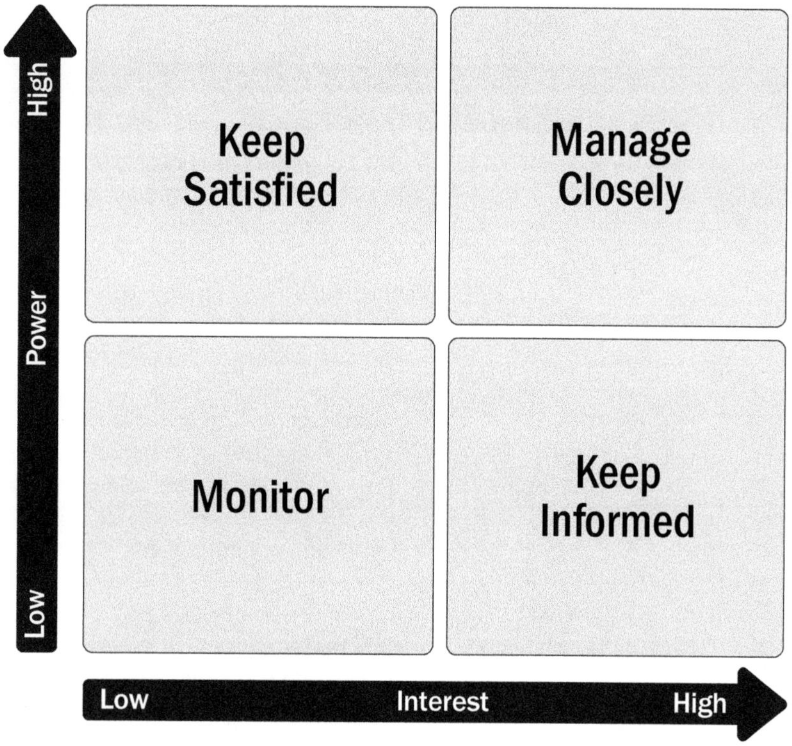

Figure 6-5. Power and Interest Map

In addition to using these tools, project practitioners who seek to gather and interpret perspectives may perform the following:

- Build diverse advisory networks and/or change agents to expand understanding beyond the immediate project team.
- Use mixed methods, such as interviews, surveys, and informal conversations, to capture both rational and emotional stakeholder responses.
- Identify key decision-makers and trace the information sources shaping their view, then offer credible alternatives where biases or blind spots appear.
- Manage pacing by slowing down when enthusiasm masks risks and accelerating when fear inhibits progress.
- Create opportunities for joint reflection to align stakeholders before acting.

Table 6-1 provides examples of how differing purposes of communication can employ various techniques to achieve intended outcomes.

6.3 Factors That Impact Project Communication

Although there may be many ways to interpret the same information, there are three factors that reliably influence the way messages are received by stakeholders: information completeness, cognitive and group biases, and sociopolitical influences. Each of these factors acts as a lens through which stakeholders interpret new information and decide how to respond.

Table 6-1. Communication Purpose, Technique, and Intended Outcome

Purpose	Technique	Intended Outcome
Build urgency for change. Inspire action through purpose and rally project teams.	"Why–How–What?"	Drive a product or service toward a meaningful outcome. Use during project kickoff or sponsor briefing.
	"And–But–Therefore"	Create a shared context; introduce a problem or challenge. Stakeholders agree on the problem and develop a solution or action as a group. Use when explaining constraints or trade-offs.
Align the team at project kickoff. Illustrate transformation by emotionally engaging the audience.	"Context–Routine–Event–Change"	Set the context, describe an observable routine or common pattern, then provoke an inciteful event, drawing the resulting consequences or resolutions for change. Use also for change request approvals, risk escalation and retrospective/lessons learned.
Enable learning after events. Respond to setbacks and support continuous improvement through reflection.	"What–So What–What Next (or Now What)?"	Implement continuous improvements by learning from past performances. By clearly stating the facts or events and explaining the relevance or impact, others can make sense of the recommended, actionable steps. Use during lessons learned or corrective action discussion.

Project practitioners who understand these factors within the context of their projects will be able to tailor communication to fit their needs, creating effective messaging strategies that build trust, manage perceptions, and maintain alignment across teams. This section describes these factors, detailing their impact on communication.

6.3.1 Information Completeness

Stakeholders depend on timely and relevant data to make informed decisions. When stakeholders are given incomplete information, they may become hesitant, suspicious, or resistant. This is particularly true when cost, schedule, or scope changes are made without sufficient explanation.

For information to be perceived as complete, it should be accurate, clear, and accessible. Sharing complete information with stakeholders supports trust, positive perceptions, and effective engagement. However, in complex projects, information is often fluid and fragmented and it may be interpreted differently depending on a stakeholder's role, context, or access level. The dynamic, unpredictable, and interconnected nature of complex projects makes sharing complete information a challenge.

Project practitioners navigating complex projects benefit from developing information-sharing approaches that consider the project environment alongside stakeholder needs. Clearly stating what is known and unknown can help build credibility within a changing environment. Carefully considering the timing of information disclosure can also influence stakeholder reactions. For example, sharing information at regularly scheduled update meetings builds the expectation of transparency while helping ensure information is framed with the appropriate context.

To provide accurate, clear, and accessible information amid complexity, project practitioners should do the following:

- Provide context alongside data points to reduce misinterpretation.
- Use confidence intervals and assumption logs to signal data uncertainty.
- Engage stakeholders in codeveloping what "complete information" means for them.

Acknowledging uncertainty is key to providing complete information within a complex context. When information is structured around stakeholder needs, aligned with decision-making cycles, and supported by transparency protocols, stakeholders become informed participants with a stronger understanding of project circumstances.

6.3.2 Cognitive Biases

As has been previously established, stakeholder interpretations and reactions are often influenced by reflexive, rather than reflective processing, developed using intuition, cognitive shortcuts, prior experiences, group norms, and emotional cues. Reflexive processing profoundly influences how communication is received and acted upon in complex projects.

Cognitive biases, which are systematic deviations from rational judgment, play a large role in reflexive processing, impacting how stakeholders process risks, interpret data, and engage in decision-making. There are several types of cognitive biases that frequently impact communication and interpretation, including the following:

- **Confirmation bias.** Unconsciously recalling information or interpretations that confirm an existing preference or mental model. For example, a chief technology officer (CTO) may dismiss ethical concerns about a new AI system because it conflicts with a desire for fast technical advancement.
- **Framing effect bias.** Allowing the presentation of information to impact its interpretation. For example, a milestone described as "80% complete" inspires confidence compared to the mathematically equivalent framing of "20% remaining." Framing effect bias can impact emotional responses and decisions, even when the underlying information is identical.
- **Anchoring bias.** Preferring early estimates or initial opinions over later evaluations. For example, an arbitrary initial deadline becomes an important reference point to define success. Anchoring can persist even after the initial information is known to be unreliable.
- **Conformity bias.** Also known as groupthink, conformity bias involves suppressing dissenting voices in the interest of maintaining consensus across a group or aligning to group authorities. For example, a project team maintains a positive outlook on a failing initiative because no one wants to challenge the dominant opinion in meetings.

These biases may have a range of different effects depending on the context. While the effects of these biases may not always be negative, they frequently distort the truth. To counter their effects, project leaders may benefit from the following:

- Embedding mechanisms for reflection into communication processes;
- Using structured templates to capture decision rationales;
- Encouraging productive disagreement and discussion among team members;

- Rotating roles, such as meeting facilitation, between team members to surface alternative views;
- Carefully reviewing any decisions made during high stress periods; and
- Creating anonymous feedback mechanisms to avoid group bias.

Additional techniques, such as red-teaming, decision logs, and devil's advocacy, can encourage diverse perspectives and support conversations about bias.

Insight

Bias is most prevalent when information is processed quickly. Building processes for reflection and adding short delays before decision-making helps reduce bias, encouraging a shift into the reflective thinking processes that create thoughtful decisions.

6.3.3 Political and Social Influences

In complex environments, particularly those involving multiple organizations or layers of management, project leaders often operate without role-based authority, relying on building trust and influence. Political and social influences are critical factors in such environments. These influences shape decision-making and stakeholder behavior and, ultimately, may determine the project's trajectory.

Political influences reflect the distribution and use of power among individuals and groups. These influences affect how decisions are made, whose voices are prioritized, and how resources are allocated. Political structures may be formal, such as roles defined in governance structures, or informal, emerging through personal networks, office politics, or organizational culture.

Social influences include stakeholder values, identities, group norms, emotional investment, and cultural dynamics. Social factors such as these may cause resistance to change, selective information sharing, or passive disengagement. In some cases, stakeholders may show outward compliance while inwardly resisting a project's direction, especially if their priorities or values are not reflected in the process. Change fatigue, uncertainty, and lack of perceived relevance can compound this effect, eroding commitment and undermining progress.

Both political and social influences can distort the way project risks and benefits are perceived.

Example scenarios

Political pressure from company leadership may cause a vice president to misrepresent project progress, presenting overoptimistic scenarios to secure support or funding.

Social pressure may lead a project team to maintain ineffective initiatives because they were launched by a well-liked coworker. These influences may cause pressure that suppresses dissent and reduces the quality of decisions. Ignoring political context or social dynamics can lead to cascading failures.

Political and social dynamics become even more pronounced in global or cross-cultural contexts, where authority may not translate uniformly and where assumptions about hierarchy, consensus, or urgency vary significantly. In these settings, the ability to lead through trust, credibility, and purpose becomes more important than formal control mechanisms.

For effective communication within an environment with significant political and social influences, project practitioners may do the following:

- Map both formal and informal stakeholder influences.
- Use culturally adapted visuals and language.
- Monitor external events, adapting messaging accordingly.
- Tailor communication approaches to fit local context and power dynamics.

The ability to recognize and navigate political and social influences creates a foundation for success. Understanding people, power, and perception is as critical as managing schedules, costs, or scope.

Combined with providing complete information and counteracting cognitive biases, consideration of political and social influences helps guide project practitioners toward developing effective communications.

Insight

Decision complexity is a factor that also influences communication. Complex decisions require open communication that is both informative and relational. Open dialogue can test assumptions, surface uncertainty, and clarify what is known and what is still emerging. Communication in these situations supports psychological safety and constructive participation as solutions evolve.

6.4 Practical Applications for Stakeholder Engagement

As established in this section, effective communication strategies are tailored to project contexts and stakeholder needs, considering the many factors that influence how people process information. Since there is no universally successful communication method for complexity, project practitioners benefit from considering effective strategies in their associated context.

This section introduces a range of complex project scenarios, labeled according to complexity types as established in Section 2, as well as their associated stakeholders. Each scenario describes the competencies and tools that could be used to communicate effectively within the project context.

6.4.1 Structural Complexity and Political and Social Influences

As an example, a multistakeholder healthcare reform project has high structural complexity. Cultural identity and group norms shape stakeholder engagement, impacting communication approaches.

The project team may map out the following information to help manage the complexity:

- **Stakeholders:**
  - Multinational team members,
  - Executives,
  - Policymakers, and
  - Community members.
- **Project team competencies:**
  - Value creation and motivational leadership,
  - Cultural and ethical competence,
  - Situational awareness, and
  - Environmental intelligence.
- **Tools to manage communication:**
  - Empathy mapping,
  - Trust-building dialogues,
  - Culturally sensitive messaging and storytelling, and
  - Stakeholder maps showing formal versus informal power dynamics across communities.

To support effective project execution, the project team may consider the following approaches:

- Question stakeholders about the factors behind their decisions. This approach allows stakeholders to examine their decision-making patterns.
- Help stakeholders pick the optimal option, even if this means choosing the least-bad option.
- In challenging times, project practitioners should pause, slow down, reevaluate, seek help, and get a second opinion.
- Document all decisions and their associated rationales.

These approaches are intended to improve stakeholder engagement. Incomplete or outdated information can create uncertainty, causing cascading errors across subsystems. When high uncertainty exists, people tend to withdraw. In these situations, more communication is needed, not less.

6.4.2 Dynamic Complexity and Cognitive Biases

In digital transformation initiatives, stakeholder expectations evolve rapidly. As an example, in a transformation project a system change introduced a high number of interconnected data failures in other systems. Complexity was introduced due to multiple reporting structures and layers of bureaucracy, requiring process changes across the supply chain.

The project team may map out the following information to help manage the complexity:

- **Stakeholders:**
  - Product owners,
  - Focus groups,
  - Agile teams,
  - Executive sponsors,
  - Business process owners, and
  - Customer-facing teams.
- **Project team competencies:**
  - Systems thinking and integration, and
  - Analytical thinking and bias recognition.
- **Tools to manage communication:**
  - Daily coordination meetings, retrospective sessions, and scenario-based planning;
  - Frequent synchronization to surface emerging risks and challenge assumptions; and
  - Visualizations, such as diagrams and maps, to illustrate complex, interconnected relationships and system dynamics.

To support effective project execution, the project team may consider the following approaches:

- Create loyalty and engagement by identifying a purpose for each stakeholder layer; for example, the individual, team, department, and organization.
- Document decision-making and rationale.
- Convert specialized, technical jargon into plain language.
- Leverage collaborative platforms, such as videoconferencing and digital whiteboards, to facilitate real-time interaction.

These approaches can be applied to address the many competing interests at stake, even when escalation paths and governance structures lack accountability. It is important to remember that teams may default to confirmation bias, interpreting feedback to support their initial assumptions.

6.4.3 Technical Complexity and Ambiguity

Using an example of a large infrastructure project involving multiple contractors and technical systems, this creates a strong need for accurate interface documentation.

The project team may map out the following information to help manage the complexity:

- **Stakeholders:**
  - System architects,
  - Integration managers,

    - Project management office (PMO),
    - Vendors, and
    - System users.
- **Project team competencies:**
    - Strategic thinking and organizational alignment, and
    - Technical literacy.
- **Tools to manage communication:**
    - Sensemaking,
    - Stakeholder engagement,
    - Weekly coordination meetings,
    - Shared dashboards, and
    - Version-controlled documentation.

To support effective project execution, the project team may consider the following approaches:

- Document the process for all decisions, including the information that informed the decision, information sources, and the logic behind the decision.
- Be aware that stakeholders may lack the data and technological literacy they need to make decisions.
- Share and document the rationale for all decisions and conclusions, even if made by using intuition.
- Guide stakeholders into continuous learning and adaptation.

These approaches can be applied to address incomplete or ambiguous information, which necessitates increased communication and shared understanding. Transparency about status, decisions, and issues builds collaboration and trust.

6.4.4 Environmental Complexity and Social Influences

In a sustainability initiative example, public sentiment and media narratives shape stakeholders' perceptions of risk and legitimacy. Supply chain disruptions across multiple locations necessitate additional risk assessment.

The project team may map out the following information to help manage the complexity:

- **Stakeholders:**
    - Multinational team members,
    - Governments,
    - Vendors, and
    - Technical experts.

- **Project team competencies:**
  - Situational awareness, and
  - Environmental intelligence.
- **Tools to manage communication:**
  - Power mapping, doubt analysis, sentiment analysis, community engagement forums;
  - A dashboard showing real-time stakeholder sentiment trends and their impacts on project decisions; and
  - Scenario planning to challenge default assumptions and encourage respectful debate.

To support effective project execution, the project team may consider the following approaches:

- Help ensure all viewpoints are represented during decision-making processes.
- Create anonymous feedback mechanisms.
- Solicit input from a wide range of people to encourage connection and commitment across groups.
- Create a culture of collaborative problem-solving.

These approaches can be applied to help address conflicts that arise when team members and stakeholders across multiple countries have different priorities, cultures, values, and communication styles. There may be experts to call upon, but they may lack the wherewithal to activate a response plan from a wide set of opinions, and there could also be resistance to expert opinions.

6.4.5 Sociopolitical Complexity

In an example situation, coalitions among the stakeholders of a public sector reform program begin to change because of social forces and political agendas.

The project team may map out the following information to help manage the complexity:

- **Stakeholders:**
  - Government officials,
  - Community leaders,
  - Advocacy groups,
  - Internal change agents, and
  - Funders.
- **Project team competencies:**
  - Systems thinking and integration,
  - Emotional intelligence,
  - Cultural and ethical competence,
  - Analytical thinking and bias recognition, and
  - Situational awareness and environmental intelligence.

- **Tools to manage communication:**
  - Power mapping,
  - Stakeholder mapping,
  - Targeted engagement plans, and
  - Monthly alignment forums.

To support effective project execution, the project team may consider the following approaches:

- Seek objective perspectives to mitigate stakeholder bias.
- Evaluate the consequences of actions to help ensure important choices are made with careful deliberation.
- Gather and review all relevant information before making decisions.

These approaches can be applied to address power relations and cultural sensitivities that need to be understood to uphold legitimacy and trust.

6.4.6 Organizational Complexity, Political Influences, and Groupthink

As an example, in a global enterprise transformation project, informal networks and office politics are influencing decision-making more than formal governance.

The project team may map out the following information to help manage the complexity:

- **Stakeholders:**
  - PMO,
  - Team members,
  - Executives, and
  - Governance or advisory roles.
- **Project team competencies:**
  - Strategic thinking,
  - Emotional intelligence, and
  - Cultural and ethical competence.
- **Tools to manage communication:**
  - Power mapping, scenario planning, transparent escalation paths; and
  - Diagram showing how informal influence flows across silos and impacts project alignment.

To support effective project execution, the project team may consider the following approaches:

- Limit the number of people with actual decision-making responsibilities and increase the number of advisors. To support cohesion and efficiency, assign decision authority to a core group that is informed by expert perspectives.

- Set clear goals and share these goals with stakeholders.
- Prioritize goals to preserve resources such as time, attention, effort, and budget.
- Document deprioritized tasks to help ensure these tasks do not take precedence over more important matters.

These approaches can be applied to help address power and organizational politics that can create challenges for making decisions. Challenges may include increased time for decision-making, project teams losing independence, and diffused responsibility across many parties. Charisma and overconfidence can also lead to unbalanced viewpoints.

6.4.7 Dynamic Complexity and Indirect Stakeholder Influence

In an example scenario for a government-funded smart infrastructure implementation project, unanticipated public opposition and shifting regulatory policies are delaying construction and requiring significant redesign. Social media, media attention, and environmental advocacy are amplifying reputational risk while the funding agency revises its requirements midproject.

The project team may map out the following information to help manage the complexity:

- **Stakeholders:**
  - Regulators,
  - Board members,
  - Investors,
  - End users,
  - Advocacy groups, and
  - Media.
- **Project team competencies:**
  - Governance and oversight,
  - Stakeholder empathy,
  - Strategic alignment,
  - Risk communication, and
  - Public affairs awareness.
- **Tools to manage communication:**
  - Stakeholder sensing,
  - Press monitoring dashboards,
  - Community listening sessions,
  - Regulatory engagement forums, and
  - Premortem risk exercises.

To support effective project execution, the project team may consider the following approaches:

- Identify and cultivate relationships with influential external stakeholders who are not yet involved.
- Build early partnerships with community representatives, legal advisors, and public affairs professionals to create readiness plans.
- Use storytelling to frame complex trade-offs in accessible language, especially when engaging public audiences or regulators.
- Conduct stakeholder sensing at regular intervals to detect shifts in sentiment, policy, or influence that could impact execution.
- Consider convening an independent group to intentionally challenge assumptions, test risks, and uncover blind spots (often referred to as a "red team" review) before publicly releasing plans.

These approaches can be applied to help address situations where stakeholders operate outside traditional project governance but still hold significant power to affect timing, funding, perception, or policy. Stakeholder influence can be indirect but consequential. Failing to anticipate stakeholder reactions can lead to misalignment with societal expectations or regulatory standards.

6.5 Summary

This section examined how communication influences understanding, alignment, and decision-making in complex project environments. The section highlighted ways that effective communication extends beyond message delivery, requiring awareness of how stakeholders perceive, interpret, and respond within dynamic systems.

This section described approaches for communicating amid complexity by:

- Explaining how stakeholder perceptions and cognitive biases shape communication outcomes;
- Exploring the influence of political dynamics, social norms, and emotional factors on message interpretation;
- Presenting techniques for simplifying ambiguity and promoting shared understanding among diverse stakeholders; and
- Introducing practical tools such as empathy mapping, power mapping, storytelling frameworks, and feedback loops to enhance engagement and alignment.

The concepts and tools discussed in this section enable project practitioners to communicate with greater clarity, empathy, and adaptability in the face of complexity.

Section 7

Decision-Making in Complex Environments

7.1 Introduction

Decision-making in complex environments is fundamentally different from decision-making in stable or complicated systems. Project decisions impact a wide range of stakeholders and functions and ultimately impact outcomes. To make well-informed decisions, project leaders employ methods and models that help them evaluate available information. However, decision-making methods and models are less effective in complex environments when relevant information is uncertain, ambiguous, evolving, or incomplete. In these circumstances, decisions often involve trade-offs, requiring a balance between immediate issues with long-term risks and objectives.

This section discusses decision-making approaches in uncertain and ambiguous environments. The following subsections are included:

- Impact of Complexity on Decisions
- The Project Practitioner's Role in Complex Decisions
- Decision-Making Frameworks and Models
- Enablers of High-Quality Decisions

Decisions encompass the strategic, tactical, and operational levels of projects. Conscientious decision-making improves the chances of overall project success.

7.2 The Impact of Complexity on Decisions

Projects require a number of decisions relating to a wide range of domains. Regardless of complexity levels, leaders and teams shall make high-impact decisions regarding areas such as strategy, operations, finances, stakeholder engagement, and risk mitigation.

In stable project environments, straightforward cause-and-effect relationships, reliable data, and established good practices support rational, structured decision-making. Complexity introduces a range of complications that disrupt traditional decision-making practices, reducing their effectiveness and requiring alternative approaches. This section describes the impact of complexity on project decisions.

7.2.1 Characteristics of Decisions Amid Complexity

Complex projects are characterized by emergent risks, nonlinear interactions, and interdependent systems that challenge established practices. These conditions make it difficult to anticipate outcomes or fully understand the implications of any single choice. As a result, decisions within complex environments may be (see Figure 7-1):

- **Nonlinear.** Avoid linear planning assumptions.
- **Ambiguous.** Apply sensemaking and experimentation.
- **Time-sensitive.** Empower fast decision-making, limit approvals.
- **Iterative.** Use inspect-and-adapt cycles.

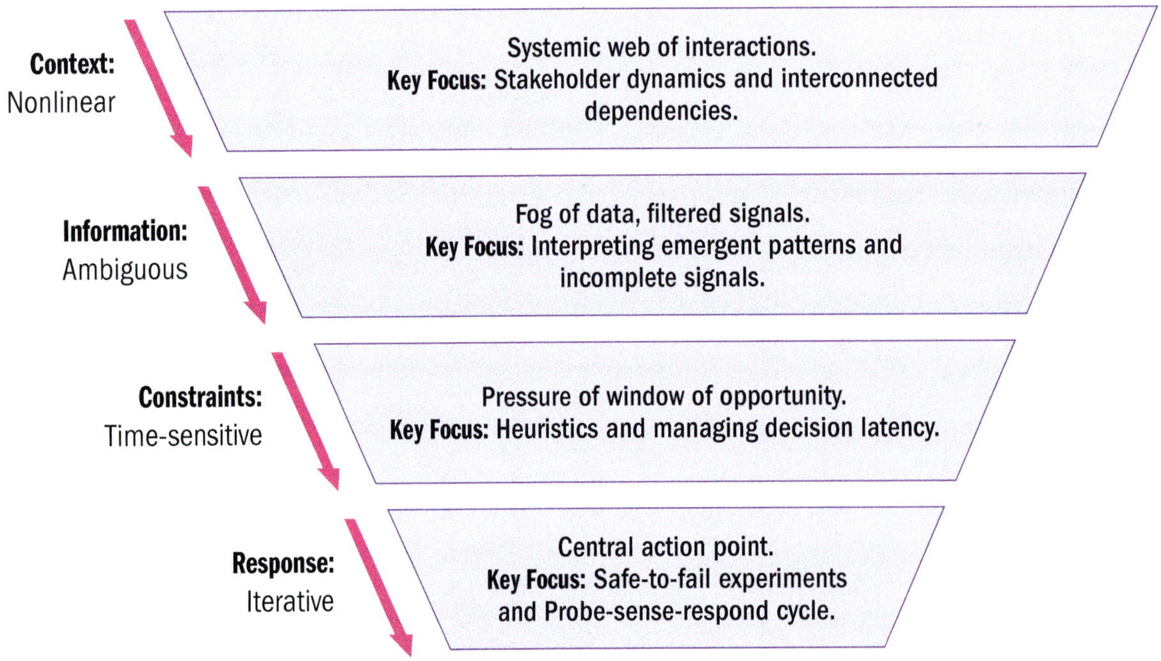

Figure 7-1. The Decision-Response Framework Layers

Figure 7-1 illustrates an example of the multidimensional nature of decision-making in complex systems. This example depicts a scenario where conditions are nonlinear and ambiguous, and leaders should prioritize time-sensitive responses through an iterative cycle of probing and sensing

7.2.2 Decisions About Risk in Complex Environments

The presence of complexity transforms the nature of project risk management. Traditional risk management, which focuses on identifying, analyzing, and planning responses for known risks, proves insufficient when faced with risks in a complex environment. Risks in complex environments may include the following:

- Emergent risks that arise unexpectedly due to the interconnected elements, ambiguity, and overall uncertainty;
- Unknown factors that cannot be predicted at the start of the project;
- Cascading effects where issues in one part of the project escalate and cascade into significant disruptions across the project system; and
- Limited predictability, because quantitative risk analysis can be less reliable due to the unpredictability of cause-and-effect relationships.

Project practitioners can evaluate and manage decisions made about risks in complex environments through the following:

- Using adaptive strategies, including continuous monitoring for signals, fostering resilience, designing safe-to-fail experiments, and emphasizing rapid response and learning from surprises;
- Making risk-informed decisions by integrating risk considerations into every decision, understanding potential impacts and designing adaptive responses in addition to preventive measures;
- Becoming accustomed to making decisions with incomplete or conflicting information, relying on sensemaking and iterative learning; and
- Designing small, controlled experiments to test hypotheses and gather data in uncertain areas, minimizing the cost of potential failure while maximizing learning.

Although making decisions amid uncertainty is challenging, avoiding decisions due to incomplete information or ambiguous circumstances leads to further disruption. Risk management approaches such as these support project practitioners in taking action when faced with unpredictable circumstances.

7.3 The Project Practitioner's Role in Complex Decisions

In addition to influencing project decisions, complexity reshapes how project practitioners engage in the decision-making process itself. Rather than relying on linear, data-driven analysis, project practitioners should integrate multiple perspectives, interpret uncertainty, and respond adaptively as conditions evolve. The project practitioner's role expands beyond traditional authority to encompass a wider range of functions, including the following:

- **Sensemaking.** Observing, interpreting, and making sense of ambiguous or conflicting information to recognize emergent patterns and underlying dynamics.

- **Facilitation.** Guiding teams and stakeholders through collaborative decision processes, encouraging open dialogue, and integrating diverse perspectives.
- **Adaptive leadership.** Modeling flexibility, supporting experimentation, and enabling distributed decision-making within teams.
- **Contextual awareness.** Continuously assessing the project's environment and tailoring decision-making approaches to the specific domain of complexity.
- **Learning support.** Creating conditions that encourage learning from both successes and failures and applying those lessons to future decisions.

Prescriptive command-and-control approaches may be ineffective in complex environments, where project practitioners should navigate interdependencies, uncertainty, and ethical considerations. Instead, effective decision-making depends on balancing authority, collaboration, and adaptability.

This section explores four aspects of the project practitioner's role that are significant in navigating complexity: exercising authority, engaging stakeholders, integrating ethics, and selecting appropriate decision-making styles.

7.3.1 Authority Within Complex Projects

In stable environments, project practitioners often operate within established organizational structures that define their scope of authority. In complex projects, this authority may be more flexible and context dependent. Project practitioners benefit from adapting their level of control to the evolving situation. The following behaviors support adaptable authority structures within complex projects:

- **Delegated authority.** Determining which decisions can be made independently and which require escalation or consultation and then delegating decision-making authority accordingly.
- **Accountability for outcomes.** Accepting accountability for both decisions and their outcomes, which includes learning from consequences and adapting future actions.
- **Empowerment.** Enabling teams with the authority needed to make timely decisions, which often requires decentralized decision-making approaches.

A fluid approach to authority supports responsiveness and resilience. However, this flexibility also depends on the project practitioner's ability to engage stakeholders effectively, as collaboration is often key to making sound decisions in complex environments.

7.3.2 Working With Stakeholders

Stakeholder engagement is central to decision-making in complexity. Diverse viewpoints can help reveal interconnections, highlight potential risks, and uncover opportunities that may not be visible from a single perspective. Effective approaches for working with stakeholders include the following:

- **Key stakeholder identification.** Recognizing those who are affected by project decisions, even if indirectly, to help ensure decisions reflect the broader system.
- **Involvement level determination.** Deciding the appropriate degree of stakeholder participation in decision-making and communicating the expected participation level to stakeholders.

- **Issue adjudication and compromise.** Facilitating dialogue and negotiation to navigate divergent stakeholder priorities and perspectives.
- **Consensus building.** Fostering collaboration to achieve alignment on decisions, enhancing commitment, and supporting adaptive implementation.

Effective stakeholder engagement strengthens decisions while building trust and shared understanding. Decision authority in complex systems is governed by the principle of subsidiarity: placing authority at the lowest level capable of making effective decisions, where context and information are most current. This shift requires moving away from hierarchical approval chains toward intent-based leadership.

7.3.3 Making Decisions Ethically

The presence of complexity amplifies ethical considerations within decision-making. In complex environments, choices can have far-reaching and often unforeseen impacts. To make decisions ethically, project practitioners benefit from the following:

- **Applying ethical frameworks.** Utilizing ethical frameworks, such as utilitarianism, deontology, or virtue ethics, to evaluate alternatives and guide responsible choices.
- **Conducting stakeholder impact assessments.** Analyzing stakeholder impacts to understand the potential positive and negative effects of decisions.
- **Upholding transparency and integrity.** Helping ensure honesty and openness even in the face of difficult trade-offs and competing pressures.
- **Taking a long-term view.** Prioritizing sustainable and responsible outcomes over short-term gains.
- **Addressing bias.** Recognizing and reducing personal and organizational biases within the decision-making process.

By incorporating these approaches within their decision-making practices, project practitioners can evaluate the ethical impact of each decision they make.

7.3.4 Decision-Making Styles

The flexibility and responsiveness needed to make decisions within complex environments can be supported by using a range of decision-making styles. Project practitioners may employ any of the following decision-making styles, depending on the context of the decision:

- **Directive.** Taking quick, authoritative action, which is appropriate in simple or low-stakes situations, when involving others creates unnecessary delays or in chaotic situations when an immediate solution is needed.
- **Consultative.** Gathering input from others before making a final decision, which is effective for high-impact decisions that involve many stakeholders.
- **Collaborative.** Engaging stakeholders in joint decision-making processes, which is beneficial in complex environments where collective insight is valuable.
- **Delegative.** Entrusting decision-making authority to team members within defined boundaries, promoting autonomy and rapid responsiveness.

- **Adaptive.** Shifting among styles as conditions change, depending on uncertainty levels, information availability, team maturity, and the impact of the decision.

Selecting and adapting decision-making styles with intention enables project practitioners to balance structure and flexibility, which is an essential capability for success in complex project environments.

7.4 Decision-Making Frameworks and Models

As established in the previous sections, complexity adds additional challenges to decision-making and requires project practitioners to adjust their decision-making strategies and approaches.

Researchers have developed models and frameworks to support project practitioners making decisions amid complexity. This section highlights prominent decision-making models within this domain, describing situations when they are appropriate to use, how they are typically implemented, and their expected impact.

Figure 7-2 shows the seven decision-making models discussed in this section.

7.4.1 Cynefin Framework for Decision-Making

Cynefin is a sensemaking framework rather than a prescriptive model. It provides a way to interpret context and guide decision-making approaches, helping project practitioners understand complexity rather than represent reality.

This framework categorizes environments into five distinct domains:

1. Clear (formerly obvious/simple)
2. Complicated
3. Complex
4. Chaotic
5. Confused (formerly disorder)

After determining the Cynefin Framework domain category, project practitioners can use the Cynefin Framework to select an appropriate decision-making strategy.

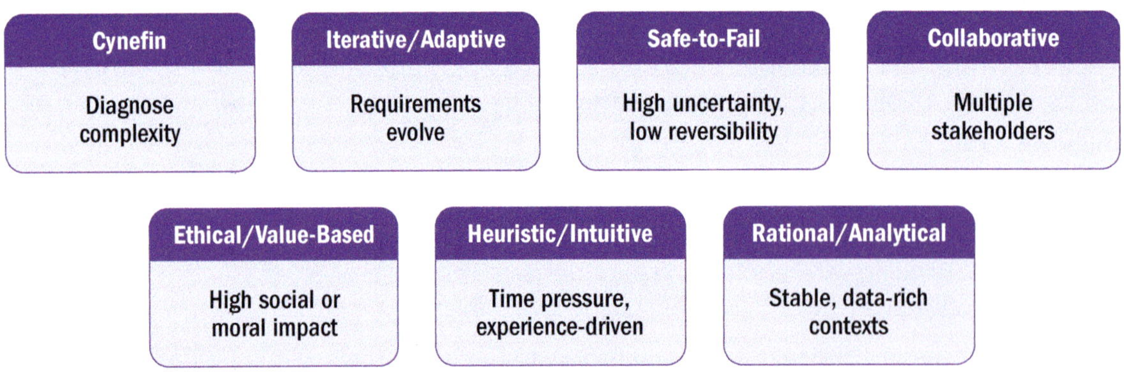

Figure 7-2. Decision-Making Approaches for Complex Environments

7.4.1.1 Implementation

Project practitioners applying the Cynefin Framework begin by assessing the situation and classifying it as one of the following domains:

- **Clear.** Stable setting with clear and repeatable cause-and-effect relationships.
- **Complicated.** Multiple valid solutions exist, requiring expert analysis and judgment.
- **Complex.** No definable cause-and-effect connection; only in hindsight do patterns become apparent.
- **Chaotic.** Absence of discernible patterns.
- **Confused.** A state of confusion in which one is not certain of the applied field.

It also recognizes liminal zones—boundaries between domains—where situations may shift as conditions evolve. Project practitioners should identify the current domain and apply the corresponding decision logic, while remaining alert to signals of transition.

This domain-identification phase allows the project practitioner time to evaluate the context before tailoring decision-making processes, achieving more informed and useful outcomes.

Each domain has a corresponding decision-making process that consists of three of the following activities:

- **Probe.** Test unknowns with miniexperiments.
- **Sense.** Read and understand signs or patterns.
- **Categorize.** Use rules that are already established.
- **Analyze.** Examine data or expert input to identify options.
- **Respond.** Act based on the understanding developed.
- **Act.** Intervene immediately to stabilize chaotic conditions.

After identifying the problem domain, the project practitioner should review the associated decision-making logic as listed in Table 7-1.

The aim in the Chaotic and Confused domains is to move the system into the Complex or Complicated regions, where meaningful sensemaking and decision-making can occur. When conditions change, transitions between domains require adaptive strategies, for example, stabilizing actions when moving toward Chaotic or safe-to-fail probes when shifting from Complex to Complicated.

In some cases, changes to the project environment may cause problems or decisions to shift between domains. These shifts can be abrupt and challenging to navigate, requiring situational awareness and the flexibility to adjust approaches.

7.4.1.2 Impact

Project practitioners who use the Cynefin Framework to guide decision-making may gain strategic benefits such as the following:

- **Contextual awareness.** Project practitioners understand their environment by breaking it down into definable domains, allowing decision-making approaches to be tailored to the specific context.

Table 7-1. Characteristics of Decision-Making in Complex Environments

Domain	Decision-Making Logic	Process Description	Project Practitioner's Focus
Clear	Sense → Categorize → Respond	Cause-and-effect relationships are clear. Apply good practices, focusing on efficiency and consistency.	Standardize, automate, monitor
Complicated	Sense → Analyze → Respond	Multiple valid solutions are possible. Use expert analysis, focusing on making informed decisions and applying good practices.	Engage experts, analyze trade-offs
Complex	Probe → Sense → Respond	Cause-and-effect relationships are unclear. Conduct safe-to-fail experiments, sense emerging patterns, and adapt, focusing on adaptability and learning.	Enable experiments, encourage learning
Chaotic	Act → Sense → Respond	Immediate action is required. Stabilize first, then adapt, focusing on rapid response and control.	Act decisively, reduce instability
Confused	Clarify → Identify Domain → Apply Proper Logic	Analyze the situation further to identify applicable domains. Apply the corresponding decision-making logic of identified domains.	Diagnose before acting

- **Risk management.** Assessing uncertainty and risk potential in various areas helps develop resilient, risk-informed methods.
- **Adaptive decision-making.** Iteration in dynamic and complex environments creates space for adaptive approaches, empowering project practitioners to employ responsive methods.
- **Communication and collaboration.** Using a common language to describe problems enhances communication and collaboration, enabling effective decision-making.
- **Strategic alignment.** Timely and contextually appropriate action supports alignment between organizational decisions and goals.

While the Cynefin Framework offers valuable guidance for navigating complex environments, it is not without risks when misapplied such as the following:

- **Oversimplification.** Project practitioners may misclassify complex situations as complicated or clear, potentially resulting in misguided decisions.

- **Overreliance on experts.** Teams that interpret the Cynefin Framework's "complicated" domain too narrowly may default to expert-driven decision-making in complex contexts, limiting diverse input and collective sensemaking.
- **Failure to adapt.** Treating domain classifications as static may anchor decisions in outdated assumptions as conditions evolve.
- **Delayed action.** Misinterpreting the Cynefin Framework's emphasis on probing and sensemaking can lead to indecision, even when action is urgently needed.
- **Misclassification.** Project practitioners who incorrectly place a situation in the wrong domain may waste effort, amplify instability, or reduce overall effectiveness.

Used thoughtfully, the Cynefin Framework supports adaptive decision-making. However, if misused, it can reinforce the rigidity it is meant to overcome.

7.4.2 Iterative or Adaptive Decision-Making Models

Iterative or adaptive decision-making models are cyclical processes where initial choices are made based on available information, then refined through experimentation, feedback, and learning.

These models were designed for changing circumstances. Decisions are understood to evolve over time and are therefore designed to be adjusted throughout the project's life cycle. These models are particularly effective when working in environments with dynamic requirements and emergent properties.

7.4.2.1 Implementation

Iterative or adaptive decision-making models are appropriate when project circumstances are dynamic. For example, frequent changes in stakeholder needs and evolving project scope are both signs that iterative approaches to decisions may be beneficial.

These models are characterized by mechanisms that support learning, responsiveness, and incremental progress in dynamic project environments, including the following:

- **Cyclical process.** Decisions are part of an ongoing loop of action, observation, and adjustment. This loop often mirrors cycles like plan-do-check-act (PDCA) or observe-orient-decide-act (OODA), emphasizing continuous flow and rapid iteration. Each cycle provides new data points for subsequent decisions.
- **Continuous learning.** New information and insights in each iteration inform subsequent decisions, helping teams detect emergent patterns and adapt strategies as the project unfolds.
- **Flexibility and responsiveness.** Plans are considered living documents, allowing teams to incorporate changes and pivot quickly in response to new data, emergent issues, or shifting stakeholder needs.
- **Incremental progress.** Projects deliver value in small, manageable steps, reducing overall risk by allowing for early validation and course correction. This approach enables early stakeholder feedback, minimizing investment in misaligned solutions.
- **Feedback loops.** Structured, informal mechanisms allow project leaders to gather performance data, stakeholder input, and environmental signals, helping ensure decisions are informed by recent feedback.

Iterative and adaptive decision-making models focus on sequential adjustments that allow project practitioners to navigate evolving circumstances. This approach acknowledges that the "right" path may not be fully knowable at the outset, thereby emphasizing agility and continuous adjustment to achieve desired outcomes.

7.4.2.2 Impact

Iterative and adaptive decision-making models foster organizational agility, resilience, and responsiveness. By emphasizing learning, experimentation, and stakeholder engagement, these models help project practitioners navigate uncertainty and identify opportunities that might not be visible at the outset. These models encourage teams to make timely adjustments based on evidence and feedback, often leading to more innovative and robust outcomes that remain aligned with evolving stakeholder needs.

Adaptive models require discipline to avoid potential pitfalls. Without clear boundaries and decision criteria, teams may experience confusion, mistaking iteration for indecision. Frequent changes can also challenge consistency, documentation, and stakeholder confidence if not well communicated or governed. However, when applied thoughtfully, iterative and adaptive models balance flexibility with focus, enabling continuous learning, early value delivery, and adaptive governance that strengthens both project outcomes and organizational capability in complex environments.

7.4.3 Safe-to-Fail Decision-Making Models

Safe-to-fail decision-making models involve designing experiments and initiatives where any potential failures are small, contained, and provide valuable insights. These models are designed for environments where outcomes are uncertain and unpredictable, allowing teams to try unproven approaches to gain information and experience that can inform higher-stakes initiatives.

7.4.3.1 Implementation

Project circumstances with high levels of uncertainty, rapid rates of change, and a lack of reliable data are good candidates for safe-to-fail decision-making models. These models rely on structured experimentation methods such as the following:

- **Bounded experimentation.** Implement small, controlled initiatives to test hypotheses or explore solutions in uncertain areas.
- **Learning orientation.** Prioritize the acquisition of new knowledge and insights from the experiment's outcome, regardless of success or failure.
- **Risk mitigation.** Design the experiment to minimize the potential for large-scale negative impacts.
- **Rapid iteration.** Facilitate quick cycles of testing, learning, and adjustment based on experiment results.
- **Feedback loops.** Establish clear mechanisms for capturing and disseminating learnings from experiments across the organization.

7.4.3.2 Impact

Safe-to-fail models enable project practitioners to generate real-world data, reduce uncertainty, and discover emergent solutions. Careful experimental design and thorough risk containment are essential to help ensure these approaches do not result in unintended negative impact. The outcome of each experiment should be carefully analyzed and considered to benefit from information gained.

By normalizing small failures as learning opportunities, these models foster a culture of innovation, resilience, and continuous adaptation, which is particularly valuable in highly ambiguous or novel project contexts.

7.4.4 Collaborative and Consensus-Based Decision-Making Models

Collaborative and consensus-based decision-making models involve multiple stakeholders in the decision process to foster alignment and commitment. They are particularly effective when decision success depends on collective acceptance.

7.4.4.1 Implementation

To foster alignment and commitment, collaborative and consensus-based decision-making models involve multiple stakeholders in the decision-making process. They are particularly effective when decision success depends on collective acceptance. These models emphasize collective ownership and shared understanding using the following approaches:

- **Inclusive participation.** Help ensure all affected or influential parties have a voice in the decision-making process.
- **Open dialogue.** Facilitate transparent and respectful communication to explore diverse perspectives and underlying interests.
- **Joint problem-solving.** Work together to identify common ground and mutually beneficial solutions.
- **Shared ownership.** Foster a sense of collective responsibility for the decision and its implementation.
- **Techniques.** Methods such as the Delphi technique or nominal group technique can structure group input and reach convergence.

By selecting the appropriate model based on the situation, these approaches enable all relevant perspectives to be considered and lead to more effective outcomes.

7.4.4.2 Impact

Collaborative and consensus-based models may lead to more robust, sustainable, and widely accepted decisions by incorporating a broader range of insights and mitigating potential resistance. However, these models can be more time-consuming and require skilled facilitation to manage potential conflicts and help ensure productive engagement.

7.4.5 Ethical and Value-Based Decision-Making Models

Ethical and value-based decision-making models focus on principles and values in addition to common goals such as efficiency or profitability. These models consider the long-term impact of decisions on various groups of people, society, and the environment, helping ensure alignment with moral and organizational values.

7.4.5.1 *Implementation*

Ethical and value-based decision-making models are best used in circumstances where there is uncertainty about ethical implications, conflicting stakeholder interests, potential for harm, or concerns about legal or policy compliance.

These models rely on inclusive and participatory practices to help ensure decisions are shaped by diverse perspectives and shared responsibility. Such practices may include the following:

- **Principle-driven decisions.** Base decisions on established ethical frameworks (e.g., utilitarianism, deontology, or virtue ethics) or organizational values.
- **Stakeholder impact.** Systematically assess the potential positive and negative consequences of decisions on all affected parties, including marginalized groups and future generations.
- **Transparency and accountability.** Help ensure ethical considerations are openly discussed and that decision-makers are accountable for the impact of their choices.
- **Long-term perspective.** Prioritize sustainable and responsible outcomes over immediate benefits.
- **Ethical matrix.** Apply this tool to systematically evaluate the ethical implications of different decision options across various stakeholder groups.

By using these practices, ethical and value-based decision-making models move beyond purely utilitarian or financial considerations by evaluating choices on fairness, responsibility, sustainability, and adherence to a defined ethical code.

7.4.5.2 *Impact*

Ethical and value-based decision-making models support complex projects with significant social, environmental, or public implications. These models help project practitioners navigate moral dilemmas, build trust, enhance organizational reputation, and help ensure projects contribute positively to society.

Implementing these models can be effective if project practitioners are careful to include all stakeholder perspectives, reflect on the impact of decisions, and inform decisions with sufficient information. When these models are used effectively, they foster responsible innovation and long-term sustainability, aligning decisions with a broader sense of purpose and integrity.

7.4.6 Heuristic and Intuitive Decision-Making Models

Heuristic and intuitive decision-making models use rapid judgments and mental shortcuts to make quick decisions that rely on experience and pattern recognition. These models can be beneficial when decisions are time-sensitive and conditions are uncertain. However, the models can be highly susceptible to cognitive biases and systemic errors.

7.4.6.1 *Implementation*

Heuristics are psychological shortcuts that reduce complex choices to simpler ones by using standard rules or pattern recognition. Intuition refers to insights generated rapidly, and often unconsciously, from accumulated experience and knowledge. Heuristics and intuition allow leaders to make rapid decisions, even in complex circumstances.

Heuristic and intuitive decision-making models may be appropriate when projects have one or more of the following characteristics:

- No clear cause-effect relationships,
- High uncertainty or ambiguity,
- Time pressure,
- Adaptive or emergent solutions are necessary, and
- Experts can recognize patterns from experience.

Because decision-making processes are subject to common cognitive pitfalls, these models are best reserved for isolated circumstances when other options are not available or for low-impact decisions.

7.4.6.2 Impact

Heuristic and intuitive decision-making models are fast, adaptable, and responsive, allowing project practitioners to act effectively with incomplete information. However, their reliance on instinct and mental shortcuts introduces significant risks. Cognitive biases, such as overconfidence, anchoring, or availability bias, can distort judgment, whereas decisions rooted in limited or irrelevant experience may lead to errors. Because intuition is inherently subjective, frequent use of these decision-making models reduces transparency and consistency across teams and organizations.

When applied with awareness and balance, heuristic and intuitive decision-making approaches complement analytical models by promoting agility and innovation, provided project practitioners remain alert to bias and validate intuition through reflection and feedback.

7.4.7 Rational and Analytical Decision-Making Models

Rational and analytical decision-making models provide a structured approach to decisions, grounding choices in stable information, including facts, logic, and evidence. Project practitioners often rely on these models to make well-informed decisions. Examples include cost-benefit analysis, decision trees, SWOT (strengths, weaknesses, opportunities, threats) analysis, and Pareto analysis.

7.4.7.1 Implementation

Rational and analytical decision-making models are most effective in project settings where the data is dependable and the objectives are clear; therefore, they have limited utility in complex projects. Before applying one of these models, project practitioners should confirm the following:

- Complete and accurate information is available to inform decision-making.
- Problems are well-defined.
- Clear performance metrics exist to evaluate progress.

After establishing that rational and analytical decision-making models are appropriate for the situation, project practitioners should proceed through versions of the following phases:

- Define the problem.
- List all possible solutions to the problem.
- Evaluate the likely outcome to each possible solution, considering benefits and drawbacks.
- Select the optimal solution based on the evaluation process.

Through this process, rational and analytical decision-making models provide a structured approach to making decisions regarding a wide range of topics.

7.4.7.2 Impact

When used correctly, rational and analytical decision-making models help reduce bias and avoid guesswork, enhancing outcomes in stable projects. These models are particularly effective when making decisions related to budgeting, risk management, and scheduling issues. The decision-modeling process also makes it easier to explain decisions to stakeholders, since the reasoning is documented and transparent.

While rational models are effective in stable environments, these models face limitations in situations where information is lacking, and possible solutions are challenging to identify. In these cases, iterative or adaptive decision-making models may be more appropriate.

7.4.8 Decision-Making Model and Framework Summary

The seven decision-making models presented in this section are each effective given the appropriate context. Table 7-2 lists situational factors encountered within projects and associates them with recommended decision-making models.

Table 7-2. Situational Factors and Decision-Making Models

Situational Factor	Recommended Decision-Making Model(s)
Diverse stakeholder perspectives	Collaborative and consensus-based, ethical and value-based
Clear cause-effect relationships	Rational and analytical, Cynefin Framework (clear/complicated)
Ambiguity and emergent patterns	Cynefin Framework (complex), iterative and adaptive, safe-to-fail
Incomplete or unreliable data	Iterative and adaptive, heuristic and intuitive, safe-to-fail
High time pressure	Heuristic and intuitive, Cynefin Framework (chaotic)
Ethical dilemmas or long-term impact	Ethical and value-based, collaborative and consensus-based
Need for learning and experimentation	Safe-to-fail, iterative and adaptive, Cynefin Framework (complex)

7.5 Enablers of High-Quality Decisions

High-quality decision-making in complex project environments benefits from a supportive organizational context. Organizational elements that enable an environment conducive to effective and adaptive decision-making may include the following:

- **Supportive leadership.** Using leadership strategies to empower teams, model vulnerability, and encourage open dialogue helps ensure diverse perspectives are considered within decision-making processes.
- **Learning culture.** Establishing a culture that allows experimentation, reflection, and iterative adjustments creates a positive environment for decision-making amid complexity.
- **Systems thinking.** Understanding the interconnectedness of project elements, recognizing feedback loops, and anticipating emergent behaviors allow project practitioners to move beyond isolated problem-solving, addressing root causes and systemic issues.

The daily practices of project practitioners can also enable high-quality decisions, helping ensure adaptive and informed choices are made consistently throughout the project life cycle. Such supportive practices may include the following:

- **Continuous planning and reforecasting.** Embed decision-making in iterative planning cycles, where forecasts are regularly updated based on new information and emergent realities, rather than relying on rigid, up-front plans.
- **Risk and opportunity management.** Continuously make risk response and opportunity exploitation decisions using methods such as involving rapid assessment, adaptive strategies, and safe-to-fail experiments.
- **Stakeholder engagement and communication.** Choose the appropriate level of transparency and collaboration for stakeholders, adapting as needed to foster buy-in and manage expectations.
- **Performance monitoring and adaptation.** Base decisions on real-time performance data and feedback loops, continuously deciding how to adjust in response to emergent patterns.
- **Learning and knowledge management.** Reflect on lessons learned and emerging insights regularly to capture knowledge for future reference and synchronize good practices across team members.
- **Leadership and team empowerment.** Adjust leadership approaches based on project needs, considering when to delegate authority and how to enable distributed decision-making and rapid response without losing cohesion.

By integrating these decision-making principles and models into daily practices, project practitioners can transform challenges into opportunities, enhancing project resilience and increasing the likelihood of successful outcomes in complex and ambiguous environments.

7.6 Summary

This section examined how decision-making shapes outcomes in complex project environments, where uncertainty, ambiguity, and time pressure demand adaptive and context-sensitive approaches.

Effective decision-making in such settings requires sound analytical methods as well as flexibility, ethical judgment, and cultural awareness.

This section provided project practitioners with a range of considerations and approaches for decision-making by:

- Establishing how complexity impacts the nature of project decisions as well as the role of the project practitioner in the decision-making process;
- Introducing decision-making models, including the Cynefin Framework, rational and analytical, iterative and adaptive, safe-to-fail, collaborative and consensus-based, ethical and value-based, and heuristic and intuitive approaches;
- Exploring the influence of information availability, cognitive biases, and cultural factors on decision quality; and
- Listing techniques and tools that enable decision-making.

The concepts and tools in this section can equip project practitioners with the knowledge to make more informed, ethical, and adaptive decisions, balancing analytical rigor with human judgment to navigate complexity with confidence.

Section 8

Leadership Strategies for Complexity

8.1 Introduction

Authoritative approaches to leadership are often ineffective in complex environments. Complexity is dynamic and unpredictable by nature, and efforts to assert firm control amid complexity often backfire. Effective leaders may instead adopt adaptive leadership approaches, which emphasize flexibility, collaboration, and learning. These approaches navigate uncertainty, foster cross-functional collaboration, and sustain team performance under shifting conditions.

This section examines adaptive leadership strategies that empower project leaders to navigate complex projects. The following subsections are included:

- Adaptive Leadership
- Psychological Safety
- Leading Cross-Functional Adaptive Teams
- Distributed Decision-Making Approaches
- Emergent Strategy Development
- Building Team Resilience
- Integration and Implementation Considerations

Many of the leadership strategies presented in this section use similar concepts and behaviors, underscoring the key aspects of leadership strategies in complex environments. Together, these topics illustrate how adaptive leadership practices translate the competencies introduced in Section 5 into the context of complex project environments.

8.2 Adaptive Leadership

Adaptive leadership is a leadership approach focused on experimentation, sensemaking, and system-wide learning, enabling individuals and teams to respond constructively to challenges that lack predefined solutions.

Unlike technical problem-solving and technical management, which focus on applying known expertise to solve defined problems, adaptive leadership addresses situations where neither the problem nor the solution is clear.

Adaptive leadership diagnoses between technical problems, which can be addressed using existing expertise and known solutions, and adaptive challenges, which require new learning, shifts in behavior, and changes in underlying assumptions. In complex project environments, prematurely classifying adaptive challenges as technical problems is a common source of failure. Effective adaptive leaders recognize situations when authority, expertise, or standard processes are insufficient on their own and instead focus on enabling learning, experimentation, and stakeholder engagement to surface viable paths forward. This distinction is foundational to navigating dynamic and sociopolitical complexity without relying on false certainty.

Characteristics of adaptive leadership include the following:

- **Situational awareness and sensemaking.** Continuously scan the environment to identify emerging changes and signals.
- **Learning orientation.** Treat uncertainty as a learning opportunity.
- **Experiment facilitation.** Design safe-to-fail experiments to gather insight without jeopardizing outcomes.
- **Stakeholder cocreation.** Engage diverse groups to develop solutions collaboratively.
- **Adaptive communication.** Communicate transparently about uncertainty while reinforcing shared confidence in project direction.

Adaptive leadership is especially valuable in contexts with dynamic, human, or sociopolitical complexity. This leadership style helps teams navigate ambiguity while maintaining alignment, momentum, and trust among stakeholders.

Example scenario

A research consortium project with multiple universities and industry partners faced collaborative challenges. Adaptive leadership approaches, including real-time learning, engaging stakeholders in solution development, and continuously adapting approaches, allowed the project leader to address these challenges while maintaining institutional confidence and working toward scientific objectives.

8.3 Psychological Safety

In the context of project management, psychological safety refers to a team environment where team members feel comfortable expressing ideas, raising concerns, taking interpersonal risks, and challenging norms without fear of punishment or humiliation.

Psychological safety fosters trust, enabling team members to admit mistakes, ask questions, and offer alternative ideas without concern for negative consequences. In complex projects, this openness allows teams to adapt quickly, learn continuously, and respond effectively to emerging challenges.

Research in organizational learning and team performance suggests that complex projects rely on deep collaboration and iterative learning. When people fear blame or retaliation, they withhold information and experimentation declines, which undermines adaptability. Psychological safety allows team members to safely surface concerns early, enabling adaptive course correction.

Creating an environment with psychological safety requires balancing high standards with high support. Teams perform best when clear expectations coexist with an environment where members feel safe taking risks. This prevents teams from mistaking psychological safety for low accountability.

8.3.1 Characteristics

Psychologically safe environments in project settings often demonstrate the following characteristics:

- **Learning culture and error recognition.** Mistakes are viewed as learning opportunities, enabling teams to identify and address problems before they escalate. Leaders celebrate issue escalation; teams discuss missteps and close calls openly. Team members are comfortable seeking help, asking questions, and requesting assistance without fear of judgment.
- **Open communication.** Team members are encouraged to communicate openly, even about challenging topics and disagreements. Issues, delays, and uncertainties are escalated as soon as they arise, allowing proactive risk management.
- **Constructive conflict.** Discussion about disagreements is constructive, focusing on ideas and solutions. Agile ceremonies, such as retrospectives, planning, and daily coordination meetings, are more productive as a result of open communication.
- **Clear, attentive, and inclusive leadership.** Project leaders are proactive by setting clear performance standards, rewarding team members for raising issues and asking for help, establishing trust through vulnerability, and engaging in inclusive decision-making processes. They notice when teams reach agreement quickly without discussion, avoid difficult topics, or defer to authority, and they act to counter these trends.
- **Collaboration and cultural sensitivity.** Team members across functions openly negotiate trade-offs and challenge assumptions to reach solutions. Project leaders and teams adapt communication and collaboration styles to accommodate diverse cultural expectations and norms.

8.3.2 Impact

Psychological safety enables project teams to function effectively in complex environments by encouraging transparency, learning, and shared accountability. Specifically, psychological safety can provide the following benefits:

- **Improves decision quality.** Psychological safety encourages consideration of diverse perspectives and constructive challenges, reducing groupthink and supporting more rigorous analysis and better outcomes.
- **Supports organizational effectiveness.** Because psychological safety operates within organizational culture, it helps teams navigate complexity arising from power dynamics, cultural differences, and competing priorities.
- **Enhances flow and predictability.** Teams that feel safe clarifying requirements and surfacing issues experience fewer disruptions and more reliable forecasts. This strengthens adaptive capacity, enabling faster recovery from setbacks and real-time refinement.
- **Surfaces critical concerns.** Open communication enables leaders to detect emerging issues early, reducing the risk that known problems remain unreported due to fear or discomfort.

8.3.3 Supportive Leadership Behaviors

Leadership behaviors that promote psychological safety may include the following:

- **Modeling vulnerability.** Leaders demonstrate openness by admitting knowledge gaps, sharing challenges, and inviting input on difficult issues.
- **Consultative decision-making.** Structured processes, such as premortems or red team reviews, give team members explicit permission to raise concerns before decisions are finalized.
- **Learning-oriented responses.** Debriefs and retrospectives focus on extracting lessons rather than assigning blame. Leaders frame mistakes as information, encouraging experimentation and supporting innovation.
- **Inclusive engagement.** Leaders help ensure all voices are heard by rotating facilitation roles, inviting input from quieter team members, and using structured feedback methods. When speaking up is met with blame, leaders intervene immediately to protect psychological safety.
- **Rewarding transparency.** Leaders publicly acknowledge team members who surface problems, reinforcing that honesty is valued even when the news is difficult.
- **Consistency and follow-through.** Leaders who maintain reliability, especially under pressure, build long-term trust and credibility.

Example scenario

During a system integration project, a team member identified a critical design flaw that would require significant rework. Instead of assigning blame, the project leader publicly thanked the individual for surfacing the issue, facilitated a collaborative problem-solving session, and implemented a structured review process to detect similar issues earlier in the future. This approach not only resolved the immediate problem but also reinforced psychological safety by demonstrating commitment to a culture of openness and continuous improvement.

8.3.4 Assessing Psychological Safety

Teams can assess psychological safety using structured methods that surface perceptions and behaviors. These methods may include:

- **Surveys.** Surveys provide baseline data and track trends over time. Questions such as "If you make a mistake on this team, is it held against you?" capture team perceptions, whereas short pulse checks after key events help detect shifts early.
- **Behavioral observation.** Leaders assess psychological safety by observing interaction patterns such as how often questions are asked, concerns are raised, and speaking time is distributed across team members.
- **Retrospectives.** Regular retrospectives can explicitly include psychological safety topics, using prompts like "Did we feel safe raising concerns during this sprint?" to normalize reflection and continuous assessment.

Psychological safety evolves as teams mature, moving from inclusion and learning safety toward contribution and challenge. Leaders can use these methods to assess a team's stage, tailoring interventions to support progression.

8.4 Leading Cross-Functional Adaptive Teams

Complexity requires teams that can think, act, and evolve together. This need is met by using cross-functional adaptive teams, which are autonomous teams with a shared mutual focus that are designed to operate across roles, disciplines, and geographies. Unlike traditional project teams that rely on static plans and hierarchical decision-making, cross-functional adaptive teams function as living systems by sensing change, learning from feedback, and adjusting structure and behavior as needed.

Well-designed cross-functional adaptive teams are effective under pressure and uncertainty, integrating diverse inputs, navigating ambiguity, and maintaining cohesion while conditions shift around them. Leaders supporting such teams cultivate conditions that support adaptability, including psychological safety, shared purpose, and relational trust.

8.4.1 Characteristics

Cross-functional adaptive teams share the following characteristics:

- **Boundary-spanning and functional integration.** People, knowledge, and capabilities are connected across the organization, integrating work and expertise that would otherwise be separate.
- **Adaptive autonomy and strategic anchoring.** Strategic guidance in the form of clear priorities and shared goals allows teams to make timely, informed decisions that are aligned with the organization's intentions.
- **Psychological safety and constructive challenge.** Team members are encouraged to question assumptions, raise concerns, and share new ideas without fear of embarrassment or retaliation, which helps teams surface risks and refine decisions.
- **Shared purpose and collective ownership.** Team goals and outcomes are determined collaboratively, which creates shared commitment and a sense of ownership among team members.

- **Enable emergent leadership and fluid role negotiation.** Team members step into leadership roles when their knowledge is most relevant to the task or challenge, which allows quick responses informed by expertise.
- **Embedded feedback loops and sensemaking practices.** Feedback is provided regularly and is incorporated into the team's working cycles, creating a culture of continuous learning.

These characteristics enable teams to function as intelligent subsystems within the broader organization. These cross-functional adaptive teams can sense, decide, and act in alignment with strategic goals, learning throughout the process.

8.4.2 Impact

Cross-functional adaptive teams are structural assets that shape how organizations respond to complexity. These teams are impactful in many different contexts, including the following:

- In structurally complex environments, the impact is a reduction in coordination overhead and the elimination of technical silos, leading to an improvement in cross-functional speed-to-market, translating across silos, and reducing misalignment.
- In dynamic conditions, where goals and timelines shift frequently, they act as agile response systems, absorbing disruption and adjusting course without losing momentum.
- In politically complex settings, they help navigate stakeholder tension and competing agendas through shared purpose and ownership.

When trusted and supported, these teams become a source of intelligence for the entire organization. Cross-functional adaptive teams do more than deliver outcomes; they help evolve how strategy is executed, how risks are managed, and how value is realized over time.

Table 8-1 illustrates how these capabilities interact with different forms of complexity and reinforce competencies introduced in previous sections.

8.4.3 Supportive Leadership Behaviors

In complex project environments, leadership is less about directing action and more about enabling clarity, cohesion, and adaptability under shifting conditions. Leaders of cross-functional adaptive teams often encounter tensions that do not have simple solutions. The following leadership behaviors help address these tensions:

- **Provide strategic alignment while supporting autonomy.** Leaders maintain alignment by clearly communicating strategic intent and priorities while preserving the team's freedom to self-organize and innovate.
- **Balance performance expectations with psychological safety.** Leaders foster a climate where team members can question assumptions and share concerns while maintaining focus on results.
- **Create accountability while enabling adaptive cycles.** Leaders support iterative learning by facilitating regular feedback, adapting plans based on insights, and helping ensure transparency about progress.

Table 8-1. Adaptive Team Capabilities for Different Complexity Types

Team Capability	Complexity Types Addressed	Impact on Project Resilience and Value	Reinforced Competency
Boundary-spanning and functional integration	Structural, organizational, technological	Aligns fragmented teams and systems, enabling coordinated insight and execution.	Systems thinking, technical literacy
Adaptive autonomy and strategic anchoring	Dynamic, organizational, environmental	Enables fast decisions in volatile environments while maintaining strategic cohesion.	Strategic thinking, situational awareness
Psychological safety and constructive challenge	Human and sociopolitical, organizational,	Promotes honest risk discussion and early problem detection.	Emotional intelligence, cultural competence
Shared purpose and collective ownership	Human and sociopolitical, organizational, environmental	Sustains alignment despite stakeholder conflict or shifting priorities.	Value creation, strategic thinking
Emergent leadership and fluid role negotiation	Structural, dynamic, human and sociopolitical	Activates relevant expertise quickly without waiting for formal approval.	Adaptive leadership, situational awareness
Embedded feedback loops and sensemaking	Dynamic, environmental, technological	Supports continuous learning and realignment as signals emerge from the system.	Analytical thinking, systems thinking

- **Maintain systemic coherence while empowering decentralized decisions.** Leaders act as integrators, connecting teams to shared priorities, facilitating cross-functional dialogue, and helping ensure local actions reinforce enterprise-level goals.

Example scenario

A digital product team operating across multiple markets faces compliance requirements, technical challenges, customer feedback cycles, and supply chain disruptions. Leadership continually shifts focus, drawing on legal insight one day and technical expertise the next. The team's effectiveness stems from its shared ability to interpret complexity; learn in real time; and move forward with clarity, confidence, and cohesion.

8.5 Distributed Decision-Making Approaches

Traditional decision-making models often falter under the pressures of complex environments. When decisions move through hierarchical layers, they may become slow, narrow in perspective, or disconnected from real-time context. Distributed decision-making (DDM) offers a flexible alternative by placing decision authority where context, expertise, and accountability reside.

Distributed decision-making is a governance and operating model in which decision authority is intentionally delegated across individuals, teams, or organizational levels, based on proximity to information and expertise. For leaders, distributed decision-making requires a mindset shift. Rather than controlling outcomes, leaders build systems that enable teams to make decisions with minimal oversight. This effort involves clarifying authority, establishing boundaries, and building trust so that distributed teams can act decisively while maintaining coherence across the organization. When implemented thoughtfully, distributed decision-making accelerates learning, reduces bottlenecks, and strengthens the organization's capacity to adapt without losing strategic direction.

8.5.1 Characteristics

Distributed decision-making approaches share the following characteristics:

- **Frame autonomy to preserve system integrity.** Teams are given the freedom to respond quickly to shifting needs, alongside clearly defined boundaries and goals to prevent fragmentation. In practice, this framing means aligning roles, codifying decision rights, and defining escalation pathways to help ensure decisions reinforce system-level objectives.
- **Accelerate decisions while embedding learning.** Teams make timely decisions informed by structured reflection. Retrospectives, stakeholder feedback, and peer reviews enable continuous learning cycles that sustain decision quality over time.
- **Align stakeholders through local context.** Decisions are informed by the realities of local context while remaining linked to enterprise-level outcomes. This balance allows teams to act independently without drifting from collective purpose.
- **Connect decision nodes through knowledge flow.** Cross-team communication mechanisms, such as shared dashboards, transparent decision logs, and real-time updates, enable collaborative learning, prevent duplication, and maintain trust across distributed teams.

8.5.2 Impact

Distributed decision-making offers structural and cultural advantages in complex environments. This approach enables teams to act immediately when conditions change, reducing decision latency at moments when responsiveness is key to delivering value. Distributed decision-making also improves how organizations detect and respond to emerging risks. In centralized systems, weak signals may remain hidden until they become systemic problems. Distributed decision-making fosters earlier detection through local experimentation and open communication, creating a culture of proactive adjustment and continuous learning.

Within distributed environments, the role of leadership evolves. Leaders shift from approving individual decisions to designing the systems and norms that guide decision quality. Leadership helps to clarify roles, reinforce purpose, and promote responsible autonomy. By creating the conditions for psychological safety, strategic alignment, and transparent feedback, leaders make distributed decision-making both coherent and adaptive.

8.5.3 Supportive Leadership Behaviors

The effectiveness of distributed decision-making depends on how leaders shape the cultural, relational, and operational conditions in which decisions occur. Supportive behaviors may include the following:

- **Clarify authority while reinforcing shared intent.** Leaders intentionally define who is empowered to make which decisions, under what conditions, and within what boundaries. Leaders sustain alignment by communicating strategic intent, contextualizing constraints, and linking local actions to organizational outcomes.
- **Model trust and normalize accountability.** Leaders build a climate where autonomy and accountability coexist. By respecting expertise, avoiding micromanagement, and supporting informed risk-taking, leaders demonstrate trust while reinforcing ownership of results.
- **Enable learning by embedding feedback.** Leaders integrate feedback mechanisms that help teams evaluate decisions, identify patterns, and adapt. By asking learning-centered questions and surfacing insights across the system, leaders can help ensure distributed decisions remain responsive and informed.
- **Integrate local action with systemic alignment.** Leaders connect empowered teams through shared purpose and continuous coordination. Leaders monitor how decisions cascade across functions, reconcile tensions between local and global priorities, and help ensure decentralized actions reinforce enterprise goals.

Example scenario

When a critical supplier had a factory closure, the product team assessed available alternatives and found a local alternative. A regional support team coordinated customer communications with the new supplier, and a finance representative assessed cost impacts. This time-sensitive change occurred without waiting for senior management approval; however, senior management was informed in a timely manner, and leadership confirmed that this change supported the overall priorities.

8.6 Emergent Strategy Development

An emergent strategy is a strategic approach that evolves through learning, adaptation, and real-time feedback rather than being planned in advance. This approach contrasts with a deliberate strategy, which is based on forecasting and formal design. Emergent strategies take shape through reflection and informed adjustment over time.

In practice, decision-making in complex environments rarely follows a purely predefined path. While organizations may establish intended directions and decision frameworks, the decisions that ultimately shape outcomes often evolve through experience, feedback, and adaptation. Distributed decision-making supports this dynamic by allowing teams to recognize emerging patterns, integrate learning into ongoing choices, and align evolving actions with strategic intent. In this way, decision-making becomes a continuous learning process rather than a one-time directive.

Developing an emergent strategy enables teams to pursue purpose-driven results amid uncertainty and ambiguity. When leaders adopt this approach, they enhance their organization's ability to observe change, interpret its significance, and adjust strategic direction accordingly.

8.6.1 Characteristics

Emergent strategies share the following characteristics:

- **Continuous sensemaking and reflection.** Strategic clarity often develops gradually. Structured reflection helps teams interpret new information, surface assumptions, and prevent small misalignments from becoming systemic issues.
- **Strategic feedback integration.** Effective teams gather, synthesize, and act on feedback from users, stakeholders, sponsors, and delivery partners. These feedback loops improve responsiveness and maintain relevance as conditions evolve.
- **Value-based alignment and recalibration.** Regular discussions of priorities and goals can help teams stay anchored in purpose while adapting to changing needs.
- **Stakeholder cocreation of direction.** Involve stakeholders to strengthen and build shared ownership, legitimacy, and responsiveness.

8.6.2 Impact

An emergent strategy replaces static, single-point planning with continuous alignment. This approach enables teams to stay oriented toward purpose while allowing processes to evolve as new insights arise.

Leaders implementing an emergent strategy shift from enforcing adherence to plans toward cultivating the conditions in which plans can emerge. This shift means designing structures for reflection, empowering decentralized action, and sustaining shared purpose amid constant change. Leaders who embrace these practices can transform uncertainty into a strategic advantage.

8.6.3 Supportive Leadership Behaviors

Leaders who enable emergent strategy act as facilitators of adaptability, creating conditions for strategy to evolve through observation, inquiry, and collaboration. The following behaviors support its implementation:

- **Normalize iteration without losing focus.** Encourage experimentation and learning, reinforcing that even unsuccessful initiatives contribute valuable insight.
- **Protect time for strategic reflection.** Build in pauses to assess progress, enabling clear-headed adaptation.
- **Facilitate dialogue across boundaries.** Create forums where diverse perspectives can be shared and synthesized, helping ensure insights from all levels inform direction.
- **Reinforce value-anchored decision-making.** Help teams connect daily choices to organizational goals, maintaining alignment even as plans shift.

Example scenario

A community healthcare organization launched an initiative to improve access to mental health services. The organization started with a broad goal focused on building the provider network and extending hours. However, as the project team engaged residents, school counselors, and clinic partners, they learned that the key to success was transportation. The team shifted their focus to coordinating mobile services and neighborhood support groups that met the overall goal for the initiative.

8.7 Building Team Resilience

Team resilience is the ability of a team to maintain functionality and cohesion while navigating disruption, change, or adversity. Resilient teams are essential for navigating complexity. These teams sustain progress under pressure and demonstrate higher levels of innovation and adaptability in uncertain environments.

8.7.1 Characteristics

Resilient teams share the following characteristics:

- **Collective adaptive capacity.** Effectively recognize, assess, and respond to challenges.
- **Stress management.** Manage pressure and constraints while preserving performance quality and a positive team climate.
- **Recovery and learning.** Recover quickly from setbacks and use failures as opportunities to strengthen adaptive capacity.
- **Communication resilience.** Maintain clear, open communication and coordination under stress or uncertainty.
- **Mutual support.** Foster a culture of trust, collaboration, and shared responsibility for overcoming challenges.
- **Purpose and identity.** Maintain a clear sense of team identity and shared purpose, even when external pressures rise.
- **Cultural and relational resilience.** Preserve healthy team culture and relationships through constructive conflict resolution and repair.

8.7.2 Impact

Team resilience is a critical success factor in complex projects, where volatility, ambiguity, and competing priorities can threaten team performance. Resilient teams maintain focus and functionality during disruption, which enables sustained progress and creative problem-solving.

Leaders and organizations that develop resilient teams may experience higher project success rates, stronger stakeholder relationships, and greater organizational learning over time. By fostering resilience, leaders can enable their teams not only to withstand challenges but to grow stronger through them.

8.7.3 Supportive Leadership Behaviors

Leaders play a key role in cultivating team resilience. The following behaviors help teams sustain adaptability, cohesion, and performance under stress:

- **Monitor stress proactively.** Track indicators of team stress and intervene early by adjusting workload, priorities, or resources.
- **Facilitate learning from challenges.** Lead structured reflection to extract lessons from adversity and reinforce creative problem-solving.
- **Coordinate support systems.** Secure consistent access to resources and align with stakeholders to protect team capacity during demanding phases.
- **Maintain positive culture.** Strengthen trust and morale through transparent communication, recognition, and effective conflict management.
- **Implement recovery strategies.** Create processes for renewal after intense periods such as recovery cycles, debriefs, and lessons learned reviews.

Example scenario

In a multisite infrastructure-upgrade project, the project practitioner fostered team resilience by establishing peer support networks across locations, scheduling brief weekly virtual check-ins to maintain connection, celebrating incremental progress, and empowering teams to make decisions within defined boundaries. These practices helped sustain engagement, cohesion, and adaptability throughout the project life cycle.

8.8 Integration and Implementation Considerations

Effective leadership in complex projects depends on how well adaptive strategies are integrated into the organization's structures, culture, and processes. This section outlines considerations for assessing readiness, implementing adaptive approaches, and addressing common challenges during integration.

8.8.1 Assessing Organizational Readiness

Before introducing new leadership approaches, project practitioners may evaluate the organization's capacity for change by examining the following:

- **Adaptive culture.** Review the organization's values and norms regarding transparency, learning, and experimentation.
- **Structural flexibility.** Determine the degree to which governance and decision-making systems support distributed and adaptive approaches.
- **Capability gaps.** Assess current team competencies and areas requiring targeted development.
- **Technological infrastructure.** Explore the availability of tools and systems that facilitate collaboration, feedback, and data-informed decision-making.

A readiness assessment enables project practitioners to tailor implementation strategies to organizational context and constraints.

8.8.2 Implementing Adaptive Leadership Strategies

Integrating adaptive leadership strategies requires deliberate, iterative effort guided by continuous feedback. Strategies may include the following:

- **Pilot initiatives.** Launch limited-scope efforts to test, refine, and demonstrate the value of new practices before wider adoption.
- **Leadership development.** Provide coaching and training that help build adaptive mindsets and behaviors.
- **Role modeling.** Encourage senior leaders to demonstrate adaptive and collaborative behaviors in visible ways.
- **Iterative rollout.** Expand implementation gradually, incorporating learning from earlier phases to refine subsequent actions.

8.8.3 Anticipating and Addressing Challenges

Project practitioners may face the following challenges when implementing adaptive leadership:

- **Resistance to change.** Established hierarchies, fear of losing control, and discomfort with ambiguity can reinforce traditional methods, leading to slow adoption.
- **Limited understanding.** Misinterpretation of adaptive principles can result in surface-level adoption without meaningful behavioral change.
- **Cultural misalignment.** Existing norms and values may conflict with the openness, experimentation, and transparency that adaptive leadership requires.
- **Resource constraints.** Limited investment in training, tools, or infrastructure can hinder sustained implementation.

Overcoming these challenges requires sustained leadership commitment, clear and consistent communication, and an adaptive mindset that treats implementation as an evolving process.

8.9 Summary

This section explored how adaptive leadership enables teams and organizations to navigate complex environments by fostering flexibility, collaboration, and learning. The section emphasized that effective leadership in complexity is less about control and more about cultivating conditions for clarity, connection, and collective adaptation.

This section characterized adaptive leadership strategies and connected them to complexity management by:

- Exploring adaptive leadership as a framework for responding to uncertainty and guiding teams through dynamic project conditions;
- Highlighting the role of psychological safety in creating environments where team members can take risks, share insights, and learn from failure;

- Outlining practices for leading cross-functional adaptive teams, emphasizing collaboration, shared purpose, and responsive coordination;
- Examining distributed decision-making approaches that enable timely, informed actions by those closest to the work and emerging information;
- Discussing emergent strategy development, showing how leaders can align evolving actions with broader organizational goals;
- Describing approaches for building team resilience, including maintaining focus, adaptability, and collective well-being under pressure; and
- Addressing integration and implementation considerations, emphasizing readiness assessment, iterative learning, and leadership commitment.

Together, these concepts translate leadership competencies into actionable approaches for navigating complexity. These competencies illustrate a shift from individual expertise to collective leadership, empowering project practitioners to transform uncertainty into opportunity and enable sustainable, adaptive success.

Part 4

Assets for Working With Complexity

Part 4 provides practical tools, techniques, frameworks, and case studies for working with complexity. The material in this part goes beyond foundational project management methods, focusing instead on approaches that are most effective in complex environments.

- **Section 9 Tools and Frameworks.** Section 9 presents seven tools, techniques, and frameworks that are especially useful when managing complex projects. The text references content from earlier sections, creating a bridge between learning and application.
- **Section 10 Case Studies.** Section 10 presents three case studies illustrating real-world complex projects. Each case is summarized and analyzed using concepts from previous sections, demonstrating how the guidance in this practice guide translates into tangible project outcomes.

Information in this part connects previous learning with tactical application to provide a richer understanding.

Section 9

Tools and Frameworks

9.1 Introduction

Navigating complex projects requires more than conceptual knowledge. Teams operating in environments marked by uncertainty, interdependencies, and emergence benefit from tested frameworks that guide analysis and response. Such tools and frameworks translate theory into practice, helping project practitioners address specific complex project challenges.

This section details tools and frameworks that support teams navigating complex situations. They are drawn from diverse domains, such as systems thinking, lean management, and military after-action processes, and they can be used individually or in tandem with one another.

The section discusses:

- Cynefin Framework
- Systems Thinking
- Kanban Framework
- After Action Review
- Design Thinking
- Complexity Heat Map
- Experiment Canvas
- Selecting Tools and Frameworks

Each section introduces the tool or framework, provides implementation guidance, and includes an example of an application. The section concludes with a discussion of how to determine the optimal tool for a particular scenario.

9.2 Cynefin Framework

The Cynefin Framework was introduced in Section 7 as a sensemaking framework that helps leaders and teams categorize projects by domain to decide on appropriate actions. This section presents structured evaluation criteria that help project practitioners categorize projects into Cynefin domains. Determining the Cynefin domain helps the team select appropriate project approaches, stakeholder engagement strategies, and response mechanisms.

Table 9-1 lists questions that help the team determine the Cynefin domain of a project.

9.2.1 Implementation Guidance

The Cynefin Framework Assessment Tool may be beneficial:

- At the initiation of a project to determine appropriate decision approaches.
- During project phase transitions, when the Cynefin domain should be reassessed.
- In the face of uncertainty when the best strategy is unknown.
- When stakeholders disagree on the optimal project management approach.
- During portfolio reviews, when determining governance requirements across initiatives.

Table 9-1. Assessment Questions

Domain	Assessment Questions
Clear	Are cause-and-effect relationships evident to everyone? Can responses be standardized? Is the situation similar to previous well-understood cases?
Complicated	Do we need expert analysis to determine the right approach? Are there multiple viable solutions requiring specialized knowledge? Can we predict outcomes with expert input?
Complex	Are relationships between actions and outcomes only clear in retrospect? Do small changes produce unpredictable results? Are multiple factors interacting in nonlinear ways?
Chaotic	Is immediate action required before analysis? Are relationships between cause and effect unclear? Is the situation rapidly changing and unstable?
Disorder	Is there a consensus on the project domain? Are there conflicting perspectives on which actions to take? What information do we need to move from Disorder to a different domain?

To apply the Cynefin Framework Assessment Tool effectively, project practitioners may follow these steps:

- **Rapid assessment.** Discuss assessment questions with project teams, reaching consensus on domain classification.
- **Response selection.** Match classified domain to appropriate practices according to the Cynefin Framework (see Section 7).
- **Adaptation monitoring.** Revisit domain assessment when significant project changes occur.

9.2.2 Example Application

A transportation infrastructure program initially classified as Complicated (expert-driven engineering) encountered community resistance and regulatory changes. Project leaders used the Cynefin Framework to reassess the domain, revealing Complex domain characteristics, unpredictable stakeholder interactions, and emergent requirements.

As a result of the domain reassessment, the team shifted from detailed up-front planning to probe-sense-respond cycles. They focused on engaging stakeholders through design thinking workshops rather than technical presentations. This domain-appropriate response reduced approval delays by 40%.

9.3 Systems Thinking

Systems thinking, as previously defined in Section 3, is a holistic approach that views projects as interconnected systems, recognizing how people, processes, technology, and the environment interact. It incorporates feedback loops, time delays, and interdependencies that shape patterns and outcomes over time.

This section introduces tools that use a systems thinking approach to determine how project elements interact, identify leverage points for intervention, and anticipate unintended consequences. These tools include:

- **Stakeholder system mapping.** Map key stakeholder groups, their relationships, and influence flows, revealing hidden dependencies and power dynamics that may affect project success.
- **Feedback loop identification.** Identify reinforcing loops (snowball effects) and balancing loops (self-correcting mechanisms) within the project ecosystem to plan interventions strategically, avoiding unintended negative consequences.
- **Leverage point analysis.** Locate high-impact intervention points where small changes produce significant system-wide improvements.

In complex projects, isolated problem-solving may create new issues elsewhere in the system. Applying systems thinking tools allow project leaders to identify hidden connections and more accurately predict the impact of interventions.

9.3.1 Implementation Guidance

The tools associated with systems thinking may be beneficial when:

- Multiple interdependent workstreams create coordination challenges.
- Solutions in one area consistently create problems elsewhere.

- Resistant stakeholders do not respond to direct engagement.
- Resource allocation decisions affect multiple project components.

To apply systems thinking tools effectively, project practitioners may follow the steps shown in Figure 9-1.

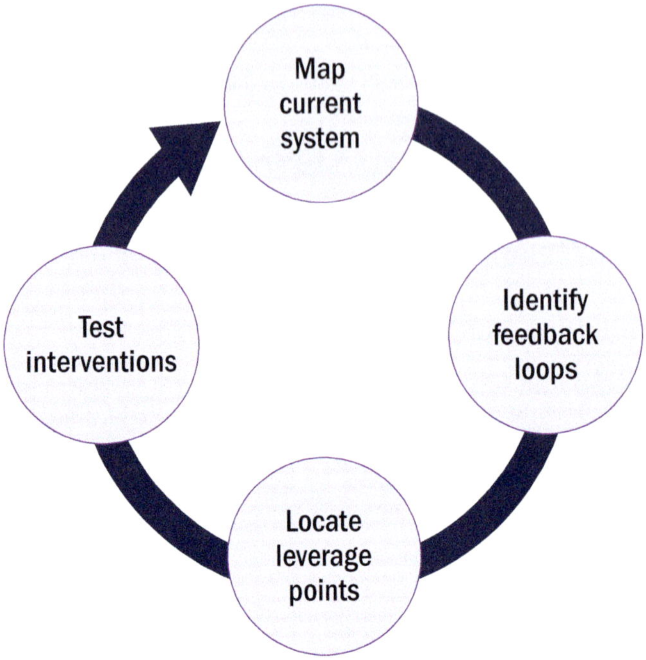

Figure 9-1. Systems Thinking Steps

- **Map current system.** Identify key elements, such as stakeholders, processes, constraints, and connections among them, using visuals to map the system.
- **Identify feedback loops.** Locate reinforcing loops (vicious or virtuous cycles) and balancing loops (resistance to change) by asking questions that help define relationships between actions and effects.
- **Locate leverage points.** Find leverage points, or places where small interventions produce disproportionate effects, by reviewing information flows, decision authorities, and incentive structures.
- **Test interventions.** Run small experiments at identified leverage points before implementing interventions to identify unpredictable results.

9.3.2 Example Application

A healthcare technology implementation faced repeated delays despite adding new staff. Systems thinking analysis revealed a balancing loop: New staff required training from experienced team members, which reduced the productive output of the experienced team members and created delays.

Team leaders determined that the knowledge transfer process was an important leverage point. They created modular training materials and peer coaching pairs, breaking the balancing loop that had reduced productivity. The technology implementation schedule was accelerated by 60% without additional hiring.

9.4 Kanban Framework

The Kanban framework, which was previously introduced in Section 4, is a visual workflow management method that uses boards, cards, and continuous flow principles to help teams limit work in progress (WIP), increase efficiency, and deliver value incrementally. Kanban methods focus on reducing lead time, the time between when a task enters the backlog and when it is completed, and cycle time, the time when an item is actively being worked on.

Kanban practice optimizes workflow by implementing work-in-progress (WIP) limits, which are constraints on how many tasks may be active within a process stage at a time. For example, a team may allow a maximum of three tasks within the "in progress" stage and two tasks within the "review" stage at any given time. These limits prevent teams from overloading any workflow stage. When a stage reaches its WIP limit, no new tasks may be started until an existing task is completed. This approach forces teams to address bottlenecks rather than accumulate queued work.

The visual element of Kanban leads it to be conflated with task boards. While kanban boards are visual, they are more than task boards. A task board is a simple way to display tasks across stages of work, whereas a kanban board implements WIP limits, makes process policies explicit, and provides a mechanism for managing flow and identifying bottlenecks. In essence, all kanban boards are task boards, but not all task boards are kanban boards. Differentiating between kanban boards and task boards enables teams to select the right tool for the needs of a specific project.

Tables 9-2 and 9-3 compare Kanban practice with the use of task boards.

Because Kanban is a visual approach, it is best understood by reviewing example boards and diagrams. Figures 9-2 through 9-4 represent a scenario in which the project team needs to produce 24 job aids.

Table 9-2 Differentiating Characteristics Between Kanban Practice and Task Boards

Characteristic	Kanban Practice	Task Board
Primary focus	Optimize flow and throughput	Status visibility and communication
WIP limits	Enforced constraints to optimize flow	Optional or undefined
Metrics	Lead time, cycle time, throughput	Task completion, status tracking
Continuous improvement	Built-in flow analysis and optimization	Ad-hoc process improvements
Complexity handling	Designed for managing uncertainty	Better suited for predictable work

Table 9-3. When to Use Kanban Practice Versus Task Boards

Context	Use Kanban Practice	Use Task Board
Work predictability	Workflows involve uncertainty and changing priorities	Work is relatively predictable with stable priorities
Constraint management	Resource constraints create bottlenecks requiring active management	Team capacity consistently matches demand
Primary need	Team needs data-driven flow optimization rather than just visibility	Primary need is status communication to stakeholders
Complexity context	Project context aligns with Complex or Complicated Cynefin Framework domains	Project context aligns with Clear Cynefin Framework domain

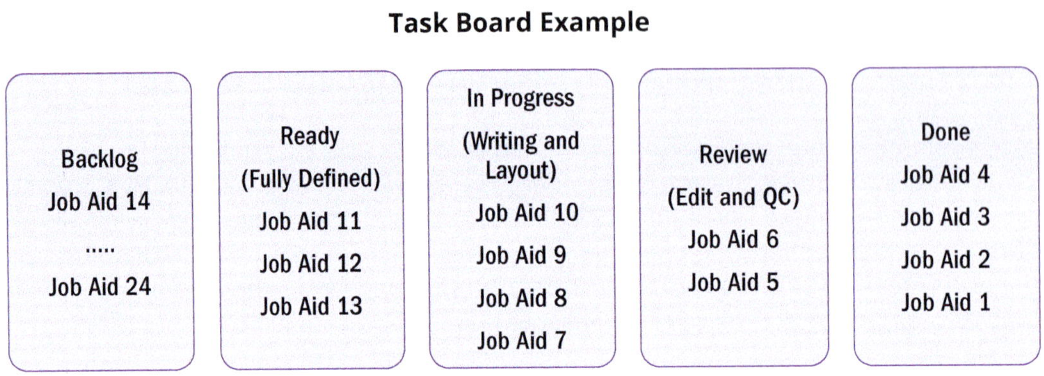

Figure 9-2. Kanban Board (Visualizing Work)

Figure 9-2 shows the task board for Day 5 of the job aid project.

Each job aid begins in the Backlog column, then is moved to the Ready column when all necessary information has been defined. When a team member begins work on a job aid, they move it to the In Progress column and write the job aid.

Once writing is complete, they move the job aid to the Review column so that it can be edited and checked for quality. After the review processes are complete, the job aid is moved to the Done column. This process is repeated for each of the job aids.

Cumulative Flow Diagram (CFD) Example

Figure 9-3 is an example of a Cumulative Flow Diagram (CFD), which is another visual tool used to monitor workflow.

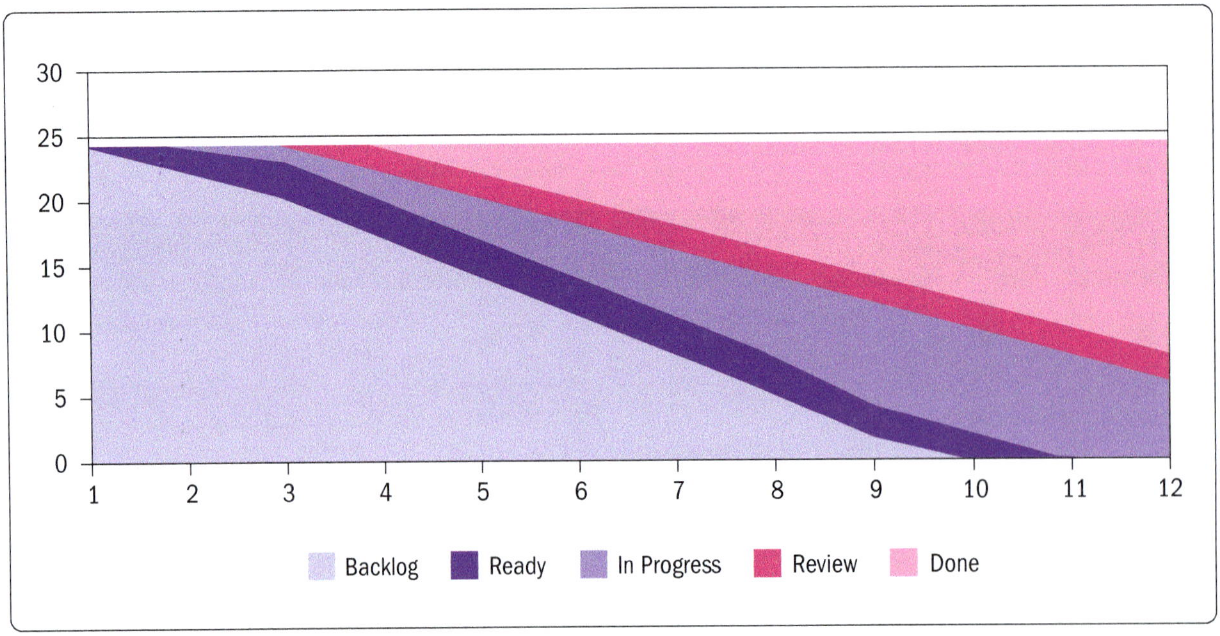

Figure 9-3. Cumulative Flow Diagram With No Work-in-Progress (WIP) Limits

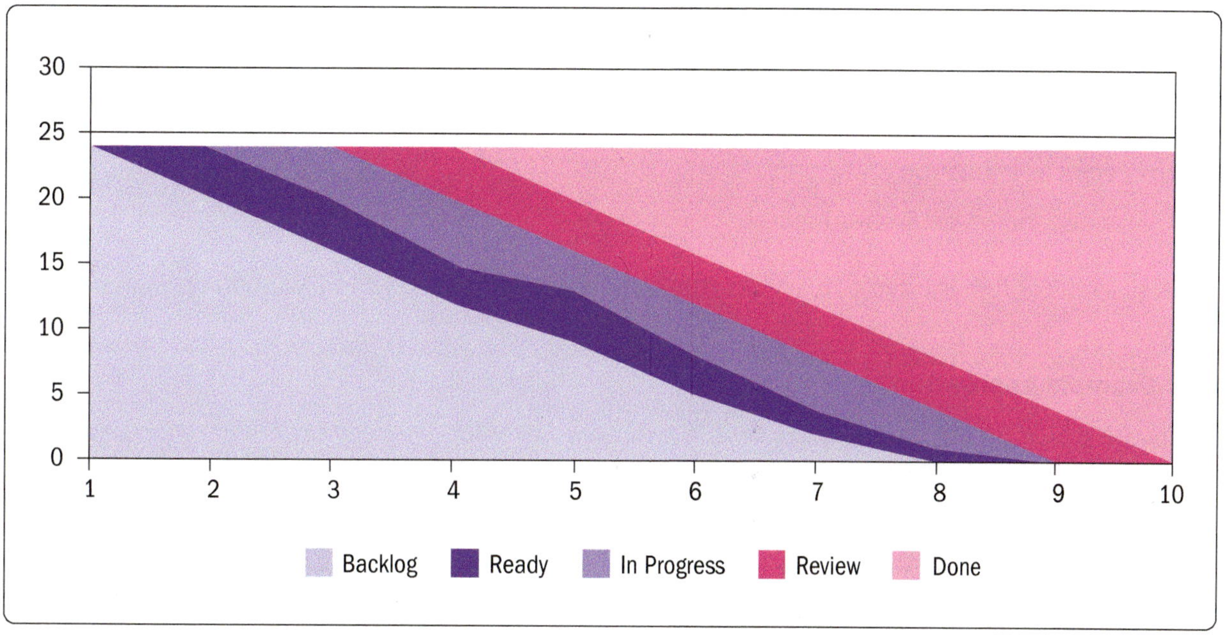

Figure 9-4. True Kanban System (With Work-in-Progress [WIP] Limits)

This CFD depicts the project on Day 12. The diagram shows that excess work has accumulated in the In Progress stage. Upon investigation, the team determines that this is due to the Review team's limited availability, which has created a bottleneck between the In Progress and Review phases.

Figure 9-4 shows a revised CFD for the same project, demonstrating how Kanban practices can be implemented to address bottlenecks. WIP limits have been implemented to help ensure no new work enters the workstream once the WIP limit is reached. The Review team's capacity has also been increased, allowing a smoother workflow and an earlier completion date for the job aids.

9.4.1 Implementation Guidance

Kanban boards work best when there is a repeatable process that can be optimized. To effectively implement Kanban practices, project teams may follow these steps:

- **Visualize current workflow.** Map realistic process stages on task board columns.
- **Establish initial WIP limits.** Set conservative constraints for each column based on team capacity.
- **Track flow metrics.** Measure the cycle time for representative work items to identify bottlenecks, using cumulative flow diagrams to reveal where work accumulates over time.
- **Adjust WIP limits.** Tighten or loosen constraints based on flow data and bottleneck analysis.
- **Hold regular flow reviews.** Examine metrics and improvement opportunities at defined intervals.

Although Kanban practices can be highly effective, they are not appropriate in all situations. Kanban should not be implemented when:

- Tasks are unique and not repeated.
- Work requires escalation for approvals.
- Projects depend on external suppliers.

These situations often involve bottlenecks that are unable to be resolved by Kanban approaches.

9.4.2 Example Application

A software development team using a simple task board to track progress experienced persistent delays. To address this, they implemented Kanban practices by adding WIP limits.

Initially, their WIP limits of three items in development and two in code review felt restrictive. However, cycle time data revealed a bottleneck moving to the code review stage. After adding a part-time reviewer and pairing junior developers for review tasks, the team eliminated this bottleneck.

As a result of implementing Kanban practices, after 1 month the average task delivery time dropped from 12 days to 6 days. This decreased the cost of development and improved ROI for the company significantly.

9.5 After Action Review

An After Action Review (AAR) is a structured reflection process conducted immediately following certain project events, phases, or milestones. By engaging in reflection while the project is active, teams are able to apply insights to subsequent project phases, adjusting approaches as needed. An AAR helps teams rapidly learn from their recent experiences, converting insights into actionable improvements that influence project outcomes.

An AAR is completed by answering a series of questions, grouped into four categories. These questions are shown in Figure 9-5 and are detailed below.

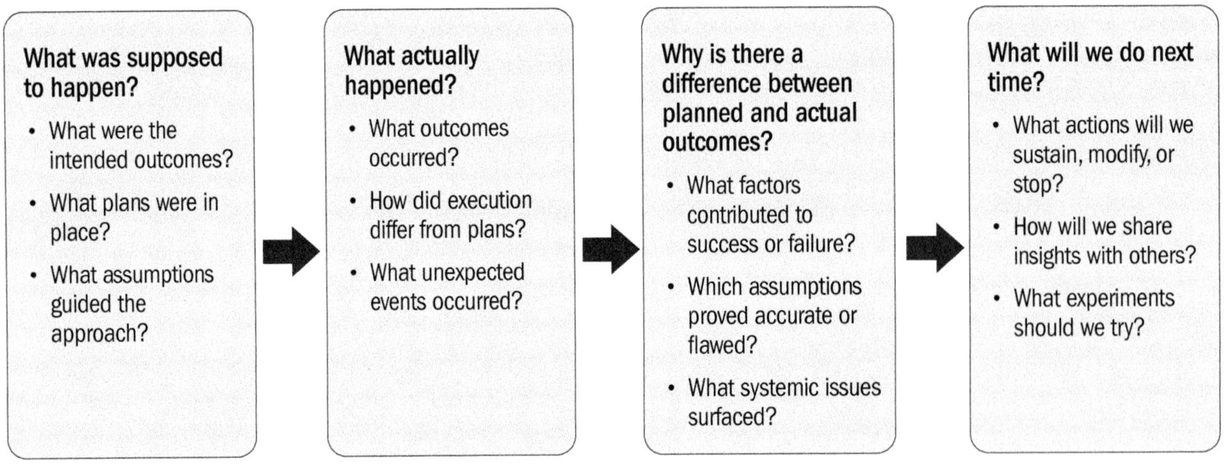

Figure 9-5. Typical Questions for an After Action Review

The Four-Question Framework:

- **What was supposed to happen?**
  - What were the intended outcomes?
  - What plans were in place?
  - What assumptions guided the approach?
- **What actually happened?**
  - What outcomes occurred?
  - How did execution differ from the plans?
  - What unexpected events emerged?
- **Why is there a difference between the planned and actual outcomes?**
  - What factors contributed to success or failure?
  - Which assumptions proved accurate or flawed?
  - What systemic issues surfaced?
- **What will we do next time?**
  - What specific actions will we sustain, modify, or stop?
  - How will we share these insights with others?
  - What experiments should we try?

After Action Reviews, which are scheduled at any point during the duration of the project, may sometimes be confused with lessons learned meetings, which typically take place after major milestones. Table 9-4 compares After Action Reviews with lessons learned sessions.

After Action Reviews are best used for rapid cycle learning during project execution, whereas lessons learned sessions support strategic pattern analysis at major milestones.

Table 9-4. After Action Review Versus Lessons Learned

Aspect	After Action Review	Lessons Learned
Timing	Immediately after events	End of project/phase
Duration	Brief focused sessions	Extended sessions
Focus	Specific recent events	Broad project patterns
Output	Immediate actionable changes	Strategic recommendations
Participants	Direct event participants	Broader stakeholder groups

9.5.1 Implementation Guidance

An AAR is appropriate at the following points within a project:

- After completing key project events, phases, or milestones;
- When teams need to adjust their approach to ongoing work;
- Following unexpected outcomes that require immediate course correction; and
- During iterative delivery cycles.

To maximize the positive impact of an AAR, project practitioners will benefit from:

- **Fostering psychological safety.** Emphasize a learning mindset and avoid assigning blame for challenges and issues.
- **Timely scheduling.** Conduct After Action Reviews shortly after the event being discussed.
- **Concise documentation.** Capture key insights by using actionable bullet points that support behavior change.
- **Assigning accountability.** Help ensure each insight has an owner and a clear implementation plan.
- **Broad summary distribution.** Distribute AAR summaries beyond the immediate team so that other project teams may benefit from the results.

9.5.2 Example Application

A hospital expansion project conducted an AAR after each design phase. Following an AAR that discussed the mechanical systems design, the team identified that coordination gaps between architects and engineers caused significant rework. The project team determined that joint design sessions were more effective at preventing misalignment than sequential reviews.

During the next project phase, which focused on electrical systems design, the team held joint design sessions. This process change eliminated two cycles of rework, saving approximately 3 weeks and US$180,000. This AAR finding was shared across the hospital's project portfolio, improving coordination on five concurrent projects.

9.6 Design Thinking

Design thinking is a nonlinear iterative process that teams use to understand users, challenge assumptions, redefine problems, and create innovative solutions to prototype and test. This customer-centric approach to problem-solving combines analytical rigor with creative exploration so teams can discover, frame, and address real customer needs.

For complex projects, design thinking helps teams move beyond technical specifications to understand the actual problems stakeholders need to be solved. Empathy—defined as understanding—as well as feeling—the thoughts and emotions of others—is a key aspect of the design thinking process.

To develop empathy for stakeholders, project practitioners may ask questions such as:

- What are stakeholders explicitly communicating?
- What might they be thinking but not saying?
- What behaviors and actions do we observe?
- What emotions and concerns are driving reactions?
- What frustrates or blocks stakeholders?
- What outcomes would delight stakeholders?

Within a design thinking approach, project teams develop empathy for their stakeholders or users before proceeding to any other project phase.

9.6.1 Implementation Guidance

Design thinking strategies may support complex projects when:

- Stakeholder requirements are unclear or conflicting.
- Technical solutions exist but lack user adoption.
- Multiple possible approaches need to be evaluated.
- Users resist the project because their needs were misunderstood.

Design thinking can be implemented within complex projects by following these six stages:

- **Empathize.** Investigating how stakeholders work, think, and feel, using tools such as observation, interviews, and surveys.
- **Define.** Articulating a concise problem statement that guides future work, framing the problem from the user's perspective.
- **Ideate.** Soliciting input from diverse participants to create multiple solution options.
- **Prototype.** Creating concrete but low-cost artifacts, such as sketches or models, to invite rapid feedback, test assumptions, and answer questions, while minimizing the cost of change. Prototypes answer specific questions.
- **Test.** Testing ideas and assumptions with potential users to reduce the risk of building the wrong solution.
- **Implement.** Delivering a solution while continuing to collect feedback to inform future design changes.

These stages are illustrated in Figure 9-6.

9.6.2 Example Application

A public transit digital payment system faced low adoption by riders even though it was technically functional. Design thinking empathy research revealed that older riders were resistant to using the

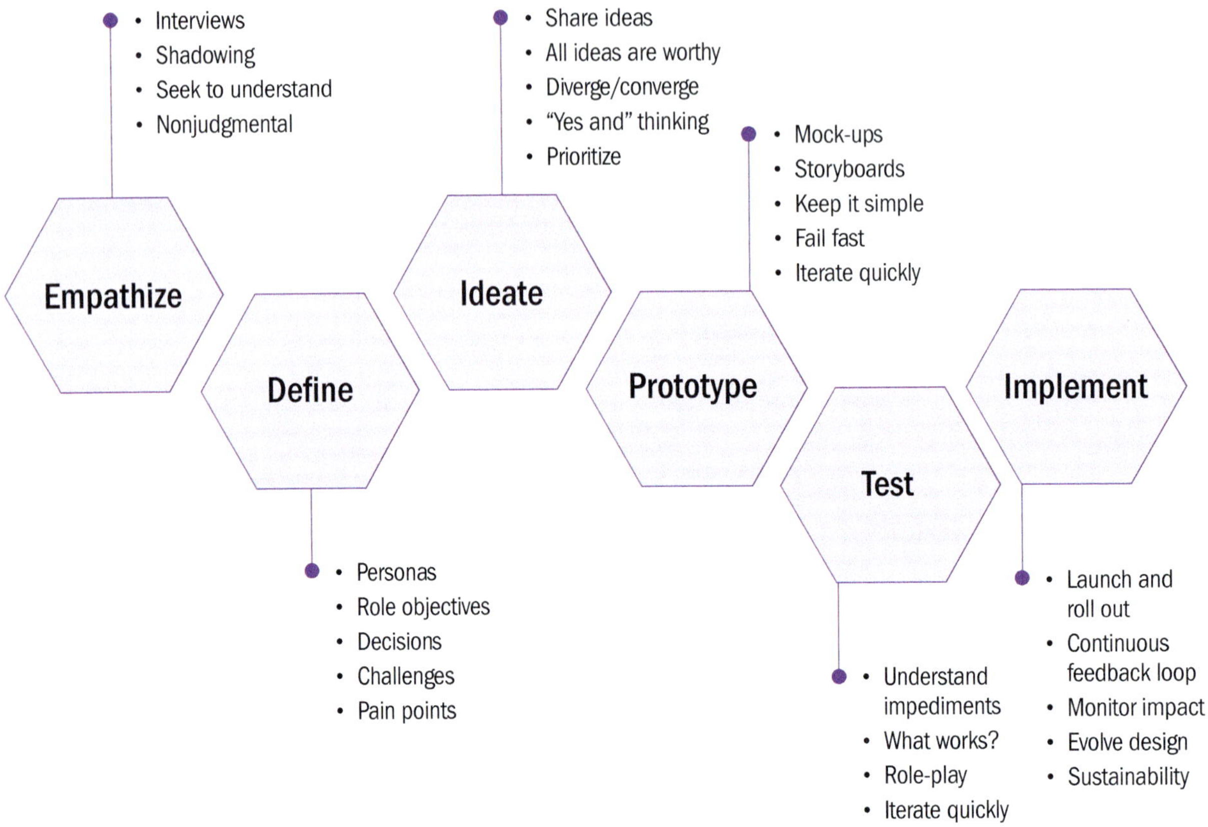

Figure 9-6. Design Thinking Process

digital payment system. These riders were not averse to the new technology. Their resistance was caused by the placement of the touchscreen, which was difficult to access while carrying packages.

The project team prototyped alternative kiosk heights and card reader positions with actual riders, eventually implementing an 18-inch height adjustment that was more comfortable for most riders. This change increased digital payment usage in those over 65 years of age from 12% to 58% within 3 months.

9.7 Complexity Heat Map

Complexity heat maps are visual tools that depict patterns of project complexity across multiple dimensions simultaneously. Reviewing these multidimensional visualizations helps teams reveal complexity patterns where enhanced practices, specialized expertise, or adaptive approaches may be required.

Heat maps can be used to evaluate the types of complexity involved in a project according to the complexity types defined in Section 2. Table 9-5 lists indicators used to assess the level of each complexity type.

Figure 9-7 shows an example of a complexity heat map. In this example, the darker the color, the higher the complexity.

Table 9-5. Complexity Type Assessment

Complexity Type	Assessment Focus	Low-Complexity Indicators	High-Complexity Indicators
Structural complexity	Component interdependencies, stakeholder count, geographic distribution	Few components, single location, clear interfaces	Many interdependent components, multisite, ambiguous boundaries
Dynamic complexity	Rate of change, feedback loops, emergent behaviors	Stable requirements, predictable responses	Rapid change, nonlinear effects, emergence
Technological complexity	Solution novelty, integration challenges, technical uncertainty	Proven technologies, isolated systems	Emerging technologies, extensive integration
Organizational complexity	Number of organizations, governance layers, decision-making processes	Single organization, clear authority	Multiorganization, distributed authority
Human/ sociopolitical complexity	Cultural diversity, change resistance, power dynamics, stakeholder conflicts	Aligned culture, stakeholder consensus	Conflicting cultures, resistance, competing agendas
Environmental complexity	Regulatory shifts, market volatility, external dependencies	Stable regulations, predictable environment	Changing regulations, volatile environment

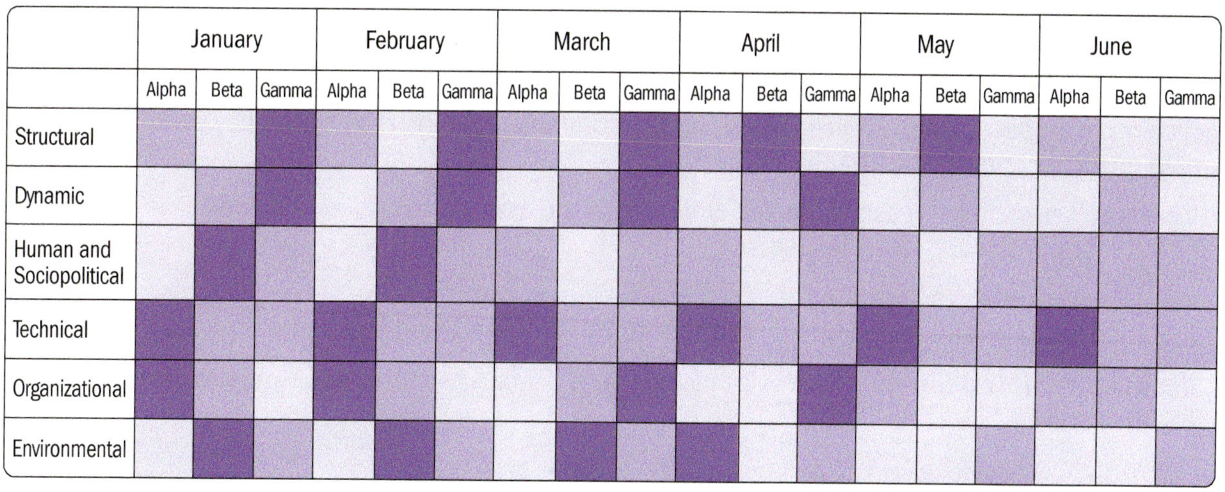

Figure 9-7. Complexity Heat Map

9.7.1 Implementation Guidance

Complexity heat maps may be beneficial in the following situations:

- Selecting the governance approach for a new project
- Informing portfolio prioritization and resource allocation
- Performing reviews to detect complexity changes
- Determining which decisions should be escalated for leadership intervention

The following steps may be completed to create and assess a complexity heat map:

- **Rate each complexity type.** Assign a rating ranging from 1 to 5 for each complexity type, considering the low and high complexity indicators in Table 9-5.
  - 1 = Very low complexity
  - 3 = Moderate complexity
  - 5 = Very high complexity
- **Create a complexity heat map.** Create a table of your ratings and use color coding (green-yellow-red) to visualize them.
- **Identify and interpret patterns.** Review the heat map and analyze patterns, for example:
  - Concentrated high complexity scores suggest that adaptive governance will be beneficial.
  - Mixed complexity scores suggest tailored complexity management may be appropriate.
  - Low complexity scores suggest that traditional project management approaches may be effective.
- **Define the appropriate response.** Use complexity heat map analysis to determine the optimal project governance approach.

To implement complexity heat map assessments effectively within an organizational context, consider the following steps:

- **Assemble an assessment team.** Include project manager, technical lead, and key stakeholders to help ensure representation of diverse perspectives.
- **Rate as a team.** Discuss each complexity type with the assessment team to achieve a consensus-based rating with supporting evidence.
- **Identify responses to complexity.** After reviewing heat map patterns, for each high-complexity dimension (≥4), work as a team to identify specific practices to address the complexity.
- **Reassess complexity regularly.** Revisit ratings on a defined cadence, adjusting practices as patterns shift.

9.7.2 Example Application

A financial services modernization project initially was rated at moderate complexity, or a level 3 rating for most complexity types. Later in the project, a complexity reassessment resulted in an increased environmental complexity level of 5 due to new compliance requirements. The human/sociopolitical complexity rating increased to level 4 due to staff resistance to organizational changes.

Reassessing the complexity heat map triggered an immediate response. The team added a compliance specialist and implemented a change management program with frontline staff engagement. This proactive response prevented an estimated 6-month delay and a US$2 million cost overrun.

9.8 Experiment Canvas

An experiment canvas is a structured template for designing, executing, and learning from small-scale tests in uncertain project environments. By using this template, teams can validate assumptions before implementing initiatives at scale. This helps reduce risk, particularly in complex projects with uncertain and emergent factors.

9.8.1 Implementation Guidance

An experiment canvas may be appropriate to use when:

- Solution effectiveness or stakeholder adoption is very uncertain.
- Multiple viable approaches need evaluation before commitment.
- Implementation is very expensive.
- Resistant stakeholders require evidence to support the project.

To use the experiment canvas, teams may follow these steps:

- **Frame hypothesis.** Articulate what is expected to happen and why, identifying three to five critical assumptions.
- **Design a minimal test.** Determine the smallest experiment that validates or invalidates assumptions.
- **Define success criteria.** List metrics and thresholds before running the experiment.
- **Execute the experiment.** Run the test and collect data.
- **Review results.** Assess outcomes by using success criteria, extracting insights regardless of the outcome.
- **Determine the next step.** Scale, pivot, iterate, or stop based on evidence.

9.8.2 Example Application

A government digital services project faced uncertainty about adoption of online permit applications. Traditionally, the project team would proceed by building the complete system at a cost of US$800,000, then collect and analyze usage metrics.

Because of the uncertainty around adoption, the project team used an experiment canvas approach to test their plans before full implementation. The team built a prototype of the online form, which they tested at a service counter with 50 users. They found that many users were unable to find the permit numbers needed to complete the form and that they did not understand the fee calculation. Only 20% of the users were able to complete the form.

Based on the results of their first experiment, the team refined the form design and ran a second experiment. Seventy-eight percent of participants successfully completed the form during the second test, validating the revised design. The experiment cost US$12,000 and allowed the team to build the full system with confidence. They achieved an 82% adoption rate, which is substantially higher than the 40% industry average.

9.9 Selecting Tools and Frameworks

Although the tools and frameworks discussed in this section provide support and structure for project leaders, choosing the appropriate tool for a specific scenario can present a challenge. This section provides guidance on how to use these tools in the context of a project.

The tools described in this section can be categorized into three critical functions:

- **Assessment tools**, which categorize complexity contexts (Cynefin Framework, complexity heat maps).
- **Process frameworks**, which reveal system dynamics and stakeholder needs (systems thinking, design thinking, experiment canvas).
- **Team-level practices**, which optimize workflow and capture learning (Kanban, AAR).

Project practitioners can combine these tools systematically by starting with an assessment, applying process frameworks to understand interdependencies, then deploying tactical practices to improve team performance.

Table 9-6 provides guidance on tool selection by recommending tools for common project scenarios, along with corresponding section numbers in this guide.

Table 9-6. Asset Selection Guide

Situation/Challenge	Recommended Assets	Why
Unclear which approach to use (predictive vs. adaptive)	Cynefin Framework (9.2) Complexity heat maps (9.7)	Categorizes context and reveals complexity patterns
Multiple interdependent workstreams are causing coordination issues	Systems thinking (9.3)	Reveals hidden dependencies and leverage points
Persistent bottlenecks are slowing delivery	Kanban (9.4)	Optimizes flow through WIP limits
Need to capture lessons while the project is active	After Action Review (9.5)	Enables real-time course correction
Stakeholder requirements are unclear or conflicting	Design thinking (9.6)	Uncovers real needs through empathy work
Need to prioritize attention across multiple complexity dimensions	Complexity heat maps (9.7)	Visualizes where enhanced practices are needed
High uncertainty about solution effectiveness	Experiment canvas (9.8)	Tests assumptions before full commitment

9.10 Summary

This section established a practical complexity management toolkit by:

- Defining seven field-tested tools and frameworks for navigating complexity in project environments
- Providing implementation guidance and example application scenarios for each tool or framework
- Helping project practitioners determine which tools to use in a scenario

The resources in this section enable project practitioners to deploy proven tools to address project challenges associated with complexity.

Section 10

Case Studies

10.1 Introduction

This practice guide covers a range of topics, including types of complexity, competencies for addressing complexity, leadership strategies, and decision-making frameworks. This section presents these topics in the context of case studies, providing insight into the practical application of theoretical concepts.

This section presents three case studies:

- James Webb Space Telescope (JWST)
- Berlin Brandenburg Airport (BER)
- Giga Yacht Project

These case studies span multiple industries, providing a broad perspective on managing complexity across domains and demonstrating how different complexity management approaches influence project outcomes. Critically analyzing each case reveals insights that deepen understanding of navigating complexity in practice.

10.2 James Webb Space Telescope (JWST)

The James Webb Space Telescope (JWST) was one of the most complex engineering projects ever executed. Building and operating the JWST required high levels of coordination, with careful management of structural precision and technological innovation under conditions of high uncertainty.

The telescope was designed to observe the earliest galaxies and search for potentially habitable planets. To observe these distant galaxies, the telescope had to operate far from Earth. At such distances, repairs were impossible, requiring every mechanism to function perfectly on the first attempt. This requirement created immense engineering challenges.

These engineering demands were compounded by organizational and political complexity. The telescope was made possible by a multiagency partnership among NASA, the European Space Agency (ESA), and the Canadian Space Agency (CSA), alongside hundreds of external contractors. Managing this ecosystem required governance structures that aligned diverse cultures, funding constraints, and priorities.

The project to build the JWST was initiated in the early 1990s. After decades of research, design, and fabrication work, the telescope was assembled in 2016 and launched on 25 December 2021. The total program cost exceeded US$10 billion, making the JWST one of the most expensive scientific projects ever undertaken.

10.2.1 Project Purpose

The project purpose was to deploy a successor to the Hubble Space Telescope, which launched in 1990 with flawed optics. The new telescope was designed to explore the universe in infrared wavelengths, with improved sensitivity and resolution relative to Hubble.

Specifically, the JWST was designed to:

- Study the early universe, observing the first galaxies and stars.
- Examine how stars and planetary systems form within gas and dust clouds.
- Analyze exoplanet atmospheres for signs of habitability.
- Study planets, moons, comets, and asteroids close to Earth.

10.2.2 Complexity Types

The JWST encountered the following types of complexity:

- **Structural.** The design included over 300 "single-point failure" mechanisms; a failure in any of them could have ended the mission.
- **Dynamic.** From project initiation in the early 1990s to the telescope launch in 2021, political climates, budgets, and technologies shifted substantially, requiring continuous adaptation.
- **Human and sociopolitical.** Thousands of staff across multiple countries worked under shifting leadership and evolving technical baselines.
- **Environmental.** Factors beyond the team's control, including space conditions and Earth-based constraints, influenced decisions.
- **Organizational.** New management approaches were required to guide teams developing novel technologies.

These dimensions of complexity interacted with one another, creating interdependencies in which small decisions in one project area could cascade into unexpected delays and costs in others.

10.2.2.1 Structural Complexity

Structural complexity, or the interconnection and interdependence of a project's components, was a major factor in development of the JWST. Space telescopes consist of many connected components that interact with one another, forming an intricate web of dependencies. Operating in space added further complexity due to harsh, unpredictable conditions and the impossibility of repairs.

Key structural complexity aspects of the JWST included:

- **Single-point failures.** The JWST contained critical systems such as sunshields and cryogenic instruments; failure of any of these would have rendered the telescope inoperable. Engineers mitigated risk through redundant mechanisms, extensive ground testing, and independent verification of components.
- **Integration challenges.** The team coordinated over 300,000 globally sourced components, including optics and electronics, each with unique environmental and calibration requirements. Phased integration tests and iterative validation helped ensure subsystems functioned together before launch.
- **Simulating space conditions.** The telescope could not be fully tested under actual space conditions. Engineers used models and simulations to run virtual tests, which allowed the team to explore "what-if" scenarios, identify potential failure modes, and optimize designs without relying on physical prototypes.

The telescope's multicomponent, tightly integrated hardware required equally tight coordination among engineers, managers, and space agencies. Extensive testing, comprehensive simulations, and collaboration across engineering teams helped ensure both hardware and human systems were aligned for mission success, effectively addressing this structural complexity.

10.2.2.2 Dynamic Complexity

Dynamic complexity arises when project conditions, requirements, or environments change faster than plans can stabilize. The JWST faced dynamic complexity throughout its long development, spanning multiple eras of technology, politics, and funding cycles. Success required adaptive planning, iterative learning, and governance structures capable of responding to uncertainty.

Key dynamic complexity aspects of the JWST included:

- **Rapidly evolving technology.** Roughly 80% of subsystems had to be invented or significantly advanced, including deployable segmented mirrors and cryogenic detectors. New interdependencies and untested behaviors required extensive prototyping and cross-disciplinary coordination.
- **Learning cycles and redesigns.** Tests often revealed flaws requiring redesign. For example, a 2018 deployment test uncovered loose fasteners and torn sunshield membranes, prompting a root cause analysis involving 400 specialists and subsequent governance improvements.

- **Changing governance approach.** Management shifted from linear, hierarchical models to adaptive approaches using iterative learning loops. Although this transition added complexity, adaptive approaches such as continuous simulations and design reviews reduced postlaunch risks.
- **Communicating challenges to stakeholders.** Clear and effective communication was critical for maintaining credibility amid the challenges caused by dynamic complexity. NASA used transparent storytelling and visual tools to frame delays as evidence of rigor and necessary investment in reliability.

Dynamic complexity demanded flexible technical and organizational responses. Adaptive governance, iterative testing, and proactive communication allowed the project teams to navigate uncertainty while advancing cutting-edge technology.

10.2.2.3 Human and Sociopolitical Complexity

Human and sociopolitical complexity arises from interactions among people, organizations, and cultural expectations. For the JWST, this complexity stemmed from collaborations between diverse organizations and contractors, high staff turnover, and intense political oversight. Sustaining a shared purpose across the project required careful coordination, cultural awareness, and knowledge management.

Key human and sociopolitical complexity aspects of the JWST included:

- **Cross-agency coordination.** The main agencies involved—NASA, ESA (European Space Agency), and CSA (Canadian Space Agency)—established an Integrated International Project Office (IIPO) to align technical baselines, key milestones, and project execution approaches while preserving agency autonomy.
- **Tailored governance approaches.** Technical decisions followed NASA documentation and sign-off standards, while implementation accommodated the iterative approach of ESA, balancing rigor with flexibility.
- **Knowledge management.** To address the long timescale of the project and resulting staff turnover, systems for documentation, mentoring, and collaboration were developed to preserve institutional memory across generations of engineers located around the world.
- **Political messaging.** Strategic communication framed the JWST as "Hubble's successor" while emphasizing the role of international collaboration, helping to maintain political support and morale.
- **Cultural integration.** Workshops and joint glossaries bridged differences in decision-making styles, facilitating rapid coordination during integration and testing.
- **Workforce well-being.** Health programs, stress counseling, and recovery cycles helped manage cognitive load and sustain performance over long durations.

Managing human and sociopolitical complexity required the combination of rigorous governance with flexibility, emotional intelligence, and proactive cultural integration. The JWST experience reinforced the importance of empowering engineers, preserving institutional knowledge, and balancing optimism with realism.

10.2.2.4 Environmental Complexity

Environmental complexity refers to uncertainty and variability in external conditions that affect a project. For the JWST, it included physical, logistical, and operational factors beyond the team's control, requiring proactive mitigation.

Key environmental complexity aspects of the JWST included:

- **Operational constraints.** Repairs were impossible after launch, which necessitated a design focus on reliability rather than repairability.
- **Logistics and supply chain.** Sensitive components manufactured across three continents required specialized shipping and transportation. Risk management included secure routes and contingency planning.
- **Pandemic disruptions.** The COVID-19 pandemic reduced the project workforce and disrupted supply chains in 2020, causing delays. NASA implemented split shifts, remote coordination, and flexible sequencing to address these challenges.
- **Risk modeling and mitigation.** The project used an integrated framework and risk matrices to manage environmental risks due to variables such as radiation and temperature. Telescope components were designed with unusually large tolerance margins to guard against postlaunch system failure.
- **Integrated environment modeling (IEM).** Simulations of thermal, contamination, and cross-domain interactions prevented cascading failures and enabled adaptive design decisions.

By actively managing environmental uncertainty through logistics planning, simulations, and contingency frameworks, the JWST team minimized risks and helped ensure reliable operation in an unpredictable environment.

10.2.2.5 Organizational Complexity

Organizational complexity arises from multiple actors, hierarchies, and interdependencies. The JWST involved three space agencies, hundreds of international suppliers, and multiple regulatory bodies. Successful governance required balancing structure with flexibility while prioritizing international collaboration.

Key organizational complexity aspects of the JWST included:

- **Multiagency coordination.** The IIPO and joint working groups coordinated project management while allowing agency autonomy.
- **Decision-making pathways.** Clear governance structures and feedback loops balanced compliance with speed, reducing bottlenecks in a highly layered bureaucracy.
- **Integration of cultures and processes.** Standardized terminology and shared governance protocols allowed improved communication across agencies, reducing misunderstandings.
- **Adaptive governance.** Adaptive governance approaches addressed tensions between centralized leadership and technical experts. Mechanisms like independent review panels and lessons learned sessions created feedback loops to adjust authority and oversight as the project evolved.
- **Trust and transparency.** "Radical Candor reviews" allowed engineers to communicate directly with leadership, improving morale and collaboration.

Navigating such immense organizational complexity required robust governance, adaptive processes, and trust-based coordination. Successfully managing these dimensions helped ensure alignment across agencies, enabling eventual launch and operation of the JWST.

10.2.3 Analysis and Insights

The JWST project demonstrates how complexity shapes the planning, execution, and outcomes of a high-stakes scientific megaproject.

This section examines the JWST through the lens of the following concepts discussed in previous sections:

- Systems Thinking and Complexity Theory (Section 3)
- Development Approaches for Complexity (Section 4)
- Competencies for Navigating Complexity (Section 5)
- Communication and Stakeholder Engagement (Section 6)
- Decision-Making in Complex Environments (Section 7)
- Leadership Strategies for Complexity (Section 8)

This analysis highlights ways the JWST team managed structural, dynamic, human, environmental, and organizational complexity throughout a multidecade, international, technologically innovative endeavor.

10.2.3.1 Systems Thinking

Systems thinking was essential for managing the interdependent subsystems of the JWST, each required to operate reliably under the extreme conditions of space.

Engineers needed a holistic perspective on how components, including optics, cooling systems, and deployment mechanisms, interacted. Systems thinking allowed them to anticipate emergent behaviors, model thousands of potential failure modes, and treat the telescope as a dynamic ecosystem rather than a collection of isolated parts.

10.2.3.2 Development Approaches for Complexity

The JWST started with hierarchical management approaches. Over time, the program tailored the development approach, combining rigorous aerospace standards with iterative prototyping. Novel technologies were developed incrementally to reduce uncertainty, whereas strict standards helped ensure consistency and mission reliability.

This combination enabled innovation while maintaining the integrity and reliability required for a one-time space deployment.

10.2.3.3 Competencies for Managing Complexity

Adaptive leadership was a critical competency for managing complexity of the JWST. This flexible approach supported high-stakes, cross-disciplinary collaboration.

For example, following a 2018 sunshield deployment test failure, leaders convened 400 specialists to conduct a root cause analysis and implement corrective actions, demonstrating adaptive leadership in practice.

Coordinating these corrective actions across agencies, contractors, and globally dispersed teams required negotiation of technical priorities, sequencing of interventions, and interface management, illustrating how adaptive leadership enables complex project success.

10.2.3.4 Communication and Stakeholder Engagement

Managing the complexity in this project required alignment across international agencies, scientists, and policymakers. Transparent communication helped the JWST project team maintain credibility during budget overruns and technical setbacks.

Leaders used regular updates, visual tools, and shared documentation to reduce misunderstandings and reinforce trust across distributed teams.

10.2.3.5 Decision-Making in Complex Environments

Decision-making involved trade-offs among cost, risk, and performance. Multiagency boards required clear evidence to justify decisions, whereas the inability to repair the telescope necessitated a conservative, evidence-based approach.

Risk assessment was embedded into daily decision-making, enabling informed choices despite uncertainty.

10.2.3.6 Leadership Strategies for Complex Projects

The JWST leaders balanced vision with technical reality and guided teams through decades of evolving requirements.

They fostered collaboration and psychological safety, allowing teams to surface risks early. Strategic leadership sustained momentum throughout the project's extended timeline.

10.2.4 Project Outcomes

The JWST fulfilled its mission on this decades-long, high-cost, complex project, achieving the following outcomes:

- Successful space telescope deployment.
- Scientific breakthroughs, providing unprecedented observations of early galaxies and exoplanets.
- Technological innovations, including segmented mirrors and advanced cryogenic instruments.

The JWST team enabled these outcomes by:

- Managing over 300 potential single-point failures through disciplined risk mitigation.
- Preserving institutional knowledge across a multidecade project.
- Establishing a blueprint for managing complex future missions.

The project also advanced scientific research globally by:

- Demonstrating that complex, one-time space deployments are achievable.
- Strengthening partnerships among NASA, ESA, and CSA.
- Reinforcing the feasibility of long-term scientific megaprojects.
- Inspiring global interest in STEM.

10.2.5 Lessons Learned

The JWST provides these key lessons for managing complex megaprojects:

- **Technology readiness.** Starting development before necessary technology has been developed introduces major schedule risks.
- **Systems engineering.** Robust integration and modeling are essential to managing single-point failures.
- **Testing.** Progressive, multistage testing helps surface unforeseen issues.
- **Transparency.** Clear communication with stakeholders maintains trust during budget escalations.
- **Collaboration.** International partnerships require strong governance and harmonized standards.
- **Flexibility.** Adaptive planning enables the project to accommodate unexpected technical discoveries.
- **Culture.** Encouraging teams to surface problems early prevents defects from becoming mission-threatening.
- **Mindset.** Designing systems that accept complexity as permanent is more effective than attempting to control it.
- **Risk management.** Continuous risk management that is embedded in daily decision-making is important in complex environments.

Successfully navigating challenges of the JWST required multidimensional approaches. Structural complexity was managed through disciplined systems engineering and configuration control, helping ensure all components functioned as a coherent whole. Dynamic complexity was addressed through iterative testing, flexible planning, and learning loops. Human and sociopolitical complexity relied on governance, collaboration, and knowledge preservation. Novel technologies were validated via incremental prototyping and risk-informed scheduling.

10.2.6 James Webb Space Telescope (JWST) Summary

The JWST project—a joint mission led by NASA with major contributions from ESA and CSA—created an infrared observatory that studies the first galaxies and stars formed after the Big Bang, planetary formation, star systems, and exoplanet atmospheres.

The JWST features innovative components, including a 6.5-meter segmented beryllium mirror and a five-layer Kapton sunshield for thermal protection. Many of its technologies were developed during the project, requiring extensive subsystem development, testing, and phased integration.

The JWST redefined space telescope capabilities, illustrating the effectiveness of international collaboration and management of complex, high-stakes systems. The project provides a blueprint for future complex missions.

10.3 Berlin Brandenburg Airport (BER)

Following the reunification of Germany in 1990, the federal government initiated a program to modernize Berlin's fragmented aviation infrastructure. The goal was to replace the city's three older airports—Tegel, Schönefeld, and Tempelhof—with one large, modern airport known as the Berlin Brandenburg Airport (BER).

Figure 10-1 shows the location of Berlin's original airports, as well as the location of BER.

BER opened in 2020, nearly 30 years after it was initially proposed. Its development spanned multiple political, economic, and technological eras. The final cost was approximately €7 billion.

Figure 10-2 shows a high-level timeline for the BER development project.

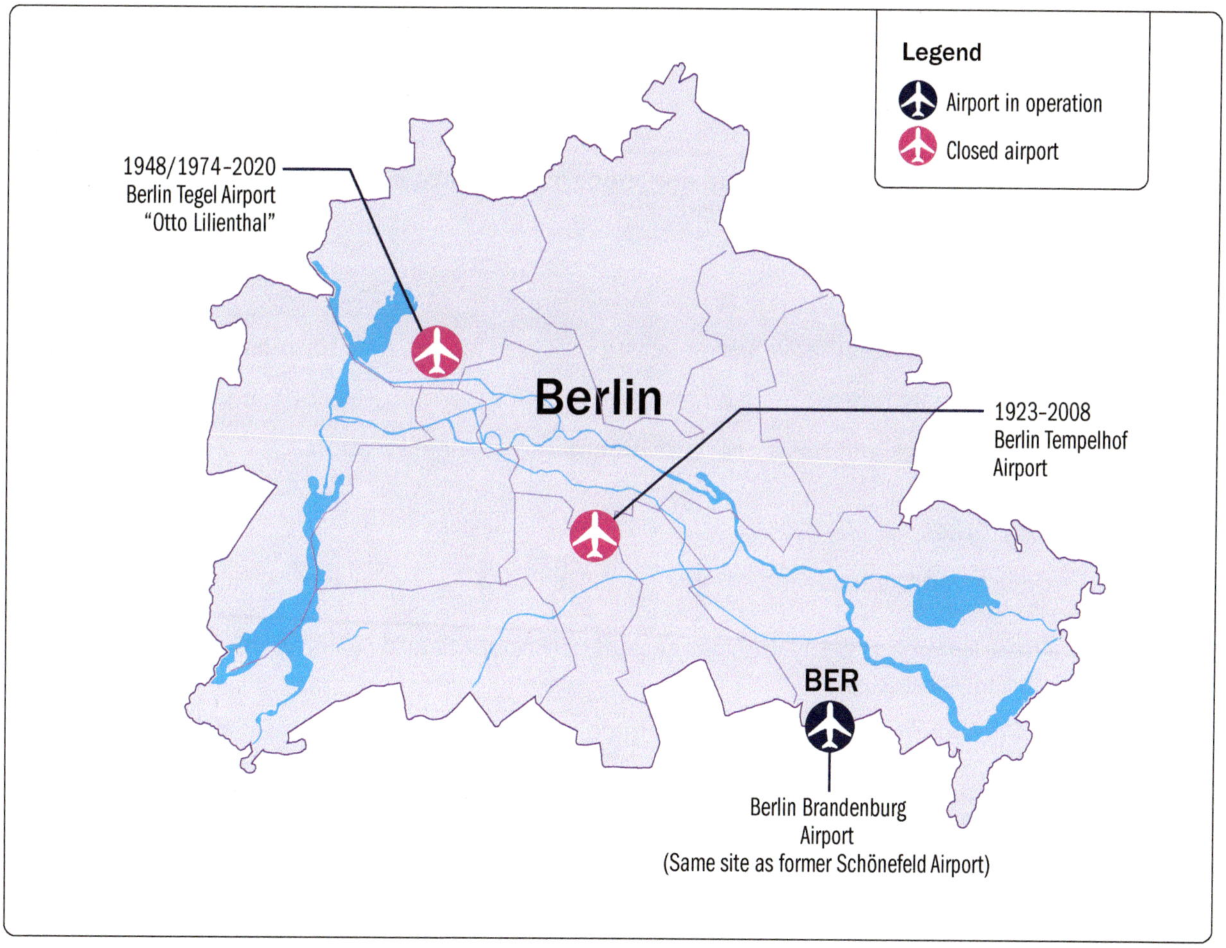

Figure 10-1. Map of Airport Locations

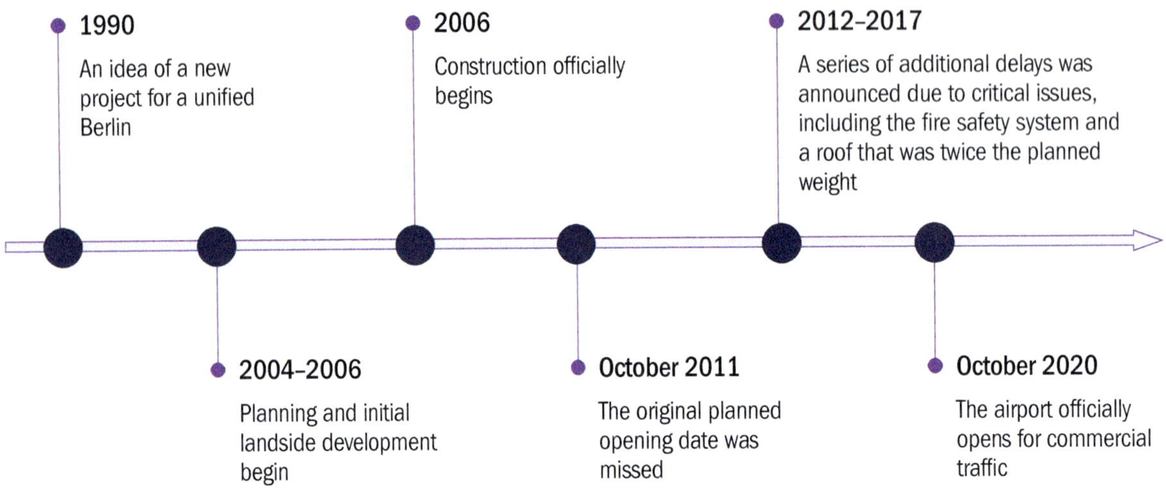

Figure 10-2. Berlin Brandenburg Airport (BER) High-Level Timeline

The BER development project demonstrates forms of complexity commonly associated with large-scale public infrastructure projects. The consolidation of multiple airports into the state of Brandenburg introduced jurisdictional and governance challenges that additional dimensions of complexity to the project.

10.3.1 Project Purpose

The main purpose of BER was to consolidate and modernize Berlin's aviation infrastructure, replacing the older airports with a state-of-the-art facility.

The project also aimed to:

- Create a European travel hub that would generate jobs and attract new businesses to the region.
- Support national unity by representing a new beginning for Germany after decades of division.
- Streamline airline logistics and passenger movement into a single location.

10.3.2 Complexity Types

The BER project displayed the following complexity dimensions:

- **Structural.** Airports contain many interdependent components and systems that need to be coordinated and integrated.
- **Dynamic.** Long development timelines exposed the project to shifting market conditions and industry models.
- **Human and sociopolitical.** Multiple public authorities and stakeholder groups created overlapping interests and decision rights.
- **Environmental.** External economic, political, and public health events influenced funding, procurement, and operations.

- **Technological.** Innovative and unproven systems introduced cascading design and integration challenges.
- **Organizational.** A fragmented contractor ecosystem complicated coordination, oversight, and accountability.

The complexity types interacted and compounded over time, increasing the difficulty of planning, execution, and governance.

10.3.2.1 Structural Complexity

Structural complexity, or the interconnection and interdependence of a project's components, was a major factor in the BER project. Building and operating BER involved numerous interdependent components, any one of which would have been complex to manage on its own. Coordinating and integrating these components simultaneously created a particularly challenging environment.

The project had to integrate existing infrastructure, such as the Schönefeld Airport runway and terminal, with new construction, including a parallel runway and two new terminals.

Additionally, they had to integrate systems to handle a diverse range of airport needs such as:

- Baggage handling;
- Fire suppression;
- IT infrastructure;
- Transportation, including a new rail line and highway; and
- Utilities, including underground water and power cables.

The inherent structural complexity of this project was further compounded by operational decisions. Authorities decided to shut down Tempelhof and Schönefeld Airports, keeping only Tegel Airport operational until the opening of BER.

This decision meant that, once BER was ready to open, nearly all commercial air traffic serving Berlin would need to transition from Tegel Airport to the new facility in a tightly coordinated operational shift.

Transitioning operations from Tegel Airport to BER was immensely complex. Immediately after Tegel Airport closed, millions of dollars of equipment were transferred across Berlin to allow BER to open the following day. Navigating the structural complexity of this maneuver required extensive planning, staging, and rehearsal.

10.3.2.2 Dynamic Complexity

Dynamic complexity arises when project conditions, requirements, or environments change faster than plans can stabilize. In the decades between planning BER and its opening in 2020, the aviation industry went through significant structural and market changes. This caused dynamic complexity, resulting in design changes that impacted budgets and timelines.

For example, the airport was initially designed using a hub-and-spoke model with extensive retail and dining establishments. During the decades of construction, the industry evolved toward direct flights and low-cost carriers. As a result, the airport design was changed midproject, adjusting terminal configurations to accommodate the shift in travel preferences.

10.3.2.3 Human and Sociopolitical Complexity

Human and sociopolitical complexity arises from interactions among people, organizations, and cultural expectations. For BER the primary source of this complexity type came from its governance structure.

The BER governance authority was distributed across multiple public stakeholders, including the Federal Republic of Germany, the State of Brandenburg, and the city-state of Berlin. This created overlapping decision rights related to airport planning, capacity, procurement, and land acquisition.

In addition to multiple government stakeholders there were other very influential groups of stakeholders, including:

- Airport labor unions
- The railway company
- Duty-free shops
- Car rental companies
- Impacted residents

The number of stakeholders involved in this project introduced a range of coordination challenges. For example, public scrutiny and political debate over site selection and approval extended over a decade.

Stakeholders from all parties had to be consulted and coordinated before reaching an acceptable result. Over 300 people were required to relocate to accommodate the selected location, and the project was required to fund soundproofing and ventilation improvements for homes in the airport vicinity.

10.3.2.4 Environmental Complexity

Environmental complexity refers to uncertainty and variability in external conditions that affect a project. The lengthy development timeline of BER helped ensure there were many sources of environmental complexity. During the span of the project, there were multiple financial upheavals, Germany transitioned to the euro, and the COVID-19 pandemic disrupted travel globally.

Each of these events influenced the development of BER. Periods of financial instability placed additional pressure on public funding and long-term financial planning. The transition to the euro had positive effects, including expanded access to materials and labor across Europe, increasing sourcing options. However, it also introduced new costs, coordination needs, and stakeholder engagement challenges associated with cross-border procurement.

Opening during the pandemic had a negative impact, as the economic downturn, citywide lockdown, and supply chain disruptions associated with the pandemic disrupted airport operations. However, the reduction in flights at the time of launch allowed issues to be addressed quickly, resulting in minimal disruptions to passengers and flights.

10.3.2.5 Technological Complexity

Technological complexity refers to the degree of difficulty encountered in selecting, implementing, and maintaining technology solutions that align with project goals and organizational capabilities. The selection of an innovative fire-suppression and smoke extraction system proved to be an unexpected source of technological complexity for BER. The design did not work as planned, which caused cascading design changes.

This redesign impacted ventilation, electrical, and control systems throughout the airport. To fix the issues with this complex and interconnected system, passenger routes, gate layouts, and the broadcast system had to be rethought, and major commercial areas were relocated. These extensive changes caused years of delay to the project.

10.3.2.6 Organizational Complexity

Organizational complexity is caused by intricate and multifaceted organizational structures. The scale of the project led to organizational fragmentation among thousands of contractors and subcontractors.

Communication gaps within these groups caused issues with installations. For example, 60 kilometers of cooling pipe was installed without thermal insulation because the functional groups involved in the work were not coordinating. Organizational complexity was compounded by high turnover in leadership and the challenges associated with maintaining oversight of thousands of individual contractors.

10.3.3 Analysis and Insights

The BER project illustrates the importance of managing the compounding effects of complexity, where one type of complexity amplifies others rather than remaining isolated.

The case demonstrates the following key concepts introduced earlier in this practice guide:

- Systems Thinking and Complexity Theory (Section 3)
- Development Approaches for Complexity (Section 4)
- Competencies for Navigating Complexity (Section 5)
- Communication and Stakeholder Engagement (Section 6)
- Decision-Making in Complex Environments (Section 7)
- Leadership Strategies for Complexity (Section 8)

10.3.3.1 Systems Thinking

Due to the project's significant structural complexity, systems thinking was essential. Of particular note are the concepts of holism and interconnectedness, which help explain how localized design and governance decisions had cascading effects across the project.

In the BER project, subsystems such as fire safety, building automation, IT infrastructure, and architectural design were deeply interdependent. Decisions made in one area frequently introduced unintended consequences elsewhere, particularly when changes were implemented late in the development process.

A systems perspective highlights how the failure to fully account for these interdependencies contributed to repeated redesigns, integration challenges, and schedule delays. This case illustrates how managing complex projects requires understanding not only individual components, but also the interactions among them and the emergent behaviors those interactions produce.

10.3.3.2 Development Approaches

Large infrastructure projects typically rely on predictive approaches to planning and development. This was especially true given that the BER project began in the 1990s, before adaptive approaches were widely adopted in project management practice.

Certain adaptive approaches may have helped address some BER challenges. Experiments, incremental testing, or early prototyping could have identified problems with the fire suppression and smoke extraction system earlier, potentially reducing the scope of later redesigns and schedule overruns.

Adaptive approaches are often effective for innovative technology development, which may also have benefited the airport's IT systems and building automation components.

10.3.3.3 Competencies

The government applied strategic thinking during planning for this project when they predicted the benefits of a centralized airport, rather than three distributed airports. Strategically locating the airport in Brandenburg helped ensure land availability for future growth.

The project team also focused on value creation for stakeholders. The experiences of travelers, businesses, and airlines were all considered in the final delivery of a major hub.

10.3.3.4 Communication, Stakeholder Engagement, and Decision-Making

Although the project team regularly communicated information about the airport's development and its complex nature, there were notable missteps related to communication and decision-making.

The airport was originally scheduled to open in the fall of 2011. However, mounting technical issues made the planned opening date increasingly unrealistic. Despite this, the airport authority delayed formally communicating the change, informing key stakeholders, including airlines, airport employees, and service providers, only shortly before the anticipated opening date.

This decision was largely politically motivated. A new regional government was inaugurated shortly before the planned opening, and authorities chose to postpone the announcement to avoid political fallout. While this approach may have reduced short-term political risk, it created significant operational challenges for stakeholders and damaged trust. This episode underscores the importance of transparent, timely communication in complex projects, particularly when delays are unavoidable.

10.3.3.5 Leadership Strategies

During the early phases of the BER project, key roles in governance and project leadership changed, which led to inconsistent oversight and coordination challenges that contributed to delays and cost overruns.

Over the past two decades, studies have increasingly highlighted the benefits of adaptive and distributed leadership approaches for large, complex, long-term initiatives with evolving and shifting external conditions.

In retrospect, the BER project may have benefited from governance and leadership practices that enabled earlier escalation of risks, greater empowerment of technical experts, and more flexible coordination across stakeholders.

10.3.4 Project Outcomes

BER began operations in October 2020, approximately 9 years behind schedule. The project was substantially over budget, reaching a final cost of approximately €7 billion compared to the original estimate of €2 billion. Much of the overrun was due to the high cost of significant redesigns, prolonged testing, and extended maintenance during schedule delays.

Although the project was delayed and over budget, BER achieved its core objective of creating an innovative aviation hub in Berlin.

Project successes include:

- BER is the primary airport in the Berlin region.
- Its rail-to-air link is a model for multimode transportation in the region.
- Passenger service ratings and operational efficiency metrics are steadily improving.

10.3.5 Lessons Learned

BER provides several lessons for navigating projects with high structural and organizational complexity:

- Systems thinking and systems engineering strategies, such as strong systems integration and early testing practices, are essential for projects with high structural complexity.
- A tailored development approach may benefit complex infrastructure projects such as BER, as both predictive and adaptive approaches have relevant management benefits.
- Governance structures balance authority, decision-making, transparency, and speed, avoiding the politics that accompany bureaucracy and promoting the transparency and decision speed of accountable governing bodies.

To apply these lessons to future projects, project leaders may benefit from shifting their thinking around structural complexity. The integration of components within a system is as important as the number of components involved. Rigorous systems engineering helps ensure that a change in one subsystem does not cause failure in another.

Innovation involves risk. Risk mitigation strategies, such as small-scale pilots or full simulations, can help identify flaws in novel systems before they are integrated into physical infrastructure, reducing the cost and delays associated with later corrections.

10.3.6 Berlin Brandenburg Airport (BER) Summary

The BER project provides a comprehensive look at the challenges inherent in multidecade infrastructure projects. By examining the complex challenges within this project, project practitioners can anticipate the compounding risks of large-scale initiatives.

This project underscores that success in complex environments depends on the continuous alignment of technical design, stakeholder governance, and adaptive management strategies.

10.4 The Giga Yacht Project

The Giga Yacht project involved the design, engineering, and construction of a private luxury yacht that exceeded 100 meters in length. The Giga Yacht project was ambitious, requiring technical advancement and enhancing organizational capability.

At the time of the project's initiation in the early 2010s, yachts of this size occupied an ambiguous space between commercial shipbuilding and bespoke, luxury craftmanship typical of yacht building. The vessel's unprecedented length required the application of large-scale shipbuilding methods while still meeting client expectations for customization, comfort, and aesthetic refinement.

The project unfolded over multiple years and involved international suppliers, multiple regulatory interpretations, and a high degree of client engagement, all of which contributed to its complexity. This case study examines how complexity was managed across structural, human, technological, environmental, and organizational dimensions during the delivery of an iconic yacht.

10.4.1 Purpose

The purpose of the Giga Yacht project was to deliver a first-of-its-kind ultra-luxury vessel while redefining technical, environmental, and experiential standards for the private yachting industry.

Specifically, the project aimed to:

- Build an iconic vessel that showcased innovation, craftsmanship, and engineering excellence.
- Minimize environmental impact by incorporating sustainable technologies such as hybrid propulsion systems and energy-efficient materials.
- Enhance onboard luxury through customized design, advanced automation, and premium amenities.
- Strengthen brand reputation and market position in the ultra-luxury maritime industry by setting new benchmarks for performance, design, and sustainability.

10.4.2 Complexity Types

Complexity of the Giga Yacht project was most visible across the following dimensions:

- **Structural.** Yachts of this size involve many complex, interconnected systems.
- **Human and sociopolitical.** Multidisciplinary teams had to collaborate closely to meet the expectations of demanding, high-net-worth clientele.

- **Environmental.** The project had to comply with a range of different regulations, including within emerging areas such as cybersecurity.
- **Technological.** Advanced and interconnected technological systems, such as hybrid propulsion and environmental controls, were complex to integrate and operationalize.
- **Organizational.** The innovative nature of this project required changes to operations and governance structure.

This section examines how the project team navigated each of these complexity dimensions.

10.4.2.1 Structural Complexity

Structural complexity arises when projects have a large number of interconnected components. Constructing the 100-meter yacht required the integration of thousands of components fabricated to precise tolerances.

Successful integration of the Giga Yacht's components required a carefully sequenced construction process:

1. The hull, which is the watertight body of the yacht, was assembled first to provide structural rigidity.
2. Mechanical, electrical, and plumbing (MEP) systems were embedded within the hull and the superstructure, which refers to the sections built above the main deck.
3. The superstructure was installed and structurally integrated with the hull.
4. Interior spaces were completed, including luxury furnishings and automated systems.

Giga Yacht components were sourced from hundreds of suppliers worldwide, including:

- Engine and hybrid propulsion components from Germany.
- Noise insulation and HVAC systems from Northern Europe.
- Luxury fittings, furniture, and electronics from Italy, France, and Switzerland.

Because systems were tightly coupled, delays or rework at any stage produced cascading effects. This made supply chain sequencing, interface management, critical path control, and buffer planning essential for maintaining schedule stability.

10.4.2.2 Human and Sociopolitical Complexity

Human and sociopolitical complexity arises from interactions among diverse stakeholders, team members, and external partners. This was a significant factor in the Giga Yacht project, which faced challenges related to:

- Coordinating multidisciplinary and multicultural teams;
- Managing knowledge across vendors, platforms, and changing personnel; and
- Aligning with the expectations of ultra-high-net-worth clients.

The project relied on multidisciplinary and multicultural teams with distinct technical languages, priorities, and professional cultures. Naval architects responsible for hull and superstructure integrity collaborated closely with mechanical and electrical engineers implementing propulsion and automation systems. These teams also coordinated with interior designers and artisans delivering bespoke luxury elements.

To address coordination challenges, leadership emphasized shared objectives related to operational performance and luxury quality. The team used cross-functional communication protocols, regular integration workshops, and centralized decision-making to align design, engineering, and craftsmanship efforts. When conflicts arose, clear escalation paths and structured conflict-resolution processes were used, supported by early-stage prototyping to demonstrate trade-offs.

Knowledge management posed challenges early in the project because critical information was dispersed across vendors, platforms, and locations. Workforce rotation during the project's multiyear duration increased the risk of knowledge loss. This was addressed by centralizing documentation, implementing collaboration tools, and introducing structured knowledge transfer and mentoring programs, which reduced rework and inconsistency over time.

Engagement with ultra-high-net-worth clients introduced additional complexity through evolving design preferences, tight timelines, and sustained pressure to deliver flawless quality. Transparent reporting, proactive stakeholder engagement, and rapid design iterations were used to balance client expectations with technical and schedule constraints.

10.4.2.3 *Environmental Complexity*

Environmental complexity refers to uncertainty and variability in external conditions that affect a project. The regulatory environment was a significant source of environmental complexity for the Giga Yacht project.

As one of the largest yachts constructed in Italy at the time, the vessel presented challenges for regulatory bodies that had limited precedent for vessels of this scale, including:

- Flag registration authorities, responsible for vessel registration and compliance with national maritime requirements.
- Classification societies, which establish and verify technical standards for structural integrity, safety, and seaworthiness.
- Safety and environmental regulators, overseeing compliance with maritime safety, emissions, and emerging cybersecurity requirements.

Regulatory requirements varied across jurisdictions and evolved over time, particularly in areas related to safety, emissions, and cybersecurity. These changes influenced both design decisions and construction sequencing.

To manage regulatory complexity, the team mapped overlapping and conflicting certification requirements from international marine authorities and coastal state regulators. They developed a harmonized compliance strategy to minimize late-stage design changes.

Regulatory oversight added further structural constraints, which influenced both design and sequencing decisions. For example, the hybrid propulsion system required demonstration of seaworthiness and compliance across multiple authorities, necessitating extensive prototyping, testing, and adaptation.

10.4.2.4 Technological Complexity

Technological complexity refers to the degree of difficulty encountered in selecting, implementing, and maintaining technological solutions that align with project goals and organizational capabilities. In the Giga Yacht project, technological complexity arose primarily from the integration of a hybrid propulsion system and advanced automated environmental controls.

The propulsion system combined conventional diesel engines with electric drives, battery banks, and power electronics within a unified control architecture. Technological challenges with this setup included:

- System integration related to weight, vibration, and power management;
- Novel interfaces among electrical, propulsion, and navigation systems; and
- High expectations for operational reliability with minimal fault tolerance.

To manage these challenges, the team relied on advanced simulation, real-time monitoring, and close coordination among propulsion, electrical, and software engineering teams.

Hybrid propulsion at this scale was relatively novel in the Italian luxury yacht context, requiring suppliers to adapt to project-specific constraints and engage in iterative integration testing. Failure diagnosis was often complex because subsystem interdependencies produced multiple contributing causes.

The vessel integrated multiple automation and sustainability systems, including:

- Energy management
- Climate control
- Wastewater treatment
- Automated lighting
- Environmental monitoring
- Onboard entertainment

These systems interfaced with sustainability technologies such as smart sensors, adaptive control systems, and energy-efficient subsystems. Integration required real-time testing during construction, iterative debugging, and close coordination among engineers, automation specialists, environmental compliance teams, and interior designers.

The high degree of interdependence among systems meant that changes in one area frequently affected others, reinforcing the need for systems engineering and disciplined change control. In one instance, automated lighting was installed prior to final interior paneling. After paneling was completed, the lighting system was found to obstruct sensor calibration, requiring removal and reinstallation.

10.4.2.5 Organizational Complexity

Organizational complexity is caused by intricate and multifaceted organizational structures. The Giga Yacht project required the company to expand its organizational capabilities by creating dedicated Giga Yacht programs.

This expansion introduced organizational complexity, including the need to:

- Create new processes, operating models, and workflows.
- Establish revised governance structures, role definitions, and reporting mechanisms.
- Expand facilities to support large-scale luxury shipbuilding.
- Recruit additional designers, artisans, and technical specialists.

The new Giga Yacht operating unit managed the simultaneous construction of multiple yachts, increasing the complexity of resource allocation, overlapping schedules, and parallel workstreams for design, construction, and testing.

To address these challenges, the organization used modular design approaches to leverage repeatable processes while accommodating client-specific requirements. Project dashboards, resource-leveling strategies, and regular multiproject review meetings were used to maintain visibility across projects.

Governance played a critical role in coordinating regulatory bodies, international suppliers and contractors, certification authorities, and client representatives. Clear decision-making hierarchies, integration boards, and technical review committees supported cross-functional decisions. Layered governance structures—including steering committees, technical boards, and PMO oversight—were used to maintain alignment and accountability.

10.4.3 Analysis and Insights

This section analyzes how the Giga Yacht case study illustrates several key concepts introduced earlier in this practice guide:

- Systems Thinking and Complexity Theory (Section 3)
- Development Approaches for Complexity (Section 4)
- Competencies for Navigating Complexity (Section 5)
- Communication and Stakeholder Engagement (Section 6)
- Decision-Making in Complex Environments (Section 7)
- Leadership Strategies for Complexity (Section 8)

10.4.3.1 Systems Thinking

From the outset, the Giga Yacht project used a systems thinking approach, treating it as an integrated maritime system. Project components, including luxury features, advanced technologies, and stringent safety requirements, interacted continuously, creating multiple layers of complexity.

By explicitly modeling the interdependencies among components, the project team anticipated how changes in one subsystem might affect others. This systems-level perspective helped prevent design conflicts and technical incompatibilities, while also revealing leverage points for optimizing performance and reducing rework.

10.4.3.2 Development Approaches for Complexity

The Giga Yacht project required development approaches capable of accommodating evolving customer expectations and rapidly advancing maritime technologies. A tailored management approach that combined traditional engineering rigor with iterative prototyping was employed and proved effective. This approach enabled the design team to refine features such as smart navigation systems, custom interiors, and sustainability enhancements through continuous stakeholder feedback.

Adopting a modular construction approach further reduced schedule risk and allowed late-stage design changes to be incorporated without disrupting the overall build process. Close coordination among shipyards, subcontractors, and design studios enhanced alignment across disciplines. Together, these adaptive development approaches increased the project's resilience in the face of high uncertainty and demanding technical requirements.

10.4.3.3 Competencies

Deep expertise in engineering, naval architecture, marine systems, structural design, and luxury interiors formed the technical foundation of the project. In addition, the team employed competencies associated with managing complex, interdisciplinary efforts, including:

- Systems thinking, to modularize and integrate diverse subsystems into a cohesive luxury yacht.
- Analytical thinking, to identify, assess, and resolve unexpected risks and issues as they emerged.
- Cultural competence, to collaborate effectively within a multinational workforce and align the working styles of engineers, artisans, and designers.
- Environmental intelligence, to track advances in materials and maritime practices and anticipate regulatory and certification requirements across multiple jurisdictions.
- Technical literacy, to integrate advanced digital systems and emerging technologies, including AI.

The strategic deployment of complexity-management competencies was critical to the project's success.

10.4.3.4 Decision-Making

Decision-making in the Giga Yacht project required careful balancing of innovation, safety, cost, and the client's highly personalized vision. Pivotal decisions that involved complex trade-offs, such as those involving material selection, energy systems, and spatial configurations, were supported by data-driven analytical models and scenario analysis.

The project also relied on iterative and adaptive decision-making models that allowed choices to be refined as design and construction progressed. This flexibility reduced the risks associated with early commitments, enabling teams to respond effectively to emerging constraints and uncertainties.

10.4.3.5 *Leadership Strategies*

Leading the Giga Yacht project required guiding cross-functional teams through a challenging environment defined by high expectations and extensive customization requests.

To navigate this challenging leadership environment, project leaders articulated a clear vision that balanced maritime engineering excellence with luxury innovation. They fostered a culture of collaboration and shared accountability among designers, engineers, and suppliers.

By setting clear standards while simultaneously encouraging experimentation and embracing uncertainty, leaders facilitated creative responses to complex technical challenges. Clear prioritization and strategic resource allocation helped maintain focus despite the project's scale and complexity.

10.4.4 Project Outcome

The Giga Yacht project successfully delivered a high-quality yacht that satisfied the customer. In addition, the project produced several broader organizational and industry-level outcomes:

- The organization established a new business unit and expanded its infrastructure and workforce, increasing capacity for future Giga Yacht projects.
- Italy reinforced its global position in luxury yacht manufacturing.
- Advanced technologies, including hybrid propulsion and high-efficiency systems, were successfully implemented.
- New jobs were created, and existing teams expanded their technical skills.
- A wide international supplier network was assembled and effectively utilized.

10.4.5 Lessons Learned

The Giga Yacht project offers a useful set of lessons learned for managing complexity in innovative and ambitious projects. These insights include the following:

- **Align client expectations early.** Structured requirements management may stabilize scope and limit disruptive late-stage changes.
- **Integrate multidisciplinary teams early.** Synchronizing teams, such as architects, engineers, and subcontractors, can support the effective integration of advanced technologies.
- **Apply rigorous systems and interface management.** Proactively managing competing spatial, technical, and regulatory constraints can prevent costly challenges.
- **Maintain continuous, transparent communication.** Facilitating connections with stakeholders helps alignment of risks and trade-offs.
- **Formalize change and risk management.** Considering possible cascading effects from changes can help anticipate challenges.
- **Help ensure leadership continuity.** Leadership collaboration across design and testing may help preserve strategic intent and support decision coherence.
- **Standardize governance and decision frameworks.** Clear governance supports collaboration across multicultural, cross-functional teams.

- **Test early and iteratively.** Early trials help ensure safety, compliance, and performance without constraining luxury design intent.
- **Balance flexibility with precision.** Clear standards balanced with open communication and flexibility enable innovation while maintaining the discipline required for safety, quality, and schedule control.

10.4.6 Giga Yacht Project Summary

Successfully delivering the Giga Yacht required disciplined systems engineering, strong collaboration, and adaptive stakeholder engagement. Treating the vessel as an interconnected set of subsystems reduced technical risk. Parallel development, prototyping, and iterative testing further mitigated the challenges of introducing cutting-edge technologies.

Equally important to project success was a collaborative culture supported by clear decision-making frameworks. These frameworks help teams navigate luxury-versus-logic trade-offs by balancing safety, sustainability, aesthetics, schedule, and budget. Integrated planning and flexible development approaches ultimately enable both technological innovation and the successful delivery of a one-of-a-kind vessel.

Integrating advanced systems and materials required extensive prototyping and testing to help ensure safety, reliability, and performance under demanding maritime conditions. By fusing engineering excellence, sustainability, and elite lifestyle design, the project ultimately delivered an innovative vessel defined by exceptional craftsmanship.

10.5 Summary

This section examined the practical application of complexity management by:

- Applying key complexity concepts—including systems thinking, development approaches, competencies, leadership strategies, and decision-making frameworks—to real-world project cases.
- Analyzing three case studies from distinct industries to illustrate how different forms of complexity manifest in practice.
- Comparing how alternative management approaches influenced project trajectories and outcomes.

Through critical examination of the James Webb Space Telescope (JWST), Berlin Brandenburg Airport (BER), and Giga Yacht project, this section demonstrates how complexity management principles translate from theory into practice across diverse domains.

Part 5

Organizational Enablers for Project Complexity

Part 5 focuses on how organizations can create environments and develop assets to transform the perspective of complexity as a risk to viewing it as a catalyst for opportunity. This section considers the governance mechanisms and organizational structure needed for organizations to sense, adapt, and respond to internal and external dynamics. Information on content and how to build a complexity playbook is presented to provide guardrails and aid in navigating complex projects. There are three sections in Part 5:

- **Section 11 Enterprise Agility in Navigating Complexity.** Presents enterprise agility as an integrated capability. Describes how leadership, structure, and culture shape the enterprise agility needed to navigate complex conditions.
- **Section 12 Organizational Learning and Adaptation.** Synthesizes strategies, cultural elements, and metrics that can forward organizations' agility and resilience so that change becomes not only a source of value but a potential competitive advantage.
- **Section 13 Complexity Playbooks.** Outlines a structured approach to developing a dynamic complexity playbook to aid decision-making and delivery. Describes typical playbook components, including visual tools and adaptable techniques that are tailored for complex project environments.

These sections extend content in previous sections that focused on individuals and teams, elevating the discussion to a strategic and enterprise-wide perspective.

Section 11

Enterprise Agility in Navigating Complexity

11.1 Introduction

Large-scale initiatives often reveal the constraints of legacy systems. As organizations attempt to deliver complex programs, they frequently encounter structural bottlenecks, outdated planning models, and governance frameworks that cannot keep pace with reality. These pressures serve as catalysts for agility, prompting leaders to reimagine how funding, accountability, and value realization are managed across the enterprise.

This section discusses agility implemented at the enterprise level, positioning enterprise agility as a fully integrated organizational capability. The following subsections are included:

- Overview of Enterprise Agility
- Supporting Complex Projects With Enterprise Agility
- Enablers of Enterprise Agility
- Frameworks for Enterprise Agility
- Support Offices Within Agile Enterprises

Agility is a defining characteristic of organizations that thrive in complexity. The enterprise agility approaches and frameworks introduced in this section provide support for organizations that seek to complete complex projects.

11.2 Overview of Enterprise Agility

Enterprise agility refers to an organization's capacity to rapidly sense, respond, and adapt to change by dynamically aligning strategy, structure, processes, people, and technology to deliver sustained value in environments with complexity and uncertainty.

Unlike team-level agility, which focuses on delivery practices, enterprise agility is embedded in how the organization thinks, governs, and operates. Enterprise agility is a system-level discipline that supports coordination, resilience, and responsiveness across interconnected teams and strategic functions.

This section describes considerations for modern organizations seeking to implement enterprise agility.

11.2.1 Characteristics of Agile Enterprises

Enterprise agility focuses on developing organizational resilience. An agile enterprise continuously senses change, interprets implications, and adjusts strategies in real time. Enterprises that demonstrate agility have the following characteristics:

- **Adaptation over speed.** Governance, leadership, funding, and culture prioritize delivering sustained value in changing circumstances over compressed timelines, accelerated workflows, and faster delivery.
- **Systemic reconfiguration.** Organizations are able to reprioritize, reallocate resources, and shift direction without losing cohesion or transparency.
- **Enabling structures.** Lightweight governance approaches, clear decision rights, and feedback loops support rapid yet responsible responses.
- **Mindset and resilience.** Teams have a collective focus on navigating complexity with purpose and focus on overcoming setbacks to achieve shared goals.

11.2.2 Systemic Enterprise Agility

Enterprise agility benefits a systemic approach that spans strategy, governance, culture, leadership, and operational infrastructure. When only delivery teams employ agile or adaptive practices, organizations may become misaligned.

Teams succeed in complex environments when they are supported by coordinated adaptation across leadership, governance, and support functions. This effort requires the following:

- **Vertical and horizontal alignment.** Organizations have shared intent, synchronized cadences, and common metrics across leadership, governance, and delivery teams.
- **Structural enablers.** Decentralized decision-making, modular team configurations, and value stream orientation help reduce friction and increase adaptability.

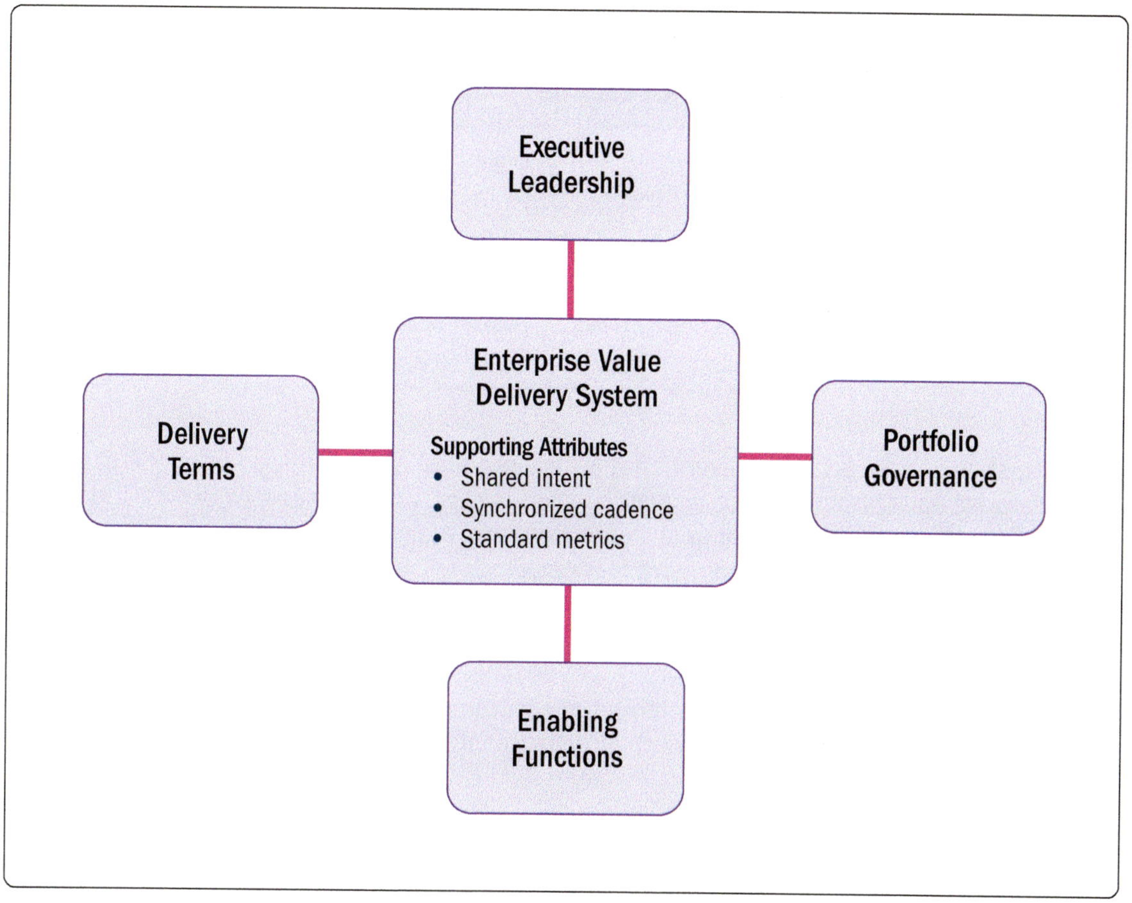

Figure 11-1. Systemic Enterprise Agility

- **Cultural enablers.** Organizations help ensure transparency, collaboration, psychological safety, experimentation, and continuous learning across all business units.
- **Evolving support functions.** Support functions may include enabling departments such as human resources, finance, legal, information technology, procurement, and compliance. Through policy design, funding mechanisms, and operational integration, these functions help prevent bottlenecks, remove systemic constraints, and enable agility to scale responsibly across the organization.

Systemic agility helps ensure all functions operate as an integrated network, reducing fragmentation and enabling coordinated change.

Figure 11-1 shows how leadership, portfolio governance, delivery teams, and enabling functions share a common foundation.

11.2.3 Enterprise Agility Versus Agile Project Delivery

Enterprise agility and agile project delivery are related, but they serve distinct purposes. Table 11-1 compares features of agile project delivery with enterprise agility.

Table 11-1. Agile Project Delivery Versus Enterprise Agility

Feature	Agile Project Delivery	Enterprise Agility
Focus	Team and project execution	Organization-wide systems and strategy
Purpose	Iterative and incremental value delivery	Aligning strategy, resources, governance, and culture for enterprise-wide responsiveness
Complexity addressed	Project-level delivery via short cycles and feedback	Stakeholder alignment, resistance to change, and competing values

As Figure 11-2 shows, agile project delivery enables adaptability within defined or evolving scope, whereas enterprise agility helps ensure project outcomes align with strategic priorities and deliver lasting value. Together, they form a complementary system. Agile delivery drives execution through iterative approaches, team collaboration, and feedback loops. This includes practices such as product backlog prioritization, continuous learning, and customer engagement critical to navigating change and managing complexity at the team level. Enterprise agility provides direction, cohesion, and sustainability by aligning strategic planning, governance, leadership, culture, and operational infrastructure. Together, they form a complementary system: agile delivery drives execution, whereas enterprise agility provides direction, cohesion, and sustainability.

11.2.4 Strategic Imperatives and Dimensions for Enterprise Agility

To implement enterprise agility, organizations should adopt strategies that facilitate repeated adaptation and innovation. These strategic imperatives help translate intentions into viable actions, even amid ambiguity and interdependence.

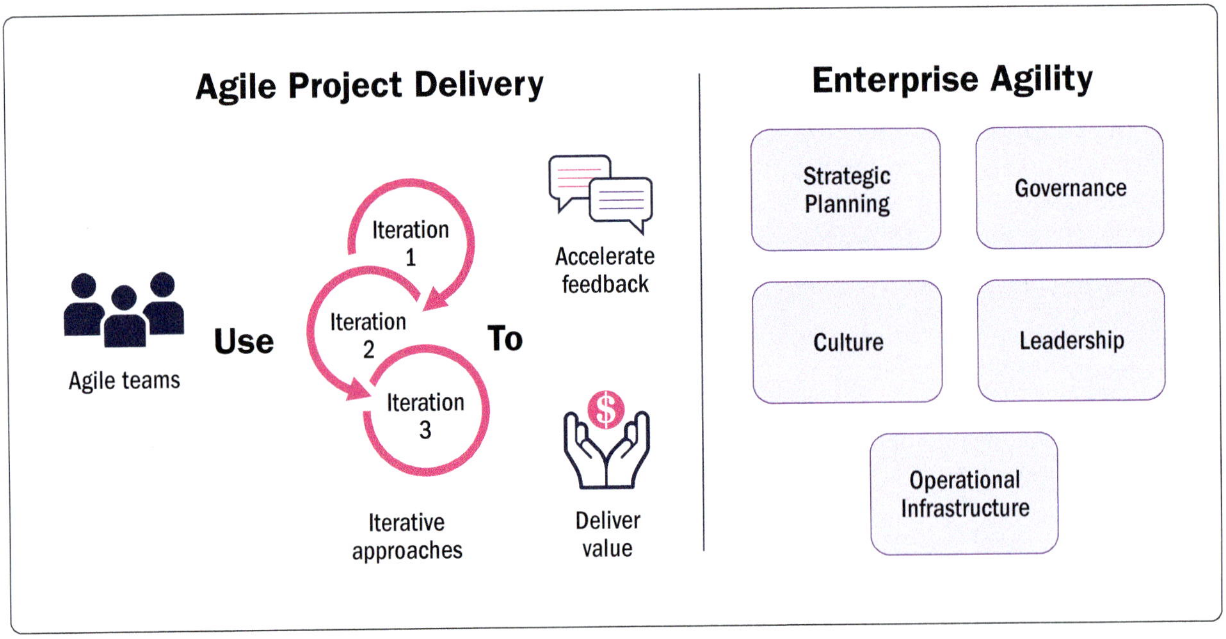

Figure 11-2. Comparing Agile Project Delivery With Enterprise Agility

To successfully move through enterprise-wide agility when faced with a complex environment, it is crucial always to ponder the following three essential questions:

- Are we doing the right thing? This type of question forces the organization to verify strategic alignment and help ensure efforts add value over the long term rather than simply checking activity in the short term.
- How fast versus how stable? In such a case, it is necessary to balance speed and resilience equally. It means that there should be a balance between speed and the ability to maintain structure and prevent chaos.
- Who defines value? This question relates to the significance of stakeholder views and customer-focused strategies. This question explains whose views contribute to the achievement criteria and how value-creation is understood.

Collectively, these are the questions that form the compass for making decisions about agility in the enterprise and help ensure agility is not simply a matter of speed but also sustainable speed, in line with definitions of value that are themselves shifting.

Table 11-2 summarizes the strategic imperatives necessary to implement enterprise ability, listing their description and the specific contributions they make to managing complexity.

Organizations should also take note of the following strategic dimensions:

- **Resource reallocation.** The ability to quickly reallocate resources for high-value projects helps ensure maximum impact and strategic alignment.
- **Innovation and experimentation.** An environment of embracing new ideas and experimental approaches leads to innovation, helping organizations uncover new solutions for complex problems.

Table 11-2. Strategic Imperatives

Imperative	Description	Purpose in Complex Environments
Strategic alignment	Continuously aligning strategy, portfolios, and execution	Helps ensure the organization adapts direction as conditions change and allocates resources and prioritizes investments to maximize customer and enterprise value across portfolios
Capability development	Building organizational learning, competencies, and adaptability	Enables sustained response to uncertainty and disruption
Collaboration and networking	Leveraging internal and external networks for value creation	Addresses complexity that exceeds individual team or unit capacity
Customer-centric approach	Defining value through customer outcomes and feedback	Helps ensure relevance and benefits realization in evolving markets
Adaptive governance	Establishing decision guardrails and escalation paths	Enables fast decisions without loss of control

- **Leadership and vision.** Agile leadership approaches help promote a compelling vision, motivate change, and exemplify agile behavior, which fosters flexibility and learning across the organization.
- **Technology utilization.** Using digital technologies and platforms facilitates collaboration, increases the speed of decision-making, and offers immediate inputs for managing complexity.
- **Integrated risk management.** Preventive identification and management of risks can enable organizations to anticipate disruptions and respond with confidence.
- **Crisis management.** When risks become issues and escalate, enterprise agility is measured by its ability to shift from risk management to crisis management, limiting subsequent losses.

Table 11-3 associates these strategic dimensions with each strategic imperative, highlighting how they interact to support planning and decision-making. Strategic dimensions indicate where complexity manifests, whereas strategic imperatives describe how project practitioners respond to these challenges.

Strategically implemented enterprise agility empowers organizations to stay focused, responsive, and resilient in the face of complexity.

11.2.5 Distributed Agility

To fully implement enterprise agility, agile approaches and mindsets should be adopted by all functions of an organization, not just delivery teams. Distributed agility involves applying agile approaches to enterprise functions and teams that have a broadly distributed impact such as human resources, compliance, finance, and governance.

Applying agile principles across these areas enhances organizational responsiveness, coherence, and value delivery. Table 11-4 lists the agile approaches that support each of these functions, as well as the way these functions contribute to complexity management.

The functions listed are illustrative examples. Additional areas, such as marketing, legal, and operations, may also adopt agile practices to enhance enterprise responsiveness.

Distributed agility encompasses not only structural changes but also cultural and behavioral changes. When support functions adopt an agile mindset, they become drivers of enterprise responsiveness.

11.2.6 Value Governance

Value governance refers to the mindset, processes, and mechanisms that help ensure organizational initiatives continuously deliver measurable business value that is aligned with strategic objectives and stakeholder needs.

Traditional governance emphasizes on-time, on-budget project delivery; risk and compliance control; and annual budgeting cycles. While these factors are important, they do not guarantee that organizations are delivering what customers need, responding to change, or maximizing return on investment.

Agile organizations integrate customer-centric value creation directly into how they make strategic decisions, govern initiatives, allocate resources, and measure success. This approach supports a dynamic, feedback-driven, and outcome-oriented organization.

Table 11-3. Strategic Imperatives and Strategic Dimensions

Strategic Dimension	Strategic Imperative				
	Strategic Alignment	Capability Development	Collaboration and Networking	Adaptive Governance	Customer-Centric Approach
Resource reallocation	Enables fluid priorities and resource realignment	Maximizes resource flexibility and mobilization of skills	Harmonizes resource sharing across networks and teams	Enables rapid adaptation while maintaining operational stability	Reallocates resources for high-impact customers
Innovation and experimentation	Drives strategic innovation aligned with evolving goals	Fosters learning and adaptive skill development	Encourages cocreation and shared experimentation	Balances exploration with disciplined delivery	Drives innovation based on customer feedback
Leadership and vision	Provides clarity and cohesion across strategic initiatives	Develops leadership competencies for agility	Promotes trust and shared vision across teams	Guides adaptive leadership across changing contexts	Aligns leadership focus with customer value
Technology utilization	Offers end-to-end visibility for strategic choices	Fosters digital competencies and operational excellence	Offers integrated systems and common platforms	Helps ensure flexible and scalable technology infrastructures	Utilizes technology for customer experience improvements
Risk management	Helps ensure strategic resilience through proactive risk planning	Strengthens risk-aware capabilities and practices	Supports collective risk identification, analysis and response	Balances proactive risk responses with continuity	Manages customer-related risks and expectations
Crisis management	Allows the enterprise to effectively respond to urgent issues	Elevates risk management capabilities and skills	Supports collective efforts to achieve the best result	Helps ensure that potential losses are mitigated as much as possible	Protects the relationships with customers

The mindset of this approach to value governance includes the following:

- **Customer-centricity.** Decisions at all levels are guided by bringing value to customers and users.
- **Outcome over output.** Results are measured by business and customer impact, not just deliverables.

Table 11-4. Agile Approaches for Managing Organizational and Project Complexity

Function	Agile Approaches	Contribution to Complexity Management
People management/ human resources	Cross-functional teams, servant leadership, continuous skills development, adaptive performance reviews	Reduces people-related uncertainty and improves responsiveness to changing project demands
Innovation management	Design thinking, Lean startup, timeboxed innovation iterations, rapid prototyping, hypothesis-driven experiments	Accelerates learning and reduces uncertainty through iterative experimentation; fosters adaptability and resilience by validating ideas early and minimizing risk of large-scale failure
Information technology/ technology enablement	Modular architecture, continuous integration, continuous delivery, DevOps, automated testing	Manages technical complexity and reduces integration risk
Procurement	Agile contracts, incremental delivery, vendor collaboration	Reduces supplier and contractual complexity
Governance, risk & compliance (GRC)	Lean governance, clear decision thresholds, fast escalation paths, empowered product ownership; risk-based monitoring, continuous risk review; adaptive compliance, real-time reporting	Provides guardrails for adaptive execution, helps ensure regulatory alignment, and enables proactive response to uncertainty and emergent risks
Finance	Iterative budgeting and forecasting, value-driven decisions, and cost transparency	Aligns financial agility with strategic priorities and dynamic conditions

- **Iterative strategy execution.** Delivering value in increments and adjusting through feedback and learning.
- **Flow-based governance.** Avoiding rigid gates or approvals supports a smooth delivery of value.
- **Cross-functional collaboration.** Soliciting input from a range of functional teams helps promote collaboration.
- **Lean budgeting and funding.** Funding is flexible and based on value stream performance rather than fixed projects.

By implementing this mindset, agile organizations can improve alignment between strategy and execution, increase customer satisfaction, and use resources more efficiently.

11.3 Supporting Complex Projects With Enterprise Agility

Enterprise agility offers strong support to teams navigating complex project environments. This support introduces adaptive mechanisms such as rolling wave planning, feedback-informed

Table 11-5. Enterprise Agility Enablers for Organizational Complexity

Enabler	Description	Complexity Management Practice
Holistic organizational alignment	Helps ensure all business functions are agile and strategically coherent, enabling coordinated decision-making and responsiveness across departments	Avoids functional silos and supports strategic coherence in dynamic, interdependent environments, reducing structural and strategic complexity through coherent priorities and coordinated decision-making
Lean governance and decision clarity	Establishes clear decision rights, escalation paths, and lightweight controls	Reduces decision latency and ambiguity in complex, fast-moving environments
Contextual ways of working	Supports situation-oriented agility by allowing teams to select their approach based on project needs, complexity, and organizational context	Enables teams to tailor agile approaches in alignment with business principles and strategic priorities, fostering adaptability without mandating a specific framework
Continuous learning and improvement	Uses feedback loops, metrics, and experimentation to refine processes and outcomes	Improves adaptability and resilience
Customer-centric focus	Aligns delivery with evolving customer needs and expectations, prioritizing value creation	Maintains relevance and value in volatile contexts by adapting to changing customer expectations
Collaborative culture	Builds trust, transparency, and adaptive capacity through teamwork and open communication, supporting cross-functional collaboration and shared ownership	Enhances problem-solving and innovation through diverse perspectives and cocreation in complex settings

governance, and responsive resource allocation. These mechanisms allow organizations to remain strategically anchored while adjusting to emerging information, changing constraints, and evolving stakeholder needs.

This section describes how enterprise agility features facilitate success within complex projects.

11.3.1 Organizational Support for Complexity

Table 11-5 describes the foundational elements of enterprise agility, then explains how these elements help organizations support complexity management in programs and projects.

11.3.2 Enterprise Agility in Practice

The following example illustrates how enterprise agility supports the implementation of complex projects.

Example scenario

A multinational organization serving diverse markets faced mounting complexity driven by decentralized infrastructures, organizational silos, evolving customer and portfolio needs, and fluctuating regulatory environments.

Recognizing that its existing models were no longer effective, the organization launched an enterprise-wide transformation guided by the strategic imperatives and enablers outlined in this section. By activating these imperatives through intentional, coordinated action, the organization reframed complexity as a driver of strategic performance rather than a constraint.

11.3.2.1 *Scenario Analysis: Strategic Imperative Implementation*

Through its imitative transformation, the multinational organization operationalized enterprise agility to address regulatory volatility, legacy systems, and dynamic stakeholder needs. Each imperative targeted a specific challenge, collectively fostering a more adaptive and resilient enterprise.

Table 11-6 analyzes how the multinational organization used strategic imperatives to address pain points, including the associated actions and results for each imperative.

11.3.2.2 *Scenario Analysis: Addressing Complexity Types*

The multinational organization's transformation initiative can also be analyzed in relation to the types of project complexity introduced in Section 2:

- **Structural and organizational complexity.** Siloed delivery and governance misalignment were mitigated through greater integration and alignment across business units.
- **Dynamic complexity.** The multinational organization adopted adaptive prioritization and real-time decision-making in response to evolving stakeholder needs.
- **Human and sociopolitical complexity.** Enabling cross-functional collaboration and strengthening psychological safety helped unite diverse stakeholder interests.
- **Technological complexity.** The organization leveraged analytics, AI technology, and cloud-based systems to enhance responsiveness and generate insights.
- **Environmental complexity.** By improving strategic responsiveness, the organization adapted to regulatory unpredictability and shifting external conditions.

The multinational organization's transformation demonstrates that when enterprise agility is embedded across leadership, teams, and systems it becomes a capability that transforms uncertainty into opportunity.

11.3.3 Adaptive Approaches for Complexity in Non-Agile Organizations

Enterprise agility provides strong support for project practitioners managing complexity. However, implementing agility at the organizational level takes time and institutional will.

Table 11-6. Strategic Imperatives, Key Pain Points, and Realized Benefits

Strategic Imperative	Pain Point Addressed	Actions Taken	Results Achieved
Strategic alignment	Fragmented execution and lack of coherence across portfolios	Clarified enterprise priorities and aligned operational capabilities	Greater strategic coherence across portfolios, resulting in measurable business growth (+20% revenue)
Collaboration and networking	Functional silos and unclear cross-team accountability	Empowered cross-functional teams and enabled real-time coordination via platforms	Higher team engagement and improved coordination +15% from the Voice of Workforce survey
Capability development	Limited adaptive capacity and outdated skill sets	Provided targeted training and coaching to teams	Accelerated adoption of emerging technologies and agile work models by 38%, as measured across business units within 12 months
Customer-centric approach	Misalignment with customer expectations and declining satisfaction	Embedded feedback loops into service design and delivery	Customer satisfaction +18%, churn −12%
Adaptive governance	Slow decisions due to rigid controls and unclear escalation	Redesigned governance for rapid decision-making while maintaining compliance	Cross-sell opportunities +22%
Technology enablement	Legacy platforms limiting insight and responsiveness	Implemented cloud-based systems and AI-powered analytics	Enhanced responsiveness and insight generation, with a 28% improvement in decision-making speed, a 35% acceleration in issuing new business quotations, and a 42% increase in idea generation for patentable innovations

Project practitioners who face complexity while working within traditional organizations can apply adaptive principles by using the following approaches:

- **Local agility.** Apply iterative planning, ongoing feedback loops, and collaboration with stakeholders inside project boundaries.
- **Influence without authority.** Advocate for agile-compatible behaviors (e.g., transparency, collaboration) even when governance is rigid.
- **Risk-based adaptation.** Use complexity-informed risk management to adjust plans and expectations dynamically.

- **Microstructures.** Create cross-functional working groups or informal communities of practice to foster agility.
- **Strategic framing.** Translate project outcomes into strategic language to gain executive support.

These approaches allow project practitioners to act as agents of agility, even in environments that are hierarchical, siloed, or resistant to change. By demonstrating the value of adaptive delivery, project practitioners can gradually influence organizational mindsets, paving the way for broader transformation.

11.4 Enablers of Enterprise Agility

Enterprise agility requires specific organizational conditions that support adaptive behavior, strategic alignment, and the continuous delivery of value in complex environments. These conditions are known as enablers.

Enterprise agility enablers are foundational capabilities, spanning leadership, structure, and culture, that allow agility to function at the enterprise level. Without these enablers, agility may remain isolated within teams or fail to scale sustainably.

This section introduces enablers that support the development and maintenance of enterprise agility. The section examines how adaptive leadership behaviors shape decision-making and learning, how structural design supports flow and responsiveness, and how cultural norms influence alignment, trust, and iteration.

11.4.1 Agile Leadership and the Adaptive Mindset

In complex project environments, effective leaders shift to agile leadership approaches, which are detailed in Section 8. Leaders following agile approaches move away from directing execution, instead creating conditions that allow others to respond, adapt, and learn.

At the center of agile leadership is an adaptive mindset, which encompasses the following attributes:

- Recognizing change as constant and ambiguity as natural;
- Guiding teams through uncertainty with learning, experimentation, and responsiveness; and
- Balancing planning with discovery and iteration.

Table 11-7 lists leadership behaviors that support enterprise agility alongside their associated benefits.

Intentional agile leadership, as implemented through these behaviors, equips teams with the abilities to think critically and act confidently in uncertainty.

11.4.2 Structural Enablers

Implementing agility at scale requires structural design that supports responsiveness, coordination, and alignment. Structural enablers reduce friction, accelerate delivery, and keep distributed teams aligned. These structural enablers may include the following:

Table 11-7. Leadership Behaviors and Benefits

Behavior	Benefit
Viewing ambiguity as a condition to navigate, not eliminate	Builds team and organizational resilience and adaptability
Distinguishing technical problems from adaptive challenges	Prevents misdiagnosis and ineffective solutions
Communicating clearly what is known, unknown, and evolving	Creates trust and informed decision-making
Encouraging dissent, questions, and experimentation	Fosters innovation and surfaces risks early
Modeling curiosity, humility, and learning	Shapes culture and normalizes adaptive behaviors

- **Cross-functional teams.** Cross-functional teams with clearly defined roles and objectives are able to integrate skills, share accountability, and deliver value, reducing handoffs and increasing speed.
- **Agile operating models.** Effective operating models define how value flows, how authority is distributed, and how information is shared. These models balance autonomy with enterprise-level alignment, including value stream orientation, iterative planning, and flexible resource allocation.
- **Scalability.** Structures should be designed to scale by incorporating decentralized governance, shared service integration, and synchronized planning cadences.
- **Information flow.** Open visibility platforms, transparent performance indicators, and collaborative tooling create a productive flow of information that supports sensemaking and helps align and inform decisions.

Table 11-8 describes the behaviors and benefits associated with structural enablers.

Table 11-8. Structural Behaviors and Benefits

Behavior	Benefit
Empowering cross-functional teams to deliver end-to-end value	Reduces delays and dependency on handoffs
Aligning work around value streams, not silos	Improves flow, responsiveness, and relevance
Granting decision authority close to execution	Enables fast, context-driven adaptation
Using modular operating models	Increases flexibility and resilience
Providing transparent collaboration tools and governance	Supports coordination, feedback, and learning

Table 11-9. Cultural Behaviors and Benefits

Behavior	Benefit
Encouraging teams to question assumptions and admit uncertainty	Surfaces risks and accelerates learning
Reinforcing purpose by using communication, prioritization, and rewards	Aligns teams even in shifting conditions
Embedding feedback loops in daily operations	Enables rapid course correction
Treating failure as a source of learning	Builds resilience and maturity
Responding to shifting priorities with confidence and clarity	Maintains performance under ambiguity

11.4.3 Cultural Enablers

Even if leadership and structure support enterprise agility, cultural factors ultimately determine whether agility scales or stalls. Essential cultural enablers of enterprise agility include the following:

- **Psychological safety.** Psychologically safe environments encourage open dialogue, risk-taking, and candid feedback. For example, teams that can surface delivery risks or challenge assumptions without fear of reprisal are more likely to identify emerging issues and adapt early.
- **Shared purpose.** Aligned goals and values provide strategic cohesion and motivation, helping teams prioritize and innovate even when plans shift. For instance, when all teams understand and believe in the customer impact they are working toward, they are more resilient in the face of rework, shifting backlogs, or stakeholder tension.
- **Feedback loops.** Feedback loops support continuous learning through metrics, retrospectives, customer input, and stakeholder feedback. Examples include sprint reviews that incorporate real user feedback, or portfolio-level cadence reviews that reshape funding and prioritization in response to outcome metrics.

Cultural enablers form the "invisible infrastructure" that sustains agility. Table 11-9 summarizes the behaviors and benefits associated with cultural enablers.

11.5 Frameworks for Enterprise Agility

Organizations undergoing agile transformation initiatives should apply agile approaches across multiple teams, departments, and even the entire enterprise. Frameworks and organizational mechanisms provide essential guidance and structure for these complex processes.

This section introduces frameworks and models that offer scalable structures to coordinate work across multiple teams, programs, and portfolios. The frameworks presented vary in design and intent, but all incorporate adaptive governance structures that promote strategic alignment, transparency, and decentralized decision-making.

Organizations seeking to implement enterprise agility may select appropriate frameworks to help maintain focus on value delivery, respond to shifting priorities, and strengthen the connection between strategic direction and operational execution.

11.5.1 Scaled Agile Framework (SAFe®)

Scaled Agile Framework (SAFe®) is a comprehensive framework that enables organizations to scale agile approaches across teams, programs, large solutions, and the entire enterprise. SAFe® consists of four hierarchical levels, discussed in Sections 11.5.1.1 through 11.5.1.4.

11.5.1.1 Team Level

The team level of SAFe® refers to agile approaches implemented within individual teams. Teams operate using adaptive approaches such as Scrum, Kanban, or ScrumXP. Key roles include the following:

- **Scrum master.** Implements agile approaches.
- **Product owner.** Owns and prioritizes the product backlog.
- **Team members.** Deliver value through completing work tasks.

Teams deliver work in short iteration cycles. Their work is coordinated with other teams to contribute to program objectives.

11.5.1.2 Program Level

The program level coordinates multiple agile teams to deliver integrated value. Agile teams are grouped into an agile release train, typically consisting of five to 12 teams, and planning and delivery occur within program increments, typically 8 to 12 weeks. Key roles include the following:

- **Release train engineer.** Facilitates agile release train execution.
- **Product management.** Owns and prioritizes the program backlog.
- **Systems architect/engineer.** Defines technical direction and the architectural runway.

The major event at this level is program increment planning, where all teams align their plans for the upcoming increment.

11.5.1.3 Large Solution Level

The large solution level coordinates multiple agile release trains and suppliers to deliver large-scale, complex solutions. Industries with large systems, such as defense, banking, and aerospace, are likely to coordinate multiple agile release trains within a solution train. Key roles include the following:

- **Solution train engineer.** Facilitates and coaches the solution train.
- **Solution management.** Defines and prioritizes capabilities, helping ensure the overall solution meets customer and business needs.
- **Solution architect/engineer.** Defines and communicates the technical and architectural vision for the large solution, with a focus on systems integration, compliance, and solution intent.

11.5.1.4 Portfolio Level

The portfolio level aligns agile execution with enterprise strategy, investment, and governance. This alignment is achieved through lean portfolio management approaches such as lean budgeting and value stream funding. Key roles include the following:

- **Lean portfolio manager.** Governs investment and strategy.
- **Epic owners.** Oversee the progress of *epics*, or large bodies of work.
- **Enterprise architects.** Help ensure technology alignment with business goals.

Success at the portfolio level is achieved by providing lightweight oversight without controlling team decisions, encouraging decentralized decision-making within an aligned structure.

11.5.2 Large-Scale Scrum (LeSS)

Large-Scale Scrum (LeSS) is an adaptive framework focused on achieving alignment while minimizing formal governance structures. Governance is embedded in the Scrum principles of transparency, inspection, and adaptation, and one product owner manages the product backlog for multiple teams.

This framework avoids adding extra layers of control or roles. Self-managing teams with high ownership and transparency are coordinated by using lightweight mechanisms such as joint sprint planning.

Key roles for LeSS overlap with the regular Scrum framework, including product owner, scrum master, and development team. However, unlike Scrum, which is designed for a single team, LeSS is intended for multiple teams working collaboratively on one product. Scaling Scrum across teams requires adaptation. However, LeSS aims to minimize those adaptations by focusing on simplicity, transparency, and learning.

11.5.3 Spotify Model

The Spotify model is a people-driven, autonomous, and flexible approach to scaling agile across large organizations. Originally developed by the music streaming company Spotify, it addresses challenges in scaling agile while maintaining high levels of team autonomy and innovation.

The Spotify model prioritizes flexibility, communication, and continuous improvement as well as fostering innovation and creativity. Governance is built around shared values, trust, and visibility, which is an approach that works well in fast-paced environments.

Key structures in the Spotify model include the following:

- **Squad.** A small, cross-functional, self-organizing team that is responsible for a specific feature or product area. Squads choose their own agile approaches.
- **Tribe.** A collection of squads that work in related areas. Tribes facilitate coordination among squads, supporting knowledge sharing.
- **Chapter.** A group of individuals from different squads with similar skills. Chapters are supported by line managers, who support development and alignment across the chapter.
- **Guild.** An informal community of interest that encourages learning, knowledge sharing, and standardization across the organization.

11.5.4 Disciplined Agile® (DA®)

Disciplined Agile® (DA®) is a tool kit that helps organizations select ways of working by tailoring and optimizing agile approaches to fit an organization's unique context, goals, and culture. Disciplined Agile® (DA®) encourages teams to make informed trade-offs depending on their situation, using process goal diagrams that help teams understand their options.

Disciplined Agile® (DA®) is not limited to individual teams; it covers the entire enterprise in the following layers:

- **Foundation.** Agile and lean approaches, principles, and roles, implemented from development to operations.
- **Value streams.** Cross-functional coordination across teams and departments.
- **Disciplined Agile Enterprise (DAE).** Aligning strategies, governance, and structures to support agility at scale.

The Discipline Agile® (DA®) tool kit guides organizations to make better process decisions through informed choice rather than prescription, empowering them to continuously learn and evolve.

Figure 11-3 compares Discipline Agile® (DA®) with other approaches.

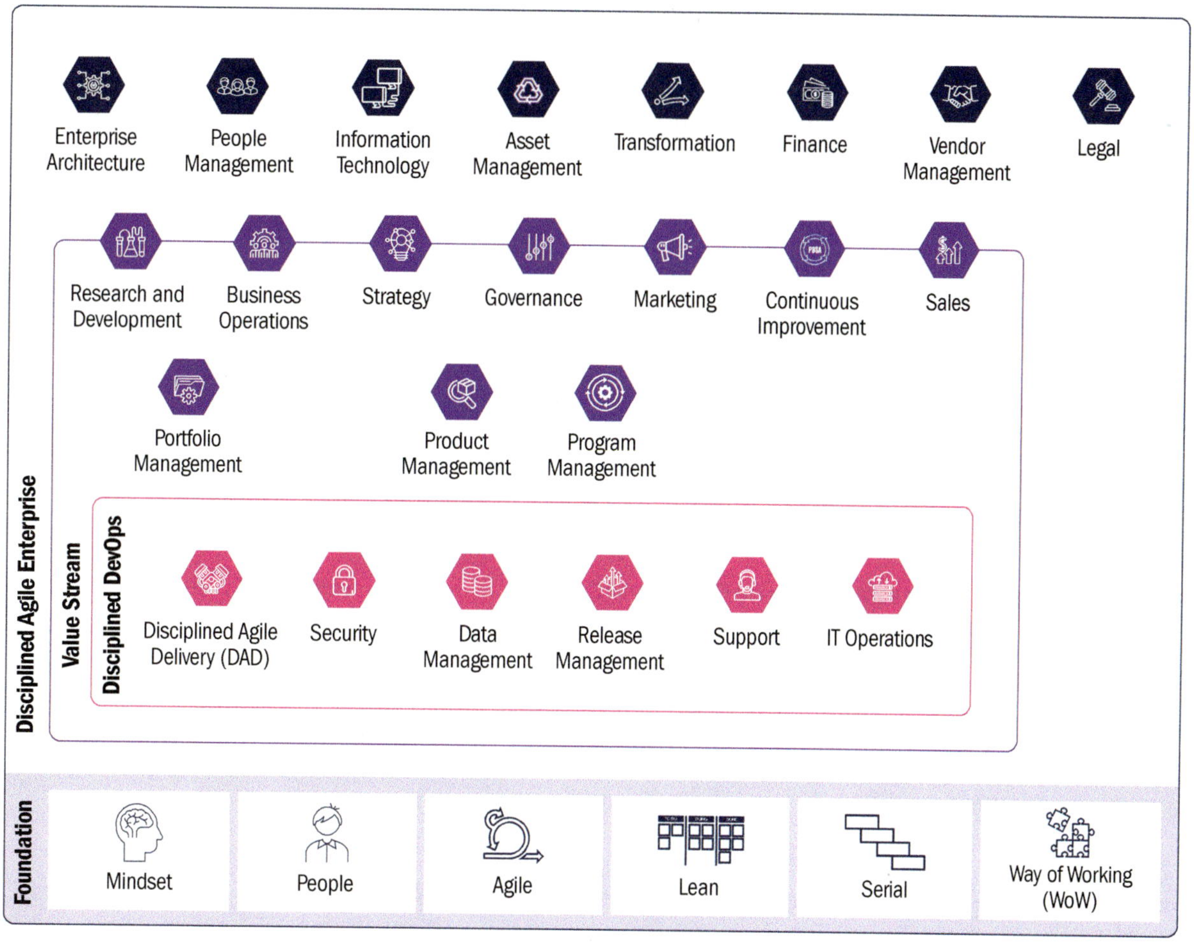

Figure 11-3. Disciplined Agile® (DA®) Compared With Other Approaches

11.5.5 Comparing Frameworks for Enterprise Agility

The effectiveness of the frameworks, tool kits, and approaches discussed in the previous section depends entirely on how they are tailored to an organization's specific environment. Factors such as delivery interdependencies, strategic ambiguity, regulatory complexity, and cultural readiness should inform how and where elements from these frameworks are applied.

Organizations may select from a range of models, frameworks, and practices to determine the best approach for their organizational context. Framework selection can be seen as a context-specific design choice, following a structured approach such as:

- Mapping the dominant sources of complexity;
- Conducting a comparative analysis of multiple frameworks or approaches; and
- Determining which features best align with strategic goals, delivery constraints, and desired feedback loops.

Rather than adopting a single framework or approach in its entirety, many organizations benefit from integrating components across approaches. These models often blend planning cadences, governance layers, backlog structures, or release strategies to help ensure fit-for-purpose agility across portfolios and functions.

Frameworks are evolving systems that will adapt to enterprise learning and ongoing feedback. Teams should regularly evaluate how well their operating model supports flow, visibility, and alignment. As complexity shifts, so should the underlying mechanisms that support agility. By using comparison-driven insights and adapting frameworks and approaches to context, organizations can create scaling architectures that enable strategic coherence without sacrificing flexibility or autonomy.

Table 11-10 compares the features of the four frameworks and tool kits discussed in this section.

11.6 Support Offices Within Agile Enterprises

As organizations scale, they often rely on a combination of strategic support offices to maintain alignment, governance, and value realization across complex portfolios. These offices may include the following:

- **Strategy office.** Defines direction, manages objectives and key results (OKRs), and aligns investment governance and portfolio planning with strategic outcomes.
- **Enterprise project management office (EPMO).** Establishes standards, tools, and oversight for project and program delivery.
- **Transformation management office (TMO).** Leads digital, agile, or enterprise transformations; drives mindset, structure, and process shifts.
- **Value management office (VMO).** Manages value streams, prioritizes portfolios, tracks benefits realization, and supports incremental funding.

Agile organizations have evolved these support offices into critical enablers of agility, driving coordination, adaptive planning, and value stream delivery. In complex project environments, the effectiveness of each office depends on the nature of the complexity being addressed. Table 11-11

Table 11-10. Four Enterprise Agility Frameworks and Tool Kits

Feature	Disciplined Agile® (DA®)	Scaled Agile Framework (SAFe®)	Spotify	Large-Scale Scrum (LeSS)
Customization	Very high	Moderate	High—encourages autonomy	Moderate
Enterprise focus	Strong	Strong	Limited—team and tribe level	Moderate
Prescriptiveness	Low	High	Low—intentionally informal	Moderate
Integration with traditional project management	Yes	Yes	No—not designed for hybrid	Limited
Role definition	Clear but flexible	Defined hierarchical roles	Light roles—informal	Simplified Scrum roles
Governance and compliance	Strong support	Strong—portfolio governance	Weak—minimal governance focus	Weak—minimal governance
Mindset and culture focus	Strong—includes mindset	Moderate—focuses on practices	Strong—emphasizes culture	Moderate—process-focused
Scaling strategy	Tailored per context	Defined layers (team to portfolio)	Tribe-based, informal scaling	One product, multiple teams

Table 11-11. Support Office Functions

Office	Function	Agile Evolution	Best Suited For
Strategy	Provides enterprise-wide visibility, long-term focus, and executive engagement	Expands to support adaptive strategy cycles and continuous prioritization	Strategic complexity, when direction or priorities shift frequently
Enterprise project management office (EPMO)	Supports consistency, accountability, and portfolio tracking	Evolves into an agile or lean PMO emphasizing iterative delivery and value realization	Delivery complexity, when multiple projects need structured coordination
Transformation management office (TMO)	Supports change enablement, communication, and cross-functional alignment	Integrates with VMOs and strategy offices to embed agility into culture and operations	Change complexity, when transformation or reinvention is the primary challenge
Value management office (VMO)	Increases transparency, agility, and customer-centricity	Serves as a lightweight, decentralized governance layer for continuous value delivery	Delivery and system complexity, when rapid reprioritization and flow are critical

summarizes the functions of each of these offices, how they evolve within agile organizations, and which complex environments they support.

Considering the function of these offices in an agile environment, along with how they address complexity, allows organizations to more effectively tailor and integrate these offices.

11.7 Summary

This section examined how enterprise agility enables organizations to navigate complexity by aligning strategy, structure, and execution through adaptive systems and behaviors. The section emphasized that implementing agility at scale requires creating conditions for continuous learning, collaboration, and value delivery across the enterprise.

This section established the impact of enterprise agility and discussed how it can be implemented by:

- Defining enterprise agility as an organization-wide capability that connects strategy, leadership, and delivery;
- Examining how enterprise agility supports complexity management by relating features of enterprise agility to complexity management needs;
- Outlining key enablers, including adaptive leadership as well as structural and cultural enablers;
- Detailing frameworks and tool kits for enterprise agility, including SAFe®, LeSS, the Spotify model, and Disciplined Agile® (DA®);
- Examining the role of strategic support offices in sustaining alignment and value flow; and
- Illustrating enterprise agility in action through a multinational organization's case study, demonstrating how adaptive governance and empowered teams can turn complexity into strategic advantage.

Together, these concepts position enterprise agility as a strategic capability for thriving in complexity. When embedded in culture, leadership, and systems, agility becomes a continuous source of innovation, alignment, and long-term value.

Section 12

Organizational Learning and Adaptation

12.1 Introduction

Successfully navigating complex projects requires teams to be flexible and able to learn from and adapt to environmental changes. Organizations can support project teams facing complexity by explicitly enabling continuous learning and adaptation. This section outlines organizational-level strategies that support learning and adaptation and includes the following subsections:

- Cultivating a Complexity-Ready Culture
- Building Adaptive Capability Across the Organization
- Measuring Complexity and Adaptive Capacity

Together, these approaches allow organizations to use change as an opportunity to create value and competitive advantages.

12.2 Cultivating a Complexity-Ready Culture

Organizations that aim to succeed in complex environments benefit from developing a complexity-ready culture. A complexity-ready culture refers to an environment that supports learning under pressure and enables continuous adjustment as conditions change.

Complexity-ready organizations emphasize responsiveness, adaptability, transparency, shared leadership, and curiosity. Leaders and team members treat failure as a source of information rather than something to conceal or punish. Attention is placed on learning from missteps and incorporating that learning into future decisions.

This section introduces the mindset, structures, and systems that support the development of a complexity-ready culture.

12.2.1 Complexity-Ready Mindset

In many organizations, complexity is framed as a problem to be reduced, controlled, or absorbed through better planning. This framing encourages short-term optimization and reactive behavior, particularly when projects encounter uncertainty or disruption.

A complexity-ready mindset reframes complexity as an environment rather than an obstacle. From this perspective, complexity is unavoidable, and building organizational capacity to learn and adapt to evolving conditions becomes essential.

Organizations focused on being complexity ready may invest in skills, systems, and culture by:

- Building competence in systems thinking, decision-making under uncertainty, emotional intelligence, and sensemaking;
- Establishing governance, funding, and information systems that support learning and revision rather than fixed plans; and
- Reinforcing behaviors that support experimentation, psychological safety, and shared responsibility for outcomes.

When complexity is treated as a source of insight rather than a liability, organizations are better positioned to adapt quickly and sustain performance over time.

12.2.2 Enabling Structures and Systems

While mindset shapes how people interpret complexity, structures and systems determine how effectively they can respond to it. A complexity-ready culture is reinforced by organizational mechanisms that make learning and adaptation possible in practice.

The following structures and systems support a complexity-ready culture:

- **Governance systems.** Adaptive governance supports learning by allowing iterative funding, staged commitments, and controlled experimentation. Decisions can be revisited based on evidence, reducing the cost of early assumptions and supporting course correction.
- **Workflows and planning systems.** Flexible workflows and scenario-based planning allow teams to reallocate resources, adjust priorities, and make decisions without excessive delay. These systems support adaptation when plans no longer match reality.
- **Feedback mechanisms.** Structured feedback loops allow teams closest to the work to surface emerging risks, opportunities, and constraints. When this information flows quickly, strategic decisions are grounded in current conditions.

Together, these structures and systems enable a complexity-ready culture in projects.

12.2.3 The Role of Leadership in Shaping Culture

Leadership plays a central role in building a complexity-ready culture by modeling adaptive behaviors that support an organizational mindset shift.

Leadership strategies that support the development of a complexity-ready culture include:

- **Enabling adaptation.** Empowering distributed teams by setting clear strategic intent and boundaries, then trusting teams to adapt within those constraints.
- **Modeling vulnerability.** Demonstrating humility and curiosity by acknowledging uncertainty and asking for help publicly. This transparency supports psychological safety, which is foundational to team learning and adaptation.
- **Investing in trust.** Supporting distributed leadership and decentralized decision-making, enabling teams to respond to change quickly, and increasing organizational speed and resilience.

By consistently adopting adaptive behaviors, leaders reinforce these behaviors across their organizations.

12.2.4 The Project Management Office as a Strategic Enabler

The project management office (PMO) can evolve to become a strategic enabler and catalyst for continuous adaptation and measurement across the organization. This is a pivotal shift that defines its modern value in complex environments. Figure 12-1 illustrates ways PMOs may evolve to support complexity.

To support a complexity-ready culture, PMOs may evolve in the following ways:

- **Integrating strategy and execution.** Aligning strategic intent with adaptive delivery, allowing priorities to translate quickly into project action.
- **Curating adaptive knowledge.** Supporting learning by collecting and sharing case studies, near failures, and examples of successful adaptation.

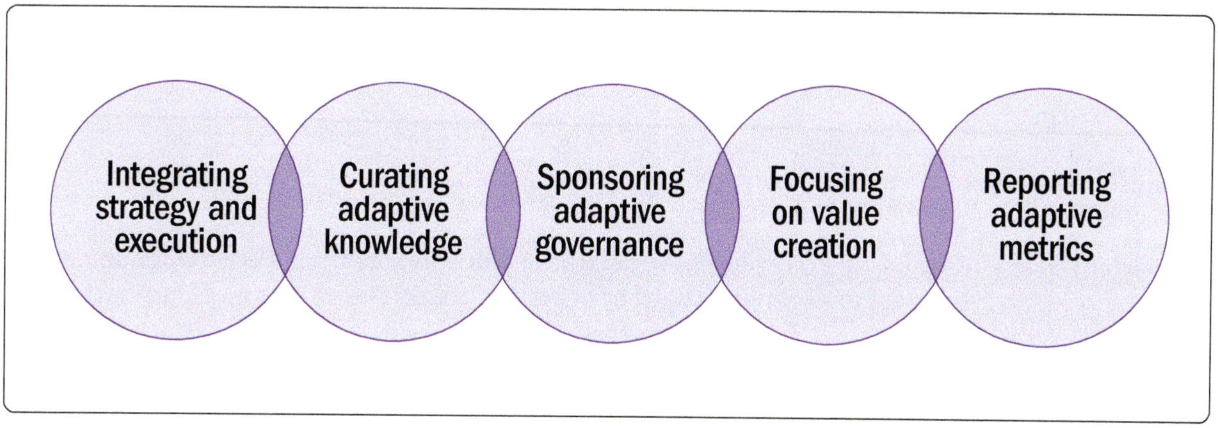

Figure 12-1. PMO Recommendations

- **Sponsoring adaptive governance.** Piloting governance approaches that support iterative funding and learning, using small experiments to demonstrate value and reduce resistance.
- **Focusing on value creation.** Designing services around the needs of internal teams and measurable outcomes, rather than enforcing uniform processes.
- **Reporting adaptive metrics.** Shifting reporting toward measures of learning speed, decision quality, and organizational health, enabling leaders to invest in capability rather than only monitor variance.

Using these approaches, PMOs can collaborate with teams across the organization to support effective navigation of complexity.

12.3 Building Adaptive Capability Across the Organization

Capability refers to the potential or capacity of an individual, team, or organization to perform a task or achieve a strategic outcome. A capability differs from a competency, which refers to demonstrated and measurable performance.

At the organizational level, capability reflects collective potential rather than specific behaviors. Adaptive capability refers to an organization's readiness to employ adaptive approaches. Organizations with adaptive capability can detect changes in the environment, identify opportunities related to those changes, and adapt internal resources, structures, and processes to pursue those opportunities.

Organizations build adaptive capability at three interconnected levels:

- Individuals
- Teams
- Across the organization

This section discusses strategies for developing adaptive capability at all three levels, strengthening the organization's ability to interpret signals, learn from experience, and respond effectively in dynamic project environments.

12.3.1 Individual Adaptive Capability

Individuals can develop adaptive capability by combining adaptive theory, experiential learning, and reflective practice:

- **Adaptive theory.** Learning the theory behind adaptive approaches as they are applied to complex projects provides an intellectual foundation.
- **Experiential learning.** Using strategies such as iterative work and controlled experimentation allows project practitioners to experience both benefits and challenges of adaptive approaches.
- **Reflective practice.** Examining decisions, assumptions, and outcomes to strengthen mental models over time.

These theoretical, experiential, and reflective practices support the development of individual adaptive competencies such as:

- **Power skills.** Emotional intelligence, inquiry-based communication, and critical thinking, which support effective engagement with uncertainty.
- **Controlled experimentation.** Engaging in small, safe-to-fail experiments that encourage exploration without risking project integrity.
- **Systems thinking.** Understanding how local actions create broader organizational effects through feedback loops and interdependencies.
- **Emotional intelligence.** Managing personal stress and influencing diverse stakeholders, particularly in scenarios defined by high uncertainty and rapid change.
- **Metacognition.** Awareness of thinking patterns and cognitive biases, helping identify when mental models no longer fit complex conditions.

Individuals who continue to learn and develop are better able to meet the cognitive demands and sustained intensity associated with complex work.

12.3.2 Team Adaptive Capability

Teams that can share insights, learn from failure, and collaborate across functions are foundational to organizational resilience. Teams may strengthen their adaptive capability through practices such as:

- **Real-time learning loops.** Conducting learning sessions regularly during projects, prompt After Action Reports, and timely retrospectives focused on learning and growth.
- **Cross-functional simulations.** Using scenario-based exercises to test adaptive responses under realistic conditions, surfacing interdependencies across roles.
- **Psychological safety.** Cultivating an environment of high interpersonal trust that allows teams to surface errors, challenge assumptions, and raise risks without fear of repercussion or blame.

These practices help ensure learning is shared and embedded in team processes rather than isolated within individuals.

12.3.3 Organizational Adaptive Capability

Organizations that thrive in complexity embed learning into strategy, operations, and leadership behavior. Learning is not used solely to improve execution, but to continually examine and evolve how the organization thinks and makes decisions.

This shift requires moving beyond single-loop learning, which focuses on improving actions, to double-loop learning, which challenges underlying assumptions, policies, and mental models. At the highest level, it includes deutero-learning: developing the organization's capacity to reflect on and improve how it learns over time.

The following approaches support adaptive capability development at the organizational level:

- **Retrievable strategic memory.** Storing lessons, patterns, and signals in accessible formats so information is shared across divisions and teams, preventing repetition of the same mistakes.
- **Organizational learning analysis.** Analyzing training initiatives to assess learning outcomes as well as the speed and efficiency of learning.
- **Capability growth metrics.** Using performance indicators to track the speed and effectiveness of adaptation.
- **Learning system awareness (deutero-learning).** Periodically reflecting on how learning occurs across the organization, evaluating what gets noticed, what gets ignored, how safe it is to challenge assumptions, and how quickly insights are translated into action. This meta-learning strengthens the organization's ability to learn under increasing complexity.

Adaptive capability at the organizational level is enabled by cross-functional knowledge sharing and learning initiatives. These mechanisms help ensure lessons from complex projects inform not only project execution but governance models and leadership norms to create a continuously learning organization.

12.4 Measuring Complexity and Adaptive Capacity

Traditional project metrics assume stable cause-and-effect relationships and predictable outcomes. In complex environments marked by volatility, emergence, and stakeholder divergence, these assumptions no longer hold, and traditional metrics may not reflect the reality of the project.

This subsection introduces metrics that provide quantitative insight into complexity and adaptive capability. These metrics can be divided into three categories:

- **Complexity metrics.** Indicators of environmental volatility.
- **Learning velocity metrics.** Indicators of how quickly the organization absorbs insight and adjusts.
- **Adaptive culture metrics.** Indicators of cultural conditions that enable candor, risk-taking, and distributed decision-making.

The metrics in this subsection are rated on a 1 to 10 scale, which allows comparisons across projects.

Figure 12-2 outlines three metric categories aligned with continuous adaptation and system health.

12.4.1 Complexity Metrics

Complexity metrics quantify the level and source of complexity in a project. Referencing these metrics helps project leaders determine appropriate governance approaches. Table 12-1 provides examples of metrics in this category.

12.4.2 Learning Velocity Metrics

Learning velocity metrics measure how quickly insight leads to action. They indicate the organization's capacity for sustained adaptation. Table 12-2 provides examples of metrics in this category.

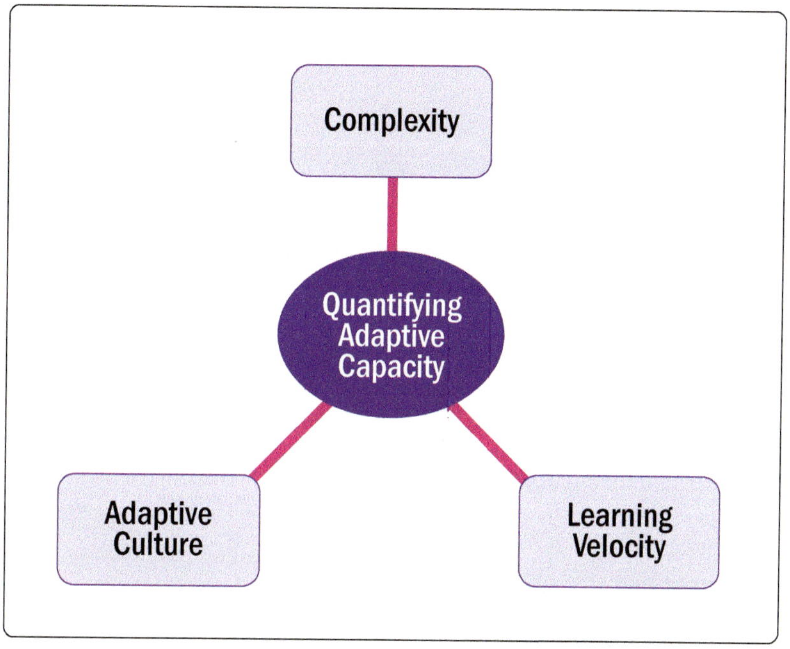

Figure 12-2. Adaptive Metrics Categories

Table 12-1. Complexity Metrics

Metric	Purpose	Key Indicator
Interdependency density	Measures the number and uncertainty of critical dependencies.	High score indicates elevated structural risk.
Requirement stability index	Tracks volatility in key requirements after discovery.	Low score indicates high dynamic complexity.
Stakeholder divergence score	Measures divergence among key stakeholders.	High score indicates stakeholder misalignment and sociopolitical complexity risk.

Table 12-2. Learning Velocity Metrics

Metric	Purpose	Key Indicator
Error-to-learning conversion rate	Percentage of failures that result in documented learning within two cycles.	Low scores indicate weak learning loops.
Cycle velocity (flow efficiency)	Measures how quickly value moves through the system, including wait time.	High scores indicate efficient flow.
Experimentation rate	Number of defined, safe-to-fail experiments per quarter.	High scores indicate learning-oriented behavior.
Improvement implementation rate	Percentage of proposed improvements that are implemented and sustained.	High scores indicate responsiveness to feedback.

Table 12-3. Adaptive Culture Metrics

Metric	Purpose	Key Indicator
Psychological Safety Score	Measures perceived safety for dissent and risk-taking.	High scores support learning capacity.
Decision latency	Time required to reach cross-functional decisions.	Low scores indicate effective decentralization.
Power skills maturity	Assesses competency in communication, critical thinking, and adaptability.	Tracks competency growth over time.

12.4.3 Adaptive Culture Metrics

Adaptive culture metrics indicate whether an organization's culture creates a supportive environment for learning, candor, and flexibility. Table 12-3 provides examples of metrics in this category.

Figure 12-3 shows an example of a dashboard using adaptive capability metrics.

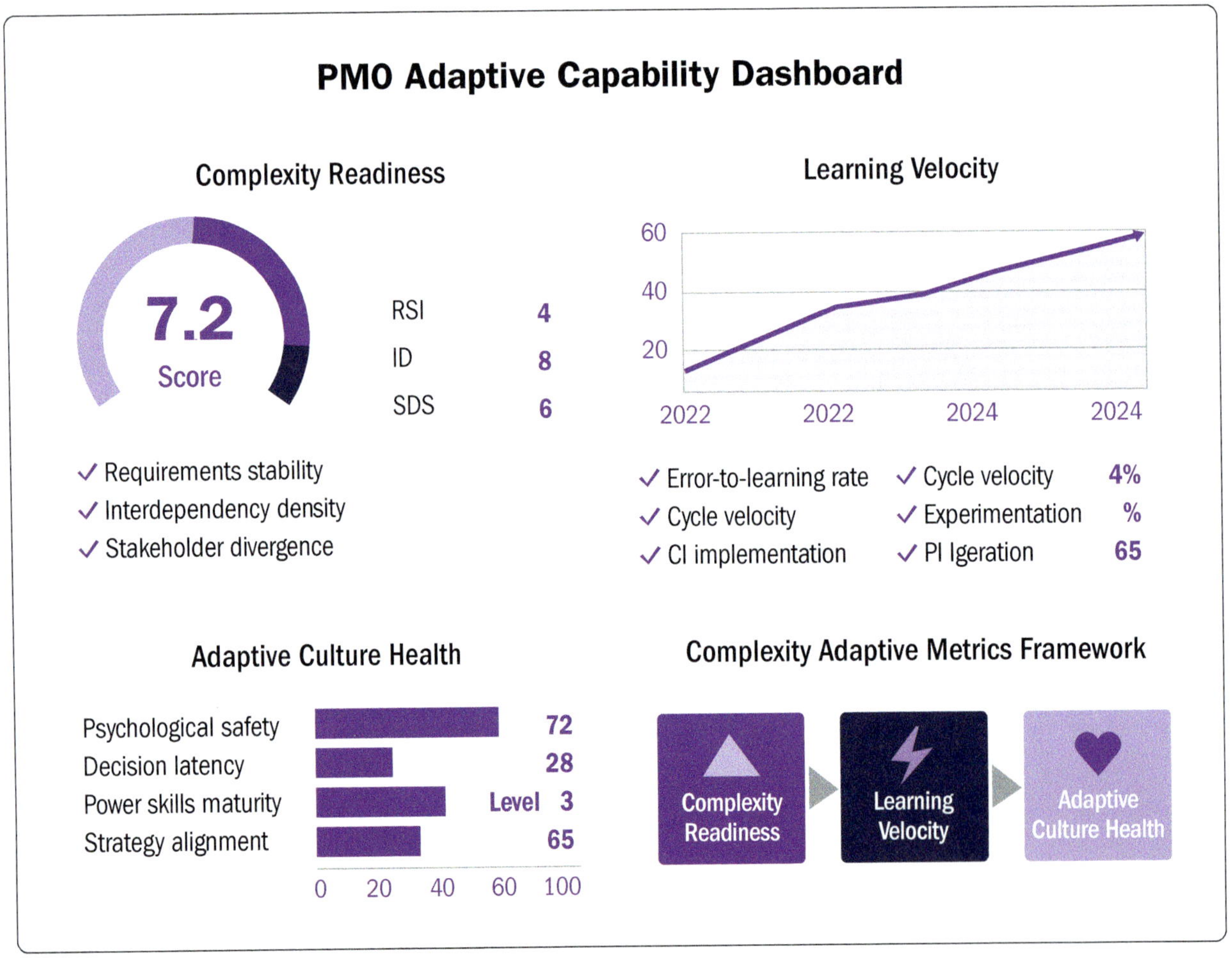

Figure 12-3. Adaptive Capability Dashboard

12.4.4 Implementing Metrics

Although these metrics are useful indicators of complexity and adaptive capability, keeping a large number of metrics updated can be challenging. Organizations seeking to use these metrics may benefit from implementing them on a small scale before employing them more broadly.

Approaches for implementing metrics on a small scale include:

- Piloting one metric, such as decision latency, on a single team for 1 month.
- Introducing a safe-to-fail experiment in one functional area.
- Using the Cynefin Framework to classify one project and adjust its governance model.
- Modeling vulnerability by sharing a recent mistake and what you learned.

These approaches help build an understanding of how adaptive metrics function in a specific organizational context.

Complexity, learning, and adaptability metrics provide an objective way to measure previously unquantifiable elements of complexity. These metrics help organizations recognize strategic value faster, strengthening organizational resilience. By tracking these metrics over time, project practitioners may demonstrate how investments in cultural health and learning capacity translate into superior project performance and sustained market leadership.

12.5 Summary

This section introduced the importance of learning and adaptation for organizations seeking to complete complex projects by:

- Describing strategies for developing a complexity-ready culture.
- Suggesting approaches for building adaptive capability across multiple levels of organizations.
- Introducing metrics that support organizations as they plan complex projects and develop adaptive capability.

The ideas, strategies, and metrics in this section support organizations seeking to use complexity to drive innovation and sustain competitive advantage.

Complexity Playbooks

13.1 Introduction

Navigating complexity in real-world projects requires decision-making under uncertainty. To support these decisions, organizations and teams can develop a complexity playbook. This section explains what complexity playbooks are, describes how they are created, and introduces strategies for designing and using them effectively in the following subsections:

- About Playbooks
- Building a Complexity Playbook
- Complexity Assessments and Frameworks
- Readiness Assessments and Frameworks
- AI-Assisted Playbook Development and Implementation

The guidance in this section helps project practitioners tailor the concepts introduced in earlier sections to their specific project contexts, translating theory into practice.

13.2 About Playbooks

A playbook is a practical guide that outlines recommended approaches, practices, and decision pathways that support consistent, effective execution in specific project situations.

Playbooks are distinct from project management plans and methodologies in the following ways:

- **Project management plans.** Document how a specific project will be executed, monitored, and controlled.
- **Methodologies.** Define standardized processes and practices.
- **Playbooks.** Help project practitioners decide which parts of a methodology to emphasize, adapt, or deemphasize based on current conditions.

A complexity playbook focuses on approaches tailored to complex project environments with emergent conditions, interconnected components, and nonlinear causality. In these environments, teams often face ambiguity about how to proceed, even when established methodologies and governance structures are available. Complexity playbooks address this gap by helping project practitioners decide how to apply available methods to their specific situation.

Complexity playbooks are intended to be referential rather than prescriptive. Teams can draw on playbook recommendations as project conditions evolve, using them to support their judgment and tailor strategies to fit specific project contexts. Used this way, a playbook functions as a sensemaking tool, a decision-support resource, and a leadership aid in situations where no single correct answer exists.

Because playbooks are not formal control documents, they can start small and evolve over time. Early versions of a complexity playbook may focus on a limited set of recurring challenges or decision points. For example, a playbook addressing project ambiguity might focus on implementing rapid learning loops or small, controlled experiments to reduce uncertainty through action.

As organizations accumulate experience and institutional knowledge, playbooks can expand to reflect more nuanced guidance and a broader range of scenarios.

13.2.1 Benefits of Using a Playbook

Developing a playbook requires an up-front investment, but the benefits compound over time, particularly in organizations that regularly manage complex work. These benefits often include:

- **Facilitating knowledge transfer.** A playbook makes tacit knowledge visible, allowing less experienced project practitioners to learn from prior successes and failures, reducing reliance on individual expertise.
- **Improving shared decision-making.** By documenting the rationale behind recommended approaches, complexity playbooks reduce the need to repeatedly justify decisions to stakeholders, lowering escalation frequency and shortening decision cycles, especially in high-pressure situations.
- **Promoting evidence-based approaches.** Under stress, teams may revert to familiar approaches, such as rigid processes and command-and-control leadership, even when evidence suggests that these approaches will not be effective. A playbook can articulate when and why flexibility is appropriate, helping project practitioners maintain effective practices when under pressure.
- **Supporting planning processes.** When complexity emerges or intensifies, the guidance within a playbook informs how the project management plan is shaped and adapted.
- **Establishing flexible guidance.** Complexity playbooks document shared decision logic and sanctioned approaches without mandating a specific method or approach, enabling project managers to adapt their plans to local conditions while staying within organizational guardrails.

Table 13-1. Playbook Roles and Responsibilities

	PMO	Project Practitioner
Creation	Designs the overall framework and defines sanctioned approaches.	Contributes experiential knowledge, lessons learned, and practical insights.
Tailoring	Establishes guardrails that define acceptable flexibility.	Adapts governance, delivery methods, and practices to the project context.
Application	Provides decision support and interpretation guidance, particularly in high-stress situations.	Applies judgment to select and adapt playbook guidance in real time.
Evolution	Aggregates feedback to refine and mature the playbook over time.	Reports outcomes, including what worked, what failed, and where gaps remain.

Similar to the playbooks used by professional sports teams, complexity playbooks equip project teams with adaptive strategies to address uncertainty and ambiguity in real-world projects. They help make good decisions scalable across the organization.

13.2.2 Playbook Roles

The ways that playbooks are developed and used will vary depending on the organizational context. In some environments, the PMO owns the design of a standardized playbook that project practitioners tailor to their projects. In others, the PMO provides governance and support, whereas project practitioners exercise greater discretion in how the playbook is applied.

Table 13-1 summarizes the roles and responsibilities assumed in this section.

Throughout this section, the PMO is positioned as the strategic steward of the playbook, whereas the project practitioner acts as the tactical decision-maker who applies it in practice.

13.3 Building a Complexity Playbook

This section introduces a seven-phase progression for creating and using a complexity playbook, guiding project practitioners from initial assessment through ongoing evolution. Figure 13-1 shows the steps involved in building a complexity playbook.

The following scenario is used to illustrate how these phases are implemented in practice:

Example scenario

A healthcare organization builds a complexity playbook to manage a digital transformation across multiple hospital sites, integrating stakeholder engagement, adaptive governance, and AI-supported decision tools. The organization is rolling out a new electronic health record (EHR) system while facing regulatory constraints, diverse workflows, and high stakeholder sensitivity.

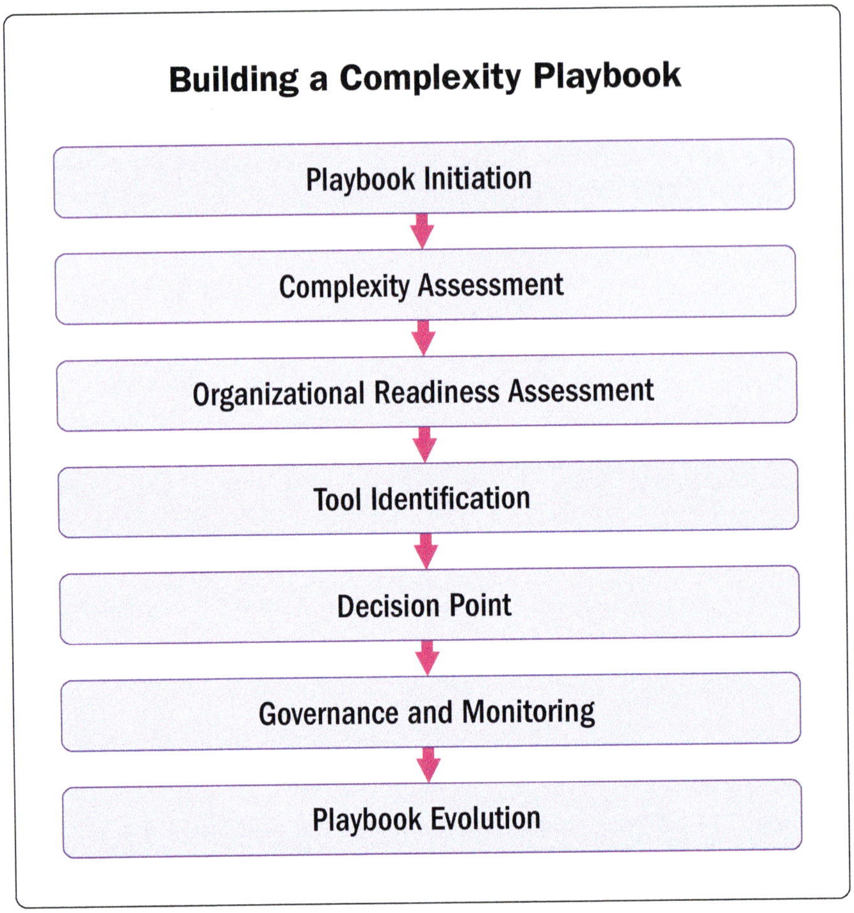

Figure 13-1. Building a Complexity Playbook

This example demonstrates how each phase translates into actionable steps, helping ensure the playbook is not only conceptual but practical for navigating complex project environments.

13.3.1 Phase 1: Playbook Initiation

Before starting a project, project leaders benefit from an initial assessment to determine whether a complexity playbook should be created and used. If the project does not demonstrate complexity as defined in earlier sections of this practice guide, a complexity playbook is not necessary, and standard processes and procedures may apply.

During Phase 1: Playbook Initiation, project leaders:

- Review the complexity factors associated with their project.
- Determine if a playbook is necessary or if standard procedures will suffice.
- If a playbook is necessary, create an initial playbook structure.

Example scenario

The project team in the healthcare organization completes Phase 1 by assessing the complexity factors of their digital transformation initiative. Because the project spans multiple hospitals, involves diverse workflows, and requires regulatory compliance, they determine that the project environment is complex.

They create a shared location to store playbook assets and draft an initial playbook shell, including a title page and a high-level outline of expected content such as complexity types and relevant tools and frameworks.

13.3.2 Phase 2: Complexity Assessment

After deciding to initiate the playbook process, the next phase focuses on a detailed analysis of the types of complexity present within the project environment. This analysis will inform later phases of playbook development, guiding the selection of tools and frameworks to include in the playbook.

During Phase 2: Complexity Assessment, project leaders:

- Identify complexity drivers such as volatility, ambiguity, uniqueness, stakeholder diversity, and technological uncertainty.
- Determine the complexity types that are likely to result from these drivers.
- Use frameworks and tools to characterize and classify the complexity drivers and types.
- Synthesize key findings and document decision-relevant insights within the playbook.

Example scenario

The healthcare organization project team uses complexity frameworks and assessments to characterize the following complexity drivers for their project:

- High stakeholder diversity
- Regulatory volatility
- Technology uncertainty

They then generate a complexity heat map to deepen their understanding of the complexity at play. Their analysis suggests that adaptive governance approaches would be appropriate and that enhanced stakeholder engagement approaches would be beneficial.

They summarize the key insights and implications of the complexity assessment and add them to the complexity playbook draft.

13.3.3 Phase 3: Organizational Readiness Assessment

Once complexity has been assessed, the playbook process proceeds to evaluate the organization's readiness to support adaptive execution. An Organizational Readiness Assessment is a diagnostic tool that evaluates how well an organization's capabilities, frameworks, and operating conditions support effective management of a complex project, and where adaptation of intervention is required.

During Phase 3: Organizational Readiness Assessment, project leaders:

- Review their organization's governance structures.
- Assess the skill sets of their project teams.
- Determine whether the organization will be able to effectively use adaptive approaches.
- Identify enablers, gaps, and constraints that should be addressed to reduce risk.
- If needed, define an action plan to build skills or adjust governance to support adaptive approaches.
- Document high-level readiness insights within the playbook.

This phase helps ensure any adaptive strategies recommended in the playbook will be implemented in a supportive environment.

Example scenario

The project team reviews the current governance structures and skill sets in the healthcare organization. This analysis reveals insufficient data security protocols and teams that lack agile competencies. Examples of their findings include:

- Data security and compliance gaps.
- Incomplete change management processes.
- Evidence that leadership does not consistently demonstrate adaptive approaches.
- Indications that key areas of the organization lack adaptive competencies.

To prepare the organization and project teams for their complex digital transformation effort, they create a comprehensive plan that includes enhanced data security protocols and targeted training on agile practices. They document this plan in the playbook at a high level, deliberately excluding sensitive or highly specific information.

13.3.4 Phase 4: Tool Identification

After complexity and organizational readiness have been assessed, the process shifts to strategy development by identifying tools and frameworks that address the needs of the project and documenting these selections in the complexity playbook.

During Phase 4: Tool Identification, project leaders:

- Translate complexity insights into practical methods and strategies.
- Identify tools and frameworks that support and address the project's complexity sources.
- Document selected tools and frameworks, along with the complexity conditions they are intended to address.

Although tools and frameworks are documented at this stage, they should continue to be assessed and adapted as project conditions evolve.

Example scenario

The project team revisits their complexity assessment and determines that the following tools may be useful for their digital transformation effort:

- Stakeholder empathy maps (introduced in Section 9) and engagement templates to address high stakeholder diversity and potential misalignment.
- Scenario planning templates and risk dashboards to navigate the uncertain technology and regulatory environments.
- Systems mapping and complexity canvas (introduced in Section 9) for navigating interdependency.
- Phased rollout planning to support organizational transitions to adaptive approaches.
- Advanced visualization tools to analyze complex relationships.

The team gathers resources related to these tools and determines how they may be adapted for the project's specific needs. They document the selected tools, along with the rationale for their selection, and share this information with stakeholders as the first substantive version of their complexity playbook.

13.3.5 Phase 5: Decision Point

After selecting tools and frameworks, project teams use decision models to determine the next steps for their projects. Decisions made in this phase are informed by insights from the previous phases and documented in the complexity playbook.

During Phase 5: Decision Point, project leaders:

- Decide whether to proceed, adjust scope, or redesign governance based on complexity insights.
- Apply structured decision frameworks to make choices within high-uncertainty and high-risk environments.
- Document key decisions and their underlying rationale in the playbook.

Example scenario

Based on insights from their complexity analysis, the healthcare project team determines a phased rollout will be more effective than a full-scale implementation of the new EHR. They use safe-to-fail decision models (discussed in Section 7) to select pilot hospitals and proceed with the phased rollout, and they document the decision criteria and outcomes in the playbook for future reference.

13.3.6 Phase 6: Governance and Monitoring

As complex projects proceed and playbook strategies are implemented, the focus shifts to governance and monitoring. Project leadership implements mechanisms that track evolving complexity as well as project performance benchmarks.

During Phase 6: Governance and Monitoring, project leaders:

- Embed feedback loops into ongoing processes.
- Implement adaptive governance approaches and control mechanisms.
- Monitor complexity signals.
- Track complexity over time.
- Document governance approaches, monitoring signals, and lessons learned in the playbook.

Example scenario

During the phased rollout of the new EHR system, the healthcare organization implements dynamic governance approaches to track complexity evolution. They monitor key complexity metrics on a monthly basis and summarize their dynamic governance approach for inclusion in the playbook.

The leadership team adjusts their approach when regularly scheduled analyses indicate that conditions have changed. For example, when the updated complexity heat map shows more than two dimensions trending upward, they convene a leadership meeting to adjust the governance model.

13.3.7 Phase 7: Playbook Evolution

A playbook is intended to be dynamic: growing and changing based on the needs of a project or organization. The final phase of playbook creation and implementation focuses on practices for adjusting the playbook over time.

During Phase 7: Playbook Evolution, project leaders:

- Review feedback from completed project phases.
- Integrate feedback into the playbook, refining tools and methods.
- Adapt strategic approaches to align with evolving practices within the organization.

Example scenario

The healthcare digital transformation project team solicits feedback from the pilot hospitals within the phased rollout. They consolidate and document these lessons learned, adding them to the playbook. They also update the guiding questions and templates for future hospital sites.

After the pilot phase, regulatory changes occur. As a result, the project team adds updated compliance resources to the playbook.

13.4 Complexity Assessments and Frameworks

Complexity assessments and frameworks are used in Phase 2: Complexity Assessment. This phase involves performing a detailed analysis of the types of complexity present within the project environment. This section introduces tools that support this analysis, alongside guidance on how they may be used to inform complexity playbook development and ongoing use.

13.4.1 Complexity Assessment Tool (CAT)

The Complexity Assessment Tool (CAT) is a means of assessing and diagramming project complexity based on structural, sociopolitical, and emergent complexity. It depicts changes in complexity over time, enabling teams to fine-tune governance and decision-making as projects evolve.

The CAT was first introduced in 2013 using the complexity categories described below. [7] These categories loosely align with the structural, human and sociopolitical, and dynamic complexity categories in this practice guide. The CAT supports structured sensemaking by helping project teams analyze and compare the levels of complexity present in a project across three principal dimensions:

- **Structural.** Complexity associated with size, variety, breadth of scope, the level of interdependence of people or tasks, or the pace of the work.
- **Sociopolitical.** Complexity associated with the project's importance, its people, power, and politics—both within the project team and in the wider stakeholder communities.
- **Emergent.** Complexity associated with the novelty of technology or process, a lack of experience, a lack of availability of information, or some combination of these.

Project practitioners provide qualitative assessments of each complexity dimension, labeling the complexity level as high, medium, or low. These assessments can be taken multiple times throughout the project and monitored by using visualizations.

CAT assessments may be revised from the original approach by assessing some or all the six complexity classifications described in Section 2. Using these classifications as inputs to the CAT provides a nuanced picture of the sources and drivers of complexity within a project. Visualizing CAT assessments by using spider diagrams allows project practitioners to track complexity changes over time.

Figure 13-2 shows a spider diagram using the complexity categories in Section 2. It shows the results of two assessments that demonstrate how the complexity profile can change over time.

13.4.2 The Complexity Assessment Tool (CAT) in Practice

In addition to its use during Phase 2 of playbook development, regular CAT assessments can support ongoing sensemaking, informing leadership approaches and decision-making as project environments evolve. To use the CAT on a regular basis, project practitioners should set up a cadence for assessment periods. For example, a project team could hold monthly meetings to reassess complexity dimensions.

CAT assessments may be determined by drawing on a variety of sources such as team retrospectives, governance analyses, and stakeholder feedback. Once this data has been reviewed and CAT ratings have been assigned, visualizing the levels for each dimension shows where complexity is intensifying

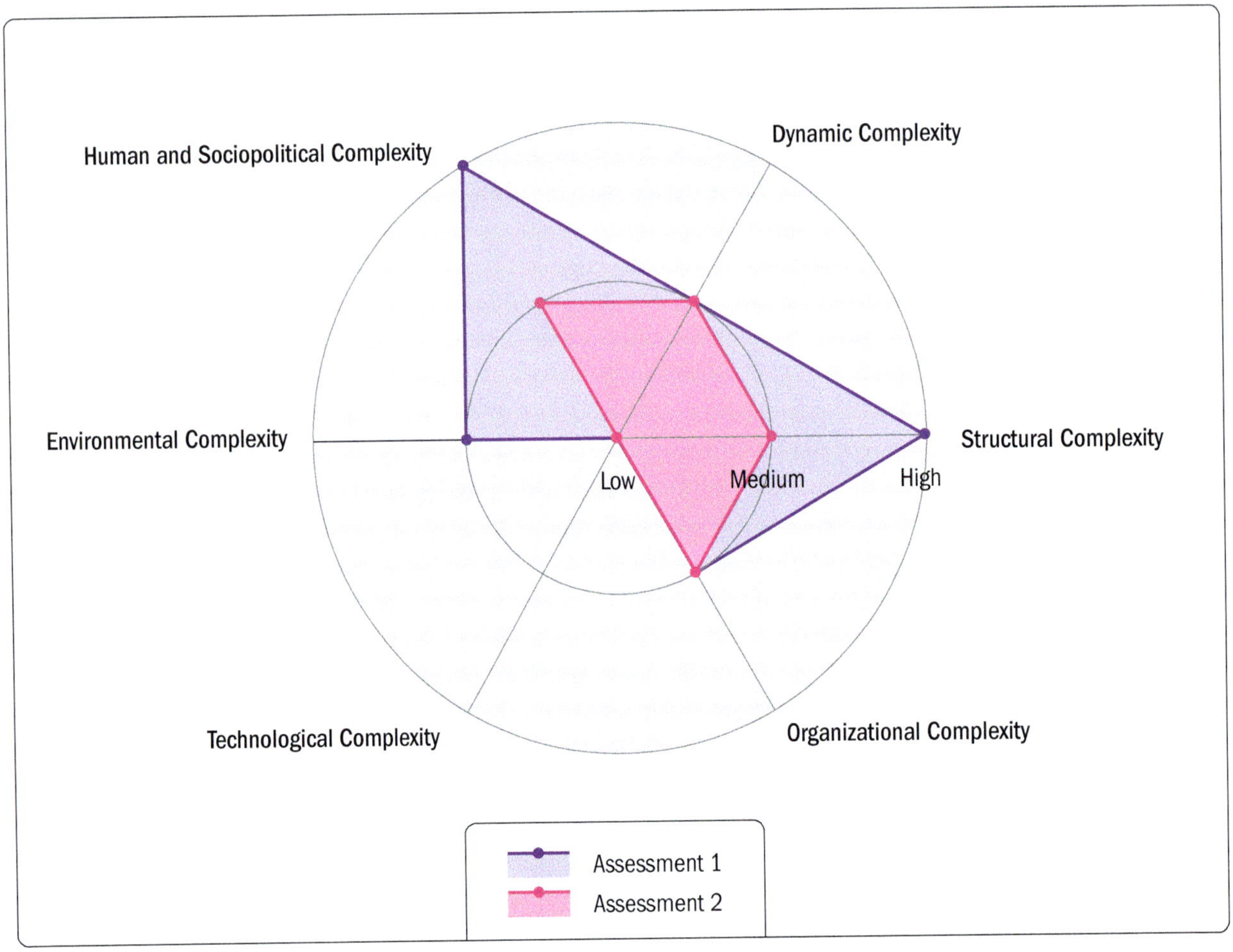

Figure 13-2. Complexity Assessment

or stabilizing. Reviewing CAT assessment trends over time will show if the project is becoming more volatile and help assess if interventions have been effective.

Reviewing CAT assessment trends helps project practitioners anticipate challenges before they escalate. When complexity dimension ratings increase over time, project leaders may consider actions such as implementing adaptive planning cycles, expanding stakeholder engagement, or conducting safe-to-fail experiments.

To promote the benefits of regular CAT assessment and review, a complexity playbook may recommend incorporating CAT assessments on a regular basis to support dynamic steering.

13.4.3 Darnell-Preston Complexity Index (DPCI)

The Darnell-Preston Complexity Index (DPCI) is a standardized assessment method that compares project complexity across multiple dimensions to help prioritize projects and determine appropriate governance and risk management approaches.

The DPCI quantifies project complexity across the following four dimensions:

- **Internal**
  - Clear objectives
  - Defined scope
  - Organizational structure
- **External**
  - Size
  - Duration
  - Resource availability
- **Technological**
  - Technology newness
  - Technology familiarity
  - Environmental
- **Legal**
  - Cultural
  - Political
  - Ecological

Factors related to each dimension are assessed and ranked on a scale of 1 to 5, where 1 indicates low complexity, and 5 indicates high complexity. Once assessed, these scores can be used to compare complexity levels across the project, helping project practitioners determine governance approaches that best fit each complexity profile.

For example, a project with high technological uncertainty and diverse stakeholders will score higher on the DPCI, signaling the need for iterative planning and adaptive decision-making.

13.4.4 Darnell-Preston Complexity Index (DPCI) in Practice

In addition to its use during the complexity assessment phase, project practitioners can use DPCI scores to determine whether a project warrants the use of a complexity playbook. For example, leadership could establish a rule that projects with a DPCI score greater than 3 on any dimension should implement adaptive approaches and follow approaches in the complexity playbook.

Example scenario

A US$250 million building expansion project required the construction of a new data center to support high-performance computing. The data center had stringent requirements related to power availability, sophisticated cooling solutions, and sustainability compliance. These technological factors, as well as schedule constraints and limited worker availability, contributed to increased complexity.

Table 13-2. Darnell-Preston Complexity Index (DCPI) Scoring Example

Dimension	Factor	Score
Internal	Organizational structure	3
External	Size	4
	Duration	4
Technological	Novel data center design	3
	Energy and cooling requirements	4
	Legacy application migration	3
Environmental	Regulatory constraints	4
	Sustainability compliance	5
Total	**Eight factors**	**30 points**
DPCI Score	Score/maximum possible score = 30/40 = **75%**	

The project team used DPCI scores to assess the complexity of the data center construction effort. Table 13-2 lists DPCI dimensions, factors, and scores for the data center project.

Each factor was rated on a scale of 1 to 5, where 1 indicates low complexity, and 5 indicates high complexity. The maximum score is determined by multiplying the number of factors by 5, which is the highest possible score.

In the building expansion project, there were eight factors, so the maximum score was 40. The project's DPCI score was determined by dividing the sum of each factor's score, 30, by the maximum possible score, 40, which gives a complexity score of 75%.

This analysis revealed high levels of complexity across multiple dimensions, which supported the use of a complexity playbook. After completing the initial phases of the complexity playbook process, project leadership recommended the following approaches:

- Move toward a flatter decision-making process by delegating decisions to those with the most knowledge about the scope, risk, and technology.
- Provide technical training for the data center design and build in buffers for unfamiliar work.
- Monitor regulatory environment and sustainability compliance weekly.
- Implement a lean change management process.
- Maintain rigorous design and configuration management processes.

These approaches helped the project team navigate multiple dimensions of complexity, successfully completing the project.

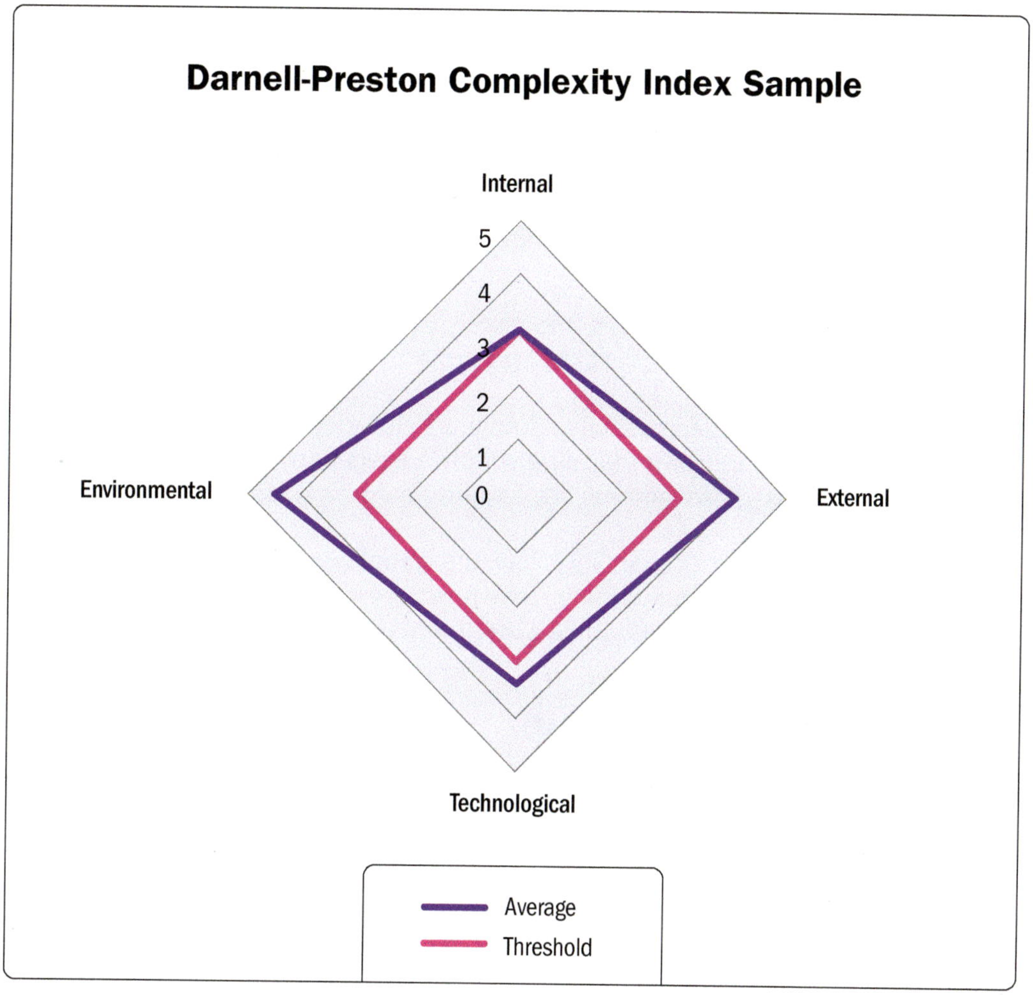

Figure 13-3. Darnell-Preston Complexity Index (DPCI) Sample

Figure 13-3 shows a complexity profile with a threshold score of 3 on each of the DCPI complexity categories and the average score for the project, providing a visual indicator where complexity is higher than the threshold.

13.5 Readiness Assessments and Frameworks

Phase 3 of the complexity playbook focuses on organizational readiness. Organizational readiness includes the governance, processes, and technologies, along with the team competencies described in Section 5.

13.5.1 Organizational Readiness Assessment

An organizational readiness assessment evaluates how well an organization's capabilities, frameworks, and operating conditions support effective management of a complex project, and where adaptation or intervention is required. This assessment helps determine whether the organizational environment can sustain the adaptive approaches recommended for a complex project by assessing readiness across the following domains:

- **Governance.** The clarity, flexibility, and effectiveness of decision-making structures, escalation paths, and accountability mechanisms, including how authority is distributed and how decisions are adjusted as conditions change.
- **Processes.** The degree to which planning, delivery, risk management, and change processes support learning and adaptation, rather than enforcing rigid compliance.
- **Technologies.** The availability, integration, and usability of tools that support collaboration, data-driven decision-making, and real-time visibility into project and organizational performance.

Assessing organizational readiness across these domains helps identify systemic enablers, gaps, and constraints that may either support or undermine adaptive execution. The assessment results often indicate whether foundational improvements are required before undertaking a complex initiative.

For example, if adaptive governance capability is low, the complexity playbook may include actions, such as clarifying decision rights, strengthening cross-functional forums, or introducing adaptive governance mechanisms before recommending experimentation or decentralized decision-making.

13.5.2 Competency Maturity Framework (CMF)

The competency maturity framework (CMF) is a structured model that assesses team capabilities (as opposed to individual competencies) across progressive maturity levels to identify strengths, gaps, and development needs.

During Phase 3 of the playbook development process, the CMF is used to evaluate whether project teams possess the adaptive skills required to operate effectively in complex and uncertain environments. Unlike role-based skill inventories, the CMF focuses on how teams behave, decide, and learn under conditions of uncertainty.

CMF assessments can be conducted using a combination of qualitative inputs (e.g., interviews, facilitated workshops, and surveys) and quantitative scoring approaches. In practice, qualitative insights are often translated into numeric ratings to enable comparison across competencies and over time. Results are typically visualized using radar charts or spider diagrams to highlight imbalances and development priorities.

In addition to supporting organizational readiness assessment, the CMF can be used for:

- Self-assessments to support individual development.
- Project reviews to evaluate readiness for complexity.
- Talent development initiatives that align learning with strategic needs.

The CMF may be scored on a quantitative scale from 1 to 5, corresponding to the following maturity levels:

- **Level 1—Ad hoc.** Capabilities are inconsistent and dependent on individual effort rather than shared practice. Teams react to issues as they arise, with limited ability to anticipate or adapt to change.

- **Level 2—Repeatable.** Basic practices exist and can be repeated, but they are applied inconsistently across teams or projects. Success depends on informal knowledge rather than shared standards.
- **Level 3—Defined.** Competencies are explicitly defined, documented, and shared. Teams apply agreed-upon practices consistently, enabling more predictable performance in moderately complex environments.
- **Level 4—Managed.** Capabilities are measured and actively managed. Teams use feedback, metrics, and reflection to improve performance and adjust behaviors in response to emerging conditions.
- **Level 5—Adaptive.** Teams demonstrate high levels of learning, flexibility, and innovation. Competencies evolve continuously through experimentation, feedback loops, and sensemaking, enabling effective action in highly complex and dynamic environments.

The CMF is most effective when used as an ongoing development tool rather than a one-time assessment. Its impact is amplified when paired with targeted interventions such as coaching, mentoring, feedback loops, and experiential learning opportunities.

13.5.3 Organizational Readiness in Practice

Evaluating organizational readiness and team competencies to identify gaps early helps prevent complexity from escalating beyond the organization's capacity to manage it. To use these frameworks effectively, project practitioners should consider the following guidance:

- **Treat governance and competencies as essential levers.** Low scores in areas such as leadership flexibility or change management often signal slow decision-making and resistance to adaptation.
- **Address gaps before implementing adaptive strategies.** Capability gaps should be addressed through targeted interventions before undertaking complex projects.
- **Integrate assessments into the project life cycle.** Update assessments at key transition points such as project initiation, major phase reviews, or shifts in project context.

The outcomes of these assessments help determine whether the organization is prepared to adopt adaptive and agile approaches as well as which playbook strategies are likely to be effective.

Example scenario

A multinational healthcare organization is preparing a cross-border digital transformation initiative involving AI, cloud migration, and regulatory compliance.

The PMO conducts a readiness assessment and competency maturity assessment, identifying key aspects of organizational readiness, including adaptive governance, distributed agility, and a collaborative culture. The key team competencies for this project are: systems thinking, cultural and ethical competence, environmental awareness, and technical literacy. The assessment results are shown in Tables 13-3 and 13-4.

Table 13-3. Organizational Readiness Assessment

	Adaptive Governance	Distributed Agility	Collaborative Culture
Organizational readiness score	2	3	4

Table 13-4. Team Competency Assessment

	Systems Thinking	Cultural and Ethical Competence	Environmental Awareness	Technical Literacy
Team score	4	2	3	5

This assessment indicates that the organization needs to improve their governance to become more adaptive. Key actions they can take include:

- Delegating decision rights based on decision type, rather than by role or hierarchy, allowing decisions to be made by those closest to the work.
- Establishing lightweight governance that is triggered by signals, not cadence.
- Empowering teams to work autonomously within established guardrails.

Taking these actions to introduce adaptive governance will likely also improve distributed agility.

The team competency assessment also revealed areas for improvement. Given that this is a cross-border project, the team will benefit from improving their cultural and ethical competence. Improving the team's environmental awareness will also be beneficial. Based on the assessment scores, the team's systems thinking and technical literacy competencies are already sufficient for the project.

13.6 AI-Assisted Playbook Development and Implementation

AI tools can support complexity playbook implementation by augmenting analysis, accelerating sensemaking, and enabling faster feedback loops. In this context, AI functions as an analytical aid, helping project practitioners interpret signals, explore scenarios, and monitor evolving conditions across the playbook life cycle.

This section describes two complementary ways AI can be applied:

- By supporting activities within each phase of the playbook development and use process.
- To inform ongoing analysis through targeted, theme-based inquiries.

It concludes with practices for responsible AI usage.

Table 13-5 AI Support Across Playbook Phases

Phase	Guiding Question	Action	Sample AI Output
Phase 1: Playbook Initiation	Is project complexity above the activation threshold?	Apply decision gate to activate the playbook.	Complexity detection or screening report
Phase 2: Complexity Assessment	How can the project's complexity be classified using assessment assets (e.g., Cynefin Framework, CAT)?	Analyze and visualize complexity.	Customized complexity heat map
Phase 3: Organizational Readiness Check	What organizational enablers and blockers are present?	Identify readiness gaps.	Readiness gap analysis
Phase 4: Tool Alignment	Which tools or templates require customization?	Configure and tailor assets.	Draft stakeholder empathy map or canvas
Phase 5: Decision Point	How does complexity inform strategic choices?	Support go/no-go or rescoping decisions.	Scenario comparison
Phase 6: Governance and Monitoring	How is complexity evolving over time?	Adapt governance mechanisms.	Alerts on volatility or risk trends
Phase 7: Playbook Evolution	How should feedback and learning be integrated?	Update and refine the playbook.	Synthesized lessons learned summary

13.6.1 AI Assistance With Playbook Development Phases

Each phase of the complexity playbook process has distinct objectives and decision points. AI can be applied differently at each phase depending on the type of judgment required, the data available, and the level of uncertainty involved.

Table 13-5 maps each playbook phase to a guiding question that frames project practitioner sensemaking, the primary action taken during that phase, and examples of AI-supported outputs that can inform (but not replace) human decision-making.

Table 13-5 is intended as an illustrative reference rather than a prescriptive workflow. Not every phase will require AI support, and the form of AI output may vary based on organizational context, data maturity, and governance constraints.

13.6.2 Guiding Questions for AI Prompts

Table 13-6 provides guidance on framing effective AI-supported inquiries by outlining recurring analytical themes that commonly arise when managing complex projects.

Table 13-6. Example Analytical Themes for AI-Supported Inquiry

Objective	Relevant Theme	Example
Monitor stakeholder volatility	Changes in stakeholder engagement over time	Generate a monthly volatility index using sentiment and interaction data.
Measure decision latency	Responsiveness of governance processes	Calculate average time between issue submission and decision approval.
Evaluate tool adaptability	Effectiveness of templates and canvases	Score adaptability of templates across project contexts.
Visualize complexity trends	Evolution of complexity over time	Create spider diagrams showing quarterly changes in complexity dimensions.

Used appropriately, these analyses can help project practitioners detect early warning signals, validate assumptions, and adjust interventions before issues escalate.

Practices for Responsible AI Usage

When integrating AI into playbook processes, project practitioners should apply explicit governance practices to help ensure responsible and effective use:

- **Human-in-the-loop validation.** AI outputs should be reviewed and validated by qualified project practitioners to maintain accountability and prevent automated errors.
- **Bias and fairness analysis.** Periodically assess AI outputs for bias (e.g., systematic favoring of specific stakeholder groups), address identified issues, and document mitigation steps.
- **Data provenance verification.** Assess the origin, quality, and limitations of input data to avoid decisions based on incomplete or unreliable information.
- **Privacy and compliance.** Help ensure compliance with applicable data protection regulations (such as GDPR) and internal privacy policies.
- **Clear accountability.** Explicitly assign decision-making responsibility to humans, even when decisions are informed by AI-generated insights.

Together, these practices help ensure that AI augments professional judgment rather than displacing it, preserving the benefits of automation while mitigating the risks of overreliance.

13.7 Summary

This section introduced the complexity playbook as a flexible and practical guide for navigating complex projects by:

- Defining complexity playbooks as iterative, adaptive, and contextualized guides for organizations and project teams operating in complex environments;

- Establishing a seven-phase process for building and implementing a complexity playbook;
- Introducing complexity assessments;
- Describing readiness assessments and team competency maturity frameworks relevant to the organizational readiness phase; and
- Providing guidance on integrating AI tools to support the development and use of complexity playbooks.

By implementing the seven-phase complexity playbook process, strategically applying relevant frameworks and assessments, and thoughtfully leveraging AI tools, project practitioners can enhance their ability to navigate and manage complex projects effectively.

References

[1] Australian Government, Department of Infrastructure and Regional Development. (n.d.). *Infrastructure Planning and Delivery Best Practice Case Studies: Channel Deepening Project – Melbourne. https://www.infrastructure.gov.au/sites/default/files/documents/best_practice_guide.pdf*

[2] Hofstede, G., Hofstede, G. J., & Minkov, M. (2010). *Cultures and Organizations: Software of the Mind* (3rd ed.). McGraw-Hill.

[3] Meadows, D. H. (1999). *Leverage Points: Places to Intervene in a System*. The Sustainability Institute.

[4] Nguyen, K., Mérindol, V., & Versailles, D. W. (2025). Empathy as the Missing Link for Seizing and Transforming Capabilities in the Open Innovation Context. *Strategic Change,* 1–13. https://doi.org/10.1002/jsc.70030

[5] Adoko, M. T., Mazzuchi, T. A., & Sarkani, S. (2015). Developing a Cost Overrun Predictive Model for Complex Systems Development Projects. *Project Management Journal*, *46*(6), 111–125.

[6] Hodgkinson, G. P., & Healey, M. P. (2011). Psychological Foundations of Dynamic Capabilities: Reflexion and Reflection in Strategic Management. *Strategic Management Journal, 32*(13), 1500–1516.

[7] Maylor, H. R., Turner, N. W., & Murray-Webster, R. (2013). How Hard Can it Be? *Research Technology Management*, pp. 45–51(July-August 2013). https://www.researchgate.net/publications/263043989

Appendix X1
Contributors and Reviewers

The Project Management Institute is grateful to all of the contributors for their support and acknowledges their outstanding contributions to the project management profession.

X1.1 Contributors and Reviewers

The following contributors had input into shaping the content of this practice guide. Individuals listed in bold served on the Development Team, and individuals listed in italics served on the Review Team. Inclusion of an individual's name in the list does not represent their approval or endorsement of the final content in all its parts.

Vahid Azadmanesh, DBA, PMP, PfMP
Joe Campa, PMI-PMOCP, PMI-CP, PMP
Luca Crocioni, PRINCE2, PMP
Oluseyi Dare, MBA, PMI-PMOCP, PMP
Ahmed Kamel Ghanem, MEM, PMP, PgMP
Jack Hsieh, PMP, PgMP, PfMP
Alex Melendez, DIT (c), MBA, PMP
Ali Mugotir, MPM, MBA, PMP
Kimthoa Thi Nguyen, DBA, PMP, PfMP
Eddy Vertil, PhD, PMI-RMP, PMP
Armijos Alfredo, PMI-RMP, PMI-PMOCP, PMP
Riyad AlMallak, PMP, PgMP, PfMP
Hanan Saad AlMaziad, PMP, PgMP, PfMP
Noura Mansour Almusharraf, PhD, PgMP, PfMP
Rajendra Aswale
Akbar Azwir, PMP, PgMP, PfMP
Kwang Gu Baek, MBA, PMP, PgMP
Tayfun Balcik
Pierre Jr Beaudry, Adm.A, MGP, PMP
Leasella Bongiovanni, CSM, PBP, PMP
Panos Chatzipanos, PhD, BC.WRE
Nguyen Si Trieu Chau, PMP, PgMP, PfMP
Louisa Dixon, MBA, PMP
Sylvie Edwards, FPMAC, PMI-RMP, PMP
Mohamed Mohsen Elfouly, PhD, PMI-RMP, PMP
Abuzar Ibrahim Ali Elgalib, BSc, MBA, PMP
Lucie Ellis, PMP, PgMP, PfMP
Jean-Luc Favrot, PMI-CPMAI, PMI-ACP, PMP
Theofanis Giotis, PhD(c), PMP, PfMP
Paul Gosnell, CRISC, CISSP, PMP
Jeff A. Harris, PMP
Murtaza Hassanali, PMI-RMP, PMP, PgMP
Farzin Hosseini, FIEI, C.Eng, PMP
Éamonn V. Kelly, DBA, GPM, PMP
Hassan Keshavarz
Jing (Julie) Li
Tong (James) Liu, PhD, Agile PO, PMP
Xinyao (Alana) Liu
Shannon McGuffey, MS, PMP
Ricardo Coutinho Mello

Peter Botond Mihok

Kunihiko Mishima

Youssef Mouzahem

Hiromi Nakatani, PRINCE2, CSP, PMP

Laura Lazzerini Neuwirth, Agile PgM, PMI-PMOCP, PMP

Donald Newberry, PMP, PgMP, PfMP

Filippo Maria Ottaviani, PhD, Eng

Zulfiqar Ali QaimKhani, PMI-CPMAI, PMP, PgMP

Rachita Ranjan, MBA, CIO.D, PMP

Ahmet Rumiye, DBA, PgMP, PfMP

Magda Scrobota, PMI-PMOCP, PMP

Mohamed Sharaby, BSc, PMI-RMP, PMP

Carlos Singh, PMP, PgMP, PfMP

Vivek Sonar, VMA, PMI-RMP, PMP

Xue Song, PhD, MPM, PMP

Frances Talbert

Khushboo Tibrewala, PMP

Meiko Tourista, CCMP, PRINCE2, PMI-PMOCP

Fede Vargas, PhD(c), DBA, PMP

X1.2 PMI Team Members

Linda R. Garber

Kelly Heuer, PhD, CAPM

Kim Marcelliano

Christie McDevitt, APR

Sarah Philbrick

Kim Shinners

X1.3 Other Key Members

Cyndi Snyder Dionisio, MBA, PMI-RMP, PMP (Chair)

Ginny Perkey (Technical Writer)

Glossary

Many of the words defined here have broader and, in some cases, different dictionary definitions. In some cases, a single glossary term consists of multiple words (e.g., distributed decision-making).

adaptive approach. A development approach in which the requirements are subject to a high level of uncertainty and volatility and are likely to change throughout the project.

adaptive governance. A flexible decision-making approach that adjusts structures, processes, and oversight in response to changing conditions so teams can navigate uncertainty and maintain effective project delivery.

adaptive leadership. A leadership approach focused on experimentation, sensemaking, and system-wide learning, enabling individuals and teams to respond constructively to challenges that lack predefined solutions.

adaptive mindset. A way of thinking that guides individuals and organizations to approach work, problem-solving, and decision-making with flexibility, grounded in agile values and principles.

After Action Review (AAR). A structured reflection process conducted immediately following key project events, phases, or milestones.

agile. A term used to describe a mindset of values and principles as set forth in the *Manifesto for Agile Software Development*.

agile maturity. The extent to which an organization has effectively adopted, internalized, and sustained agile principles, values, and practices across its teams, processes, and culture.

agile project delivery. An iterative and incremental approach to managing and executing projects that emphasizes customer collaboration, adaptive planning, continuous feedback, and value-driven delivery through cross-functional, self-organizing teams.

agile transformation. The process through which an organization fundamentally changes its structures, processes, culture, and mindset to adopt and scale agile principles and practices across all levels of the enterprise.

agility enablers. The foundational capabilities, practices, structures, and cultural elements that support and accelerate an organization's ability to adopt, sustain, and scale agile principles and behaviors across the enterprise.

ambiguity. A state of being unclear, having difficulty in identifying the cause of events, or having multiple options from which to choose.

anchoring. A cognitive bias where people rely too heavily on the first piece of information encountered (the "anchor") when making decisions.

assumption. A factor in the planning process considered to be true, real, or certain, without proof or demonstration.

attribute. A distinguishing feature or characteristic ascribed to a person or thing.

benefits realization management. A structured approach that helps ensure portfolios, programs, and projects deliver measurable benefits aligned with organizational strategy while enabling adaptive decision-making to preserve long-term value.

capability. The potential or capacity of an individual, team, or organization to perform a task or achieve a strategic outcome.

causal loop diagram. A visual tool used in systems thinking to represent the feedback structures within a system.

collective ownership. A shared sense of accountability for outcomes and a mutual commitment to team goals and decision-making.

competency. The combination of conditions and characteristics of knowledge, skills, abilities, and behaviors that enables superior performance.

competency maturity framework (CMF). A structured model that assesses team capabilities across progressive maturity levels to identify strengths, gaps, and development needs.

complex adaptive systems (CAS). Systems composed of interconnected agents whose behavior evolves through feedback, learning, and interaction with a dynamic environment.

complexity. A characteristic of a program or project or its environment that is difficult to manage due to human behavior, system behavior, and ambiguity.

complex project environments. Projects involving interdependent variables, dynamic conditions, and multiple stakeholders, making outcomes unpredictable.

Complexity Assessment Tool (CAT). A tool that depicts different types of complexity over time, enabling teams to track changes and fine-tune governance and decision-making as projects evolve.

complexity heatmap. A visual assessment of project complexity across multiple dimensions.

complexity theory. The study of how complex systems, composed of many interacting components, exhibit unpredictable emergent and nonlinear behavior.

confirmation bias. A type of cognitive bias that confirms preexisting beliefs or hypotheses.

connectivity. The intricate web of components, where changes in one area can significantly impact other areas.

cultural competence. The ability to navigate diverse cultural contexts and organizational boundaries by confronting challenges, taking risks, and learning from mistakes.

cultural enablers. The shared values, beliefs, behaviors, and mindsets within an organization that support, reinforce, and accelerate the adoption and sustainability of agile principles and adaptive ways of working.

Cynefin Framework. A sensemaking framework that helps leaders and teams categorize situations into domains (clear, complicated, complex, chaotic, and confused) to decide on appropriate actions.

Darnell-Preston Complexity Index (DPCI). A standardized assessment method that compares project complexity across multiple dimensions to help prioritize projects and determine appropriate governance and risk management approaches.

decision ecosystem. The interconnected roles, norms, governance structures, and communication channels that shape how decisions are made and coordinated across a system.

decision rights. Clearly defined roles and responsibilities specifying who is empowered to make which decisions, thereby reducing ambiguity and delays.

design thinking. A nonlinear iterative process that teams use to understand users, challenge assumptions, redefine problems, and create innovative solutions to prototype and test.

deutero-learning. Learning how to learn; developing the ability to reflect on and improve one's learning strategies.

distributed decision-making (DDM). A governance and operating model in which decision authority is intentionally delegated across individuals, teams, or organizational levels, based on proximity to information and expertise.

dynamic complexity. The challenges arising from changing interdependencies, emergent behaviors, and nonlinear cause-and-effect relationships that evolve throughout project life cycles.

emergence. The appearance of new patterns, properties, or behaviors that arise from interactions within a system, but cannot be explained by the parts in isolation.

emergent leadership. Leadership that arises dynamically in response to contextual needs, rather than from formal authority, often shifting fluidly among team members.

emergent strategy. A strategic approach that evolves through learning, adaptation, and real-time feedback rather than being planned in advance.

emotional capability. An organization's ability to recognize, understand, and manage members' emotions through norms and routines that support change.

emotional intelligence. The ability to identify, assess, and manage the personal emotions of oneself and other people, as well as the collective emotions of groups of people.

empathy. Understanding, as well as feeling, the thoughts and emotions of others.

empathy map. A visual tool used to synthesize insights about a stakeholder by capturing what they think, feel, say, and do, to build shared understanding and inform decisions, communication, and design choices.

enterprise agility. An organization's capacity to rapidly sense, respond, and adapt to change by dynamically aligning strategy, structure, processes, people, and technology to deliver sustained value in complexity and uncertainty.

environmental complexity. The external forces and contextual conditions that influence the ability to plan, execute, and deliver projects successfully.

ethical competence. The ability to protect organizational reputation and build trust by applying ethical reasoning and articulating persuasive arguments within and beyond the organization.

experiment canvas. A structured template for designing, executing, and learning from small-scale tests in uncertain project environments.

feedback. A process where a system's output is looped back as an input, influencing future behavior.

feedback loops. Structured mechanisms that allow teams and organizations to continuously monitor outcomes, extract learning, and adjust behavior in response to changing conditions

holism. An approach that emphasizes understanding systems as a whole, rather than only analyzing their individual parts.

human and sociopolitical complexity. The intricate web of people dynamics that emerge when diverse stakeholders, team members, and external partners interact throughout a project.

hybrid approach. A combination of elements from both agile and predictive approaches that is useful when there is uncertainty or risk around the requirements.

interconnectedness. The condition in which elements of a system are linked, with changes in one part influencing other parts of the system overall.

Kanban. A visual workflow management framework that uses boards, cards, and continuous flow principles to help teams limit work in progress, increase efficiency, and deliver value incrementally.

lean-agile. A combined mindset and approach that integrates the principles of lean thinking and agile approaches to maximize value delivery, minimize waste, and enable adaptive, customer-focused, and flow-based organizational performance.

lean management. A systematic approach to optimizing operations by eliminating waste, streamlining processes, and maximizing value.

nonlinear. A type of relationship or behavior where outputs are not directly proportional to inputs.

nonlinear causality. A relationship in which cause and effect are not directly proportional, where small changes can produce disproportionately large effects.

organizational complexity. The intricate and multifaceted nature of modern organizations.

organizational readiness. The degree to which an organization's structures, leadership, culture, and systems are prepared to adopt and sustain complexity-informed leadership strategies.

organizational readiness assessment. A diagnostic tool that evaluates how well an organization's capabilities, frameworks, and operating conditions support effective management of a complex project, and where adaptation or intervention is required.

pattern recognition. Identifying recurring themes, systemic issues, and causal patterns across project situations and stakeholder interactions.

playbook. A practical guide that outlines recommended approaches, practices, and decision pathways to support consistent, effective execution in specific project situations.

predictive approach. A development approach in which the project scope, time, and cost are determined in the early phases of the life cycle.

program. A group of related projects and program activities managed in a coordinated manner to obtain benefits not available from managing them individually.

project. A temporary initiative in a unique context undertaken to create value.

psychological safety. A team environment where team members feel comfortable expressing ideas, raising concerns, taking interpersonal risks, and challenging norms without fear of punishment or humiliation.

purposeful systems. Systems in which individual elements (often people or organizations) work together to achieve a shared goal or objective.

reductionism. An approach that explains a system by breaking it down into its individual components.

reflective system. Higher forms of cognition such as logical reasoning, planning, and hypothesis.

reflexive system. Automatic and basic forms of cognition such as implicit stereotyping, automatic categorization, and empathy.

risk mitigation. A risk response strategy that involves decreasing the probability of occurrence or impact of a threat.

safe-to-fail experiments. Controlled trials designed to test new ideas in uncertain environments without risking major failure or project disruption.

scaling agility. The application of agile principles, practices, and mindsets across multiple teams, departments, or the enterprise in a coordinated and aligned manner to deliver complex solutions and strategic business outcomes. *Also known as agile at scale.*

Scrum. A lightweight, agile project management framework used primarily for iterative and incremental product development, especially in software.

Scrumban. A hybrid project management framework that combines elements of both Scrum and Kanban.

sensemaking. Interpreting complex or ambiguous situations to build shared understanding and guide effective action.

situation diagnosis. Distinguishing between technical and adaptive challenges to determine the appropriate leadership approach.

situational awareness. The ability to interpret shifting conditions, anticipate their impact, and make informed decisions to mitigate issues and risks in dynamic environments.

stakeholder divergence score (SDS). A measure that indicates the degree of misalignment among key stakeholders on project objectives, priorities, and success criteria.

stakeholder volatility index (SVI). A composite measure that tracks how frequently and significantly stakeholder influence, expectations, engagement, or position change over the course of a project.

stock-and-flow models. A representation of how quantities (stocks) accumulate or deplete over time through rates of change (flow).

strategic coherence. The degree to which actions, structures, and decisions across the organization remain aligned with evolving strategic intent.

strategic flexibility. The ability to modify strategies, priorities, and actions as new information or environmental conditions emerge.

strategic intent. A clearly communicated purpose or directional ambition that aligns distributed actions without dictating specific execution paths.

strategic learning. The practice of using outcomes, feedback, and experimentation to iteratively refine strategic direction and decision-making.

structural complexity. The degree to which a project contains numerous, interrelated components.

structural enablers. Organizational design elements—such as roles, teams, governance, processes, and workflows—that support, facilitate, and sustain agile ways of working and adaptive behavior across the enterprise.

synthesis. The process of combining separate elements or perspectives to form a more complete understanding of a system.

system. A set of interrelated components working together toward a common purpose, often characterized by feedback loops, boundaries, and emergent properties.

systemic alignment. The degree to which distributed decisions and actions reinforce overarching organizational goals and values.

systems thinking. A holistic approach that views projects as interconnected systems, recognizing how people, processes, technology, and the environment interact, and how feedback loops, time delays, and interdependencies shape patterns and outcomes over time.

tacit knowledge. Personal knowledge that can be difficult to articulate and share such as beliefs, experience, and insights.

team resilience. The ability of a team to maintain functionality and cohesion while navigating disruption, change, or adversity.

technological complexity. The degree of difficulty encountered in selecting, implementing, and maintaining technology solutions that align with project goals and organizational capabilities.

technical readiness review. A structured evaluation that examines whether the technical elements of a project, such as designs, requirements, and supporting systems, are sufficiently mature to progress to the next phase of work.

uncertainty. A lack of understanding and awareness of issues, events, path to follow, or solutions to pursue.

value. The excess of monetary and nonmonetary benefits over investment that is gained from achieving the goals of a portfolio, program, or project.

value governance. The mindset, processes, and mechanisms that help ensure organizational initiatives continuously deliver measurable business value, aligned with strategic objectives and stakeholder needs.

volatility. The possibility for rapid and unpredictable change.

water-Scrum-fall. A hybrid project management approach that combines elements of the traditional waterfall approach with the iterative and flexible nature of Scrum.

Index

Note: Page numbers in *italics* refer to figures.

E

U

V

W